THE JESUS HOAX

HOW ST. PAUL'S CABAL FOOLED THE WORLD FOR TWO THOUSAND YEARS

THE JESUS HOAX

HOW ST. PAUL'S CABAL
FOOLED THE WORLD
FOR TWO THOUSAND YEARS

David Skrbina

Expanded 2nd Edition

Creative Fire Press
— 2024 —

CREATIVE FIRE PRESS

Creative Fire Press is a division of The Walden Group, a non-profit educational publisher.

Library of Congress Cataloging-in-Publication Data

Skrbina, David
*The Jesus Hoax: How St. Paul's Cabal Fooled the World for
   Two Thousand Years*

p. cm.
Includes bibliographical references

ISBN 979-8987-7263-58
(pbk.: alk. paper)

1. Christianity, history of

Printing number: 9 8 7 6 5 4 3 2 1

Printed in the United States of America on acid-free paper.

DEDICATION

To my friend E. M.: Christian, rationalist, and seeker of the truth

CONTENTS

THE JESUS HOAX

HOW ST. PAUL'S CABAL FOOLED THE WORLD FOR TWO THOUSAND YEARS

CHAPTER 1
SETTING THE STAGE

> "For I tell you that Christ's life of
> service was on behalf of the Jews…"
> —Paul (Romans 15:8)

Jesus of Nazareth, known as Jesus Christ, known as the Son of God, known as God himself, is widely acknowledged to be one of the most famous individuals in history. We know his story: Born of a virgin, he performed numerous miracles and made many divine pronouncements during his short, 33-year life. He spoke of a dedication to God, of a spiritual inwardness, of love and forgiveness. He suffered greatly for his beliefs, and asked his followers to likewise suffer for theirs. He promised redemption from sin and eternal blessings from God. Ultimately he gave his life for the salvation of mankind. His bodily resurrection and ultimate ascension into heaven were proof of his promise. In the end, his teachings led to the foundation of one of the great religions of the world.

That Jesus should be counted among the most famous people in history is hardly surprising. *Time Magazine* ranked him #1 in all of history, and a slightly more technical study done by MIT University ranked him #3 (behind Aristotle and Plato). His followers literally number in the billions. There are about 2.4 billion Christians on Earth today, roughly 1/3 of the planet, making Christianity the #1 religion globally. The United States is strongly Christian; about 70% of Americans call themselves Christians, which encompasses some 250 million people. It's clear that Jesus, as the nominal founder of the Christian church, is among the most important and influential persons who ever lived.

But some historians and researchers have made a startling claim: that Jesus, the Son of God, never existed. They say that Jesus Christ was a pure myth. Is that even possible? Surely not, we reply. This most-influential founder of the most-influential religion of Christianity surely had to exist. And he surely had to be the miracle-working Son of God that is proclaimed in the Bible. How could it be otherwise? we ask. How could a venerable, two-thousand-year-old religion, with billions of followers throughout history, be based on someone who never existed? Impossible! Or so we say.

If that were the case, if Jesus never existed, imagine the consequences: an entire religion and the active beliefs of billions of people, all in vain. All of Christianity based on a myth, a fable, even—as I will argue—a lie. Why, that would be catastrophic. The Crusades, the religious wars, the burning of heretics, the Inquisition, the countless lives led in hope of heaven and fear of hell—all in vain.

Or consider a slightly less radical but still earth-shaking possibility: that Jesus existed, but he was just a man. Some argue that he was an entirely ordinary—and entirely mortal—teacher of morality. What if Jesus was just a simple preacher, a Jewish rabbi (as he is called in the Bible), who spoke in defense of the poor and the underprivileged, and through his various social agitations, managed to get himself executed by the Roman authorities? And what if his body was unceremoniously buried in some non-descript grave somewhere in Palestine, never to be seen again?[1] What if there were no virgin birth, no star of Bethlehem, no miracles, no raising of the dead, no walking on water? What if there was no bodily resurrection, and no ascension into heaven after 40 days (as it says in Acts)? Well, that would be nearly as bad as if Jesus never existed at all. All of Christian history would still be founded on a myth or on a lie. It would still be a sham. And all the efforts of Christians worldwide, throughout all of history, would still be in vain. This would be a devastating conclusion; and this is the view that I will defend in this book.

Let me start with a basic question: "Did Jesus exist?" Note that it's very important to distinguish between the two conceptions of Jesus. If someone asks, "Did Jesus exist?" we need to know if they mean (a) the divine, miracle-working, resurrected Son of God (sometimes called the *biblical Jesus*), or (b) the ordinary man and Jewish preacher who died a mortal death (sometimes called the *historical Jesus*). Christianity requires a biblical Jesus, but the skeptics argue either for simply a historical Jesus—which would mean the end of Christianity—or worse, no Jesus at all.

---

[1] Or perhaps it has been found! I elaborate on this fascinating prospect in Chapter 3.

It is my purpose in this book to argue that the miracle-working, ascended-to-heaven, Son-of-God Jesus never existed. I will, however, accept the historical Jesus: the Jewish preacher, the rabbi, who lived and taught at that time, who was a social agitator that incited his fellow Jews against the Romans, and who therefore got himself crucified. (Crucifixion was generally reserved for crimes against the Roman State.) I can't be certain, of course, but unlike the other Jesus skeptics, I have some reasons for thinking that a mortal, historical Jesus did exist. But I agree with the skeptics that the miracles, the resurrection story, and most of his alleged sayings were pure literary construction, pure myth.

It is my further purpose to explain how and why the biblical Jesus myth—bluntly, the Jesus *lie*—came to be constructed, and how it came to influence world history. It is a shocking story, frankly, and one that has only been hinted at before. Bits and pieces of this counter-narrative have been discovered and examined throughout history, but the whole picture has never been clearly pieced together until now. In recent years, political correctness and contemporary liberal dogma both have conspired to suppress any such discussion. The media have no interest in examining this alternate story, for reasons that I will explain. Western governments have little incentive, and much disincentive, for promoting open talk of this issue. Christians obviously don't want to hear any talk of a Jesus myth, nor—as I will explain—do Jews or Muslims. In short, hardly anyone in power, and many ordinary people, have no desire to consider the radical thesis that Jesus Christ, Son of God, never existed. And yet it is of untold importance.

Now of course, I cannot technically prove my thesis. I cannot give an ironclad, bullet-proof argument that the Jesus story was a hoax. Part of the problem is the notorious difficulty of "proving a negative"—that is, it can be difficult or sometimes impossible to prove that some alleged event did *not* happen. The other issue is that the circumstances of that place and time are so obscure, and our hard knowledge so limited, that little of anything can be stated with certainty.

But I am not alone in this shortcoming. No Christian can prove the biblical account of events, either. Their entire case rests on the Bible, but this document is riddled with difficulties, as I will show. And it obviously is biased, since it (the New Testament) was written by followers of Jesus who were hardly objective and who obviously had a large incentive to support the conventional view. So, in a sense, both the Christian and I are on equal footing; neither of us can definitively prove our case. But the weight of evidence, and archeological history, and common sense are on my side. They all point to the very strong likelihood that a divine Jesus never existed, and that his story was constructed for very specific reasons and purposes.

But there is an additional problem for defenders of Christianity. It is a common rule of argumentation that whoever makes the more extraordinary claims holds the primary burden of proof. To makes claims about a virgin birth, or a miracle-working Son of God, or being risen from the dead, are, to say the least, extraordinary claims. Therefore, in any debate about Jesus' existence, it is the Christian, and not the skeptic, who holds the burden of proof. If I claim that the biblical Jesus did not exist, and a Catholic theologian claims he did, then I merely need to show the implausible and unlikely nature of such an event, along with a lack of any corroborating evidence. The theologian, by contrast, must give definitive, positive evidence that such a miracle man actually existed, and did and said what is claimed in the Bible. Indeed, if Jesus was the Son of God— or perhaps even *God himself*—then the Christian theologian has a *very* high bar to cross. My standard of proof is much lower, and therefore much more achievable. In other words, it is much, much easier for me to 'win' such a debate. I think this will become clear as my argument proceeds.

Two Defenses, Refuted

When confronted with the case against Jesus, and the strong likelihood of his mythological nature, Christians typically find themselves unable to rationally defend their version of events. Sensing defeat, they may retreat to one of two commonly-held views that they see as their ultimate safe havens. It's worth mentioning these briefly now, at the outset, in order to get them out of the way.

First: "Christianity relies on faith, not reason. Therefore, rational arguments against it, or against Jesus, have no effect. We simply *believe* the Christian story, and that's good enough."

This is a very convenient 'get out of jail free' card that religious people like to play. But it doesn't work. It's worth noting that all of Western civilization is based on the idea of rationality and reason, from its very inception in ancient Greece around 600 BC. Reason is older than Christianity, and is the foundation of everything that we have achieved. It's not that faith has no place, but if we allow faith to override reason in our ideological thinking, we surrender the very basis of our own culture. It's self-defeating and self-destructive.

Furthermore, many of the most famous Christian theologians in history were eminently rational; Augustine, Anselm, Thomas Aquinas, Martin Luther, and John Calvin, to name a few, were all justly famous for their reason-based arguments. A true Christian should never have to surrender reason, even in the name of faith.

Additionally, even if we want to place an emphasis on belief, *we still need to have a reason to believe.* If our beliefs aren't rational, we are liable to believe in absolutely anything: pixies, magic dragons, unicorns, you name it. We might start burning people as witches, or try casting out demons, or drinking deadly poisons, or rely strictly on prayer to heal serious diseases. A society ruled by non-rational beliefs is a very dangerous one; I have a hard time believing that people would truly want to live in such a society.

Second: "It doesn't matter if the Jesus story is true. Jesus' life and teachings still help people to live better lives and become better people."

This is tantamount to surrender. The entirety of the Christian faith is based on the idea that Jesus was the Son of God, that he actually came to Earth to save us, and that he actually died and was bodily risen. The whole religion collapses into absurdity if the Jesus story is false. If Jesus' resurrection promises us eternal life, and if non-believers are threatened with eternal damnation, this only matters *if he actually existed*, and *if he was right*. Christianity makes astonishing, monumental claims: about eternal life, eternal damnation, the existence of God, and so on. And it does so on the basis of one man: Jesus of Nazareth. If that man never existed, or if he existed but was an ordinary rabbi who died a mortal's death, not to be resurrected, then the Christian religion is meaningless. It's all just fairy tales and wishful thinking—or worse, as I will explain.

Furthermore, can it really be beneficial to accept a myth as truth? Can one really live a happy, successful, and meaningful life dedicated to a false story, or to a lie? Take the case of Santa Claus. This story may be useful to keep naughty little children in line, but it works only because of their ignorance and naiveté. Even if we could keep up the charade for years, would it be ethical to do so? Surely not; ultimately it would lead to terrible outcomes—not the least of which, when the child, now grown to adulthood, finds out he has been lied to his whole life.

And what if there were a whole society of Santa-believers; can we envision them leading a truly good life? Would they be able to construct and sustain a vibrant, healthy, successful society? Of course not. It should be self-evident that a life based on self-deception or falsehood can never turn out well.

Granted, certain ideas attributed to Jesus could be considered beneficial: the Golden Rule, loving thy neighbor, aiding the poor, human equality, the virtue of hope. (Recall, however, that the 10 Commandments are from the Old Testament; they are, strictly speaking, Judaic rather than Christian. In fact, some say that Jesus came and *negated* the Old Testament!) But one doesn't need to be a Christian to love thy neighbor, or to aid the poor, or to treat others kindly. There are independent and thoroughly rational reasons to do these things, as many other philosophers and religious figures have noted, both before and after Jesus. The fact that some people find these things helpful in no way justifies a general belief in the Christian story.

And then we have the fact that many of the so-called Christian virtues turn out to be false, misleading, or downright dangerous—as I will explain. This adds another whole layer of problems to the Christian story.

I therefore conclude that it does matter, profoundly, if the Jesus story is true or false. Anyone, any alleged Christian, who tries to claim otherwise can hardly be taken seriously.

A Few Questions about God

Jesus, we are told, was God.[2] Skepticism about Jesus therefore naturally leads to skepticism about God—that is, the Judeo-Christian God as conceived in the Old Testament, who created the world in six days, who created Adam and Eve, who caused the Great Flood, who sent his only son to save mankind, and who loves each and every one of us. Generally speaking, in this book I will ignore questions about God's nature and existence, in order to focus on the Jesus story and its origins. Technically,

---

[2] See Philippians 2:6; Colossians 1:15; John 8:42, 8:58, 10:30, and 14:9.

God's existence is independent of Jesus' existence. Even if Jesus were a total myth, there could still be, in theory, a God. Orthodox Jews believe in God but not Jesus. Muslims believe in God (Allah) but not a divine, son-of-God Jesus who died and was risen. The two issues are distinct.

That being the case, I will say just a few words here about God, and specifically about what is rational and what is irrational about him.

It is common knowledge that there have been many religions in world history—more than 4,000, by some estimates. Each of these has a different conception of God or the gods. Clearly, the vast majority of them must be in error. More likely, all of them are in error. As the saying goes, "They can't all be right, but they can all be wrong." Odds are that every religion has seriously defective beliefs about God or the gods, to the point where we can say almost nothing conclusive about the divine. We cannot even be sure that gods exist.

Even within Christianity there is a vast range of beliefs and practices. For example, *The World Christian Encyclopedia* infamously notes that, globally, there are some 33,000 "distinct denominations" of the Church, including 242 Catholic, 9,000 Protestant, and over 22,000 "independent." This is a huge diversity within what is nominally one religion. Obviously they have many commonalities, given that they all call themselves Christian; but equally obviously, there is a lot of disagreement between these groups—all of whom claim to use the same Bible. Once again, they can't all be right, but they can all be wrong.

If we set aside atheism for a moment, it has been argued that all the world religions could agree on just two propositions about God:

1)   God is the Supreme Being or ultimate reality.
2)   God is that which is most revered.

Despite the vast and irreconcilable difference amongst religions, virtually everyone could likely accept these two claims. If we stuck to just these two views, there would be no religious disagreements, no religious wars, no religious strife at all.

But of course, with just these two claims, one cannot construct a functioning religion—one that builds temples, grows in numbers and wealth, and projects power around the world. You can't have "the Church" without a lot more to God than that. That's why the various religions have been compelled to add additional qualities to God, to create additional stories about him, to bring him to Earth, to create demands on people, to inflict fear and awe, and so on.

We can do a bit better than these above two characteristics, however. Perhaps surprisingly, there are a number of qualities that we can attribute to God without being irrational, *provided* that we are careful how we define them. For example, God can logically, rationally, and consistently be said to have the following properties:

- God is uncreated.
- God is perfect.
- God is eternal.
- God is omnipresent.
- God is one.
- God is a mind or spirit.

Rational thinkers and philosophers throughout history have attributed some or all of these to a divine Being. They are not contradictory, they are not illogical, and they do not lead to irreconcilable paradoxes.

But even these are not enough for most religions. These still don't allow anyone to build up a church, a complex doctrine, or to exert power over people. Therefore, theologians have introduced yet additional qualities, ones that do allow for conventional religion:

- God is a 'person' (someone who loves, forgives, punishes, etc).
- God 'speaks' to humans.
- God is omniscient.
- God is omnipotent.
- God is supernatural.
- God does good acts.
- God saves some and condemns others.

These qualities cause major problems. While I can't detail it here, they lead to all sorts of problems: contradictions, paradoxes, absurdities, and sheer mysteries.

The biggest problem of all comes when we believe that God is a *moral being*: someone who is good, kind, benevolent, just, etc. This notion is central to Christianity but it leads directly to what we call the Problem of Evil.[3] In short, the problem is this: The world is plagued by all varieties of evils, including murder, rape, war, violence, illness, disease, accidents, famine, earthquakes, tsunamis, hurricanes. These cause massive human suffering and death, every day. But the world is allegedly overseen by a benevolent and loving God who wishes well for us humans, who are, after all, created in his image. This moral God, furthermore, is all-powerful; he can instantly do whatever he wishes. How is it, then, that humans suffer such vast and unending evils? God has the power to halt or prevent every conceivable evil. And yet he does not. Why?

Suffice it to say that there is no rational answer to this question. It seems that God either does not really care about our suffering—in which case he's not all good—or he's not really able to do anything about it—in which case he's not all powerful. In other words, God is either *not* a moral being, or he's *not* all-powerful (or neither!). He clearly can't be both good and powerful at the same time. And yet that's exactly what Christianity, and many other religions, want us to believe. It's an unsolvable dilemma. The Problem of Evil has no answer.

Apart from the Problem of Evil and other paradoxes, we have the simple observation that there is no evidence of God. He doesn't come and speak to us anymore. He doesn't appear in burning bushes or clouds of smoke and fire. He doesn't send down his sons (or daughters) to enlighten us anymore. Science has no need to postulate God, since everything that happens is covered by the laws of physics. Biblical-scale miracles no longer happen—meaning, major events that don't have straightforward scientific explanations. Why is God hiding?[4]

Because he remains hidden, people cannot agree on God, and hence they fight and die in his name. Why would he allow this to happen? Of the more than 4,000 religions, at least 3,999 of them are wrong about God; how can we tell which is right? Or what if they are all wrong? What if we think we are doing the right thing, but God is secretly angry

---

[3] The Problem of Evil was famously criticized by philosopher David Hume in part 10 of his *Dialogues Concerning Natural Religion* (1778). More recent critiques include John Mackie's article "Evil and omnipotence" (1955), and in a more popular vein, B. C. Johnson's essay "God and the problem of evil".

[4] It does no good to say that God is "testing" us. He created us how we are, and he knows the future, therefore it can't be a test.

with us? What if all those who rigorously attend church every Sunday are, in God's eyes, unthinking sheep who will ultimately be punished? How can we ever really know what God likes, or doesn't like? We have no answers to these questions, and we never will. It does no good to say, "Well, God is mysterious." This is another religious cop-out. It's a meaningless statement that can be used to cover over any inconvenient problem. It's another sign of intellectual and moral surrender.

The only reasonable conclusion is that God—if he exists at all—is limited in many ways. He can be a kind of ultimate reality, and we can indeed revere him. He can have any of the first set of properties shown above, but none of the second group. But even these "acceptable" qualities are arbitrary human constructions. We choose them because we like them, but that's it. We have no real reasons, no evidence, to make any such claims. Based on the actual evidence, it seems that there is no God at all.[5] But if it makes us feel better to invent him, and give him a few, limited qualities, there is little harm in doing so.

Enough about God. My focus here is Jesus, and we have many interesting things to learn about him.

The Problem of the Experts

When we try to make a rational and critical inquiry into Jesus, we are immediately confronted with a serious issue, namely, "the problem of the experts." This problem has several different aspects, all of which make it very hard for the average reader to ascertain the truth.

While there are exceptions, writers on Christianity tend to fall into three groups: *academics*, *journalists*, and *independent researchers*. In all three cases, we have reasons for concern. Consider first the academics. The vast majority are either (a) faculty of a religious-based school or institution, or (b) members of a religious studies department in an ordinary, secular university. In either case, if they are experts in Christianity, nearly all are Christians. This obviously colors their outlook, imposing severe constraints on the kinds of ideas that they will consider and the conclusions that they will reach. Of the few non-Christian academic writers on

---

[5] With the possible exception of *pantheism*, which declares that the universe in its entirety is God. But I set that aside for now.

Christianity, many are Jews (e.g. Daniel Boyarin, Hyam Maccoby, Martin Buber, Paul Goodman, Alan Dershowitz), and a few (e.g. Reza Aslan) are Muslims—and these carry their own baggage. For obvious reasons, open-minded, critically-thinking, non-religious faculty members rarely become experts in Christianity.

Then look at journalists, who have their own set of issues. Journalists like to portray themselves as unbiased and neutral, and as a result, we typically do not know their religious affiliation; this is particularly problematic here. Also, journalists typically have no advanced degrees, and thus do not really understand how to do serious academic research. They may have a fulltime job with a newspaper or other media outfit, but they often write books "on the side," either as a second source of income or to bolster their job credentials. Either way, they don't really care that much about serious academic research. Their chief motive is income, not truth. Because of this, they are under strong pressure to stick to fairly conventional views about religion (or whatever topic they write on). They don't have the freedom to follow the facts where they might lead, or to expound on some politically-incorrect theory. Their employers would certainly take a dim view of their careers if such journalists decided to publish something outside the conventional bounds.

Finally, we have our independent researchers. They typically suffer from all the above problems: they (often) have no advanced education; they usually have an inadequate grasp of how to do detailed and careful research; they have their own (unknown) religious bias; and they likely have a need to sell books for income. Again, this imposes all sorts of restraints on the conclusions that they might reach.

Of course, everyone has a kind of bias about religion. Even the atheists and professional skeptics have hidden or unexamined assumptions. So be it. The best we can hope for is that our experts are open and honest about their biases, which will allow us, the readers, to better judge their analysis and their writings.

I too have my biases, I'm sure. But let me be as transparent as I can. I was "raised" Presbyterian but rarely attended and never committed to the church, ever. I have been a religious skeptic since my early teens, and I recall debating my religious classmates even in middle school. I hold advanced degrees in mathematics and philosophy, and I spent 15 years teaching philosophy at a campus of the University of Michigan. I'm not an atheist, but my religious stance changes depending on the circumstances; sometimes I'm an agnostic, sometimes a pantheist, sometimes a polytheist. In no sense am I a Christian, a Muslim, or a Jew. Nor is anyone in my immediate family. I like to think that I am as unbiased as possible—perhaps more so than nearly any present-day writer on Christianity. I am currently an independent lecturer and researcher with sufficient finances that I do not need to sell books to make a living. I write what I think is true and important. I follow the facts wherever they lead, and I try to make the most reasonable and most plausible conclusions from those facts. Whether these facts result in a useful and honest book on Jesus, I leave it to the reader to decide.

Another Jesus Skeptic?

As one can obviously see by now, I am a 'Jesus skeptic.' But I'm far from the first, of course. There have been many such skeptics in the past, and their numbers appear to be growing. In recent times this group has been referred to as "Christ Mythicists," meaning those who deny the existence of the biblical, divine Jesus (though not necessarily the historical human Jesus). Christ Myth Theory, or CMT, is also popular with atheists in general, since it feeds into their view that God too does not exist.

So, why this book? Why do we need yet another Jesus skeptic?

To answer this question, let me give a brief overview of some of the prominent skeptics and their views. I will argue that their ideas, though on the right track, are woefully short of the truth. They lack the courage or the will to look hard at the evidence, and to accept the most likely conclusion: that Jesus was a deliberately constructed myth, by a specific group of people, with a specific end in mind. None of the recent Christ mythicists or atheist writers have, to my knowledge, articulated the view that I defend here.

But let me first offer a quick recap of the background and context for the idea of a mythological Jesus. The earliest modern critic was German scholar Hermann Reimarus, who published a multi-part work, *Fragments*, in the late 1770s. Strikingly, his view is one of the closest to my own thesis of any skeptic. For Reimarus, Jesus was the militant leader of a group of Jewish rebels who were fighting against oppressive Roman rule. Eventually he got himself crucified. His followers then constructed a miraculous religion-story around Jesus, in order to carry on his cause. They lied about his miracles, and they stole his body from the grave so that they could claim a bodily resurrection.[6] This is quite close to what I will call the 'Antagonism Thesis'—that a group of Jews constructed a false Jesus story, based on a real man, in order to undermine Roman rule. But there is much more to the story, far beyond that which Reimarus himself was able to articulate.

In the 1820s and 1830s, Ferdinand Baur published a number of works that emphasized the conflict between the early Jewish-Christians—significantly, *all* the early Christians were Jews, as I will explain—and the somewhat later Gentile-Christians. This again is a key part of the story, but we need to know the details; we need to know why the conflict arose, and what were its ends.

In 1835, David Strauss published the two-volume work *Das Leben Jesu*—"The Life of Jesus." He was the first to argue, correctly, that none of the gospel writers knew Jesus personally. He disavowed all claims of miracles, and argued that the Gospel of John was, in essence, an outright lie with no basis in reality. Again, this is very much on the right track, but we can now add many more details.

German philosopher Bruno Bauer wrote several important books, including *Criticism of the Gospel History* (1841), *The Jewish Question* (1843), *Criticism of the Gospels* (1851), *Criticism of the Pauline Epistles* (1852), and *Christ and the Caesars* (1877). Bauer held that there was no historical Jesus and that the entire New Testament was a literary construction, utterly devoid of historical content. Shortly thereafter, James Frazer published *The Golden Bough* (1890), arguing for a connection between all religion—Christianity included—and ancient mythological concepts; this also is true, and there is a good explanation for it.

It was about at this time that another famous Christian skeptic emerged: Friedrich Nietzsche. In his books *Daybreak* (1881), *On the Genealogy of Morals* (1887), and *Antichrist* (1888) he provides a potent

---

[6] This possibility is actually described in Matthew (27:64 - 28:15). The Gospel says, "this story [of the stolen body] has been spread among the Jews to this day." This is fascinating; it suggests that "Matthew" (true identity unknown) was worried that people might not accept the miraculous resurrection and might simply believe the most obvious conclusion: that someone took the body away, in order to later claim a resurrection.

critique of Christianity and Christian morality. Nietzsche always accepted the historical Jesus, and even had good things to say about him. But
he was devastating in his attack on Paul and the later writers of the New
Testament. He viewed Christian morality as a lowly, life-denying form
of slave morality, attributed not to Jesus but to the actions of Paul and the
other Jewish followers. Along with Reimarus, Nietzsche provides the
most inspiration for my own analysis.

Into the 20th century, we find such books as *The Christ Myth* (1909)
and *The Denial of the Historicity of Jesus* (1926), both by Arthur Drews,
and *The Enigma of Jesus* (1923) by Paul-Louis Chouchoud. All these
continued to attack the literal truth claimed of the Bible. It was also
around this time that a Jewish writer, Marcus Eli Ravage, wrote an important, two-part series of articles that drew upon Nietzsche's claims but
put them into accessible language for a broad audience. Arguing that
Christianity was "a subversive Jewish conspiracy," Ravage explained
how this invented and toxic ideology went on to subvert the Roman Empire. Though offering no new evidence, his two essays nonetheless
reached a mass audience that would have remained largely ignorant of,
say, Nietzsche's writings.[7]

More recently, we have critics such as the historian George Wells
and his book *Did Jesus Exist?* (1975). Here he assembles an impressive
amount of evidence against an historical Jesus. Bart Ehrman has called
Wells "the best-known mythicist of modern times," though in later years
Wells softened his stance somewhat; he accepted that there may have
been an historical Jesus, although one that we know almost nothing
about. Wells died in 2017 at the age of 90. Similar arguments were offered by philosopher Michael Martin in his 1991 book, *The Case against
Christianity*. Though a wide-ranging critique, he dedicated one chapter to
the idea that Jesus never existed; Martin died in 2015.

Among living critics, we have such men as Thomas Thompson,
who wrote *The Messiah Myth* (2005); he is agnostic about an historical
Jesus but argues against historical truth in the Bible. By contrast, Earl
Doherty (*The Jesus Puzzle*, 1999), Tom Harpur (*The Pagan Christ*,

---

[7] The two essays were "A real case against the Jews" and "Commissary to the
Gentiles," published in *Century Magazine*, in January and February of 1928.
Both essays are reproduced in *Classic Essays on the Jewish Question* (2022, T.
Dalton, ed.; Clemens & Blair).

2004), and Thomas Brodie (*Beyond the Quest for the Historical Jesus*, 2012) all deny that any such Jesus of Nazareth ever existed. Richard Carrier, in his book *On the Historicity of Jesus* (2014), finds it highly unlikely that any historical Jesus lived.

Perhaps the most vociferous and prolific Jesus skeptic today is Robert Price, a man with two doctorates in theology and a deep knowledge of the Bible. Though agnostic on the historical Jesus, Price argues that much of Christian theology is a synthesis of pre-Christian mythology, and hence devoid of truth content. He thus qualifies as a proponent of the "Christ Myth" thesis. His extensive writings include *Deconstructing Jesus* (2000), *The Incredible Shrinking Son of Man* (2003), *Jesus Is Dead* (2007), *The Christ-Myth Theory and Its Problems* (2012), and *Killing History* (2014). Price's central points can be summarized as follows:

1) The miracle stories have no independent verification from unbiased contemporaries.
2) The characteristics of Jesus are all drawn from much older mythologies and other pagan sources.
3) The earliest documents, the letters of Paul, point to an esoteric, abstract, ethereal Jesus—a "mythic hero archetype"—not an actual man who died on a cross.
4) The later documents, the Gospels, turned the Jesus-concept into an actual man, a literal Son of God, who died and was risen.

I find some truth in all these claims, as I will show. But there is much more to the story than Price is willing to entertain. Perhaps this relates to his personal situation. Price seems to rely heavily on book sales and speaking fees for income; he is very much in "the Jesus business." I can't help but think that this affects what he says and writes. He also has indicated in recent podcasts that he supports the Zionist cause (of a Jewish homeland in Palestine, at the expense of the native Palestinians); furthermore, he seems be philo-Semitic in the extreme. Again, these things are consistent with his guarded stance in his books, and are very much in line with my brief analysis above.

These men, then, are perhaps the most authoritative critics of the traditional account of Jesus. They know their stuff, and they know how to do research. But of course, this does not make them right, or even guarantee an open and honest assessment. It does ensure a clever and learned critique, though.

There are many other books attacking the Jesus story, but the vast majority are written by marginally qualified individuals. Some are atheists, some are members of competing religions, some are just out to sell books. Most lack the advanced degrees that would indicate an ability to do careful, detailed research. I leave it to the reader to investigate these as desired.[8] A word of caution to the reader: Examine the qualifications of the writer before buying the book!

Finally, with the exception of Nietzsche, all of the above individuals exhibit a glaring weakness: they are loathe to criticize anyone. No one comes in for condemnation, no one is guilty, no one is to blame for anything. For the earliest writers, I think this is due primarily to an insecurity about their ideas and a general lack of clarity about what likely occurred. For the more recent individuals, it's probably attributable to an in-bred political correctness, to a weakness of moral backbone, or to sheer self-interest. In recent years, academics in particular are highly reticent to affix blame on individuals, even those long-dead.[9] This is somehow seen as a violation of academic neutrality or professional integrity. But when the facts line up against someone or some group, then we must be honest with ourselves. There are truly guilty parties all throughout history, and when we come upon them, they must be called out.

Consider this: There are very good reasons, as I will show, for believing that none of the Jesus miracle stories are true. And yet someone, at some point later in time, wrote them down *as if they were true*. The conclusion is clear: *someone lied*. When you write obvious falsehoods and portray them as literal truth, that's a lie. The questions then are, Who lied? When? and Why? I will address these matters in due time. For now, I simply note that *none* of our brave critics, our Jesus mythicists, seem willing to pinpoint anyone: not Paul, not his Jewish colleagues, not the

---

[8] A few such recent titles include: *Nailed*, by D. Fitzgerald (2010); *Jesus Christ, A Pagan Myth*, by S. Dalton and L. Dalton (2008); *Jesus Never Existed*, by K. Humpreys (2014); *Caesar's Messiah*, by J. Atwill (2005); *The Christ Conspiracy*, by Acharya S (1999); *There Was No Jesus*, by R. Lataster (2013); *Atheist Manifesto*, by M. Onfray (2007).

[9] There are exceptions, of course. Hitler, Nazis, or Islamic "terrorists" are still open targets, for example.

early Christian fathers—no one. A colossal but evidently bogus story has been laid out about the Son of God come to Earth, performing miracles, and being risen from the dead, and yet—no one lied? Really? Can we believe that? Was it all just a big misunderstanding? Honest mistakes? "Noble" lies? No thinking person could accept this. Someone, somewhere in the past, constructed a gigantic lie and then passed it around the ancient world as a cosmic truth. The guilty parties need to be exposed. Only then can we truly understand this ancient religion, and begin to move forward.

Let me now lay out the basic facts of Christian history, as we understand them today. I use the word "fact" advisedly, because it is very hard to determine such things with certainty, and there are skeptical voices on nearly every issue. Still, in the next chapter I will present the most widely-accepted information that we have that relates to the origins of Christianity and to the tales of Jesus. Today, thanks to on-going scientific research and archeological analysis, we know much more about those ancient times than in decades past, and we can have much more confidence regarding what did, or did not, happen.

CHAPTER 2

JUST THE FACTS...

"Inside every Christian is a Jew."
—Pope Francis (16 June 2014)

There is so much obfuscation and mystery surrounding Jesus and the Bible that it can be almost impossible to get a straight story on things. It's true that little can be said with certainty. But as with any historical situation, some things about Christianity are generally accepted as true and others are considered highly likely by a majority of experts. This being the case, let me lay out the least contentious and most widely-accepted facts about this religion. These facts will serve as a foundation to later claims about what is likely to have occurred, and what is unlikely.

As we all know, Christianity is more properly understood as Judeo-Christianity. Therefore we must begin with an account of early Judaism and the history of the Jewish people. These facts have a direct bearing on the formation of Christianity and its aftermath, to the present day.

Consider, first of all, the ancient origins of Judaism and the corresponding events of the Old Testament (OT), otherwise known as the Jewish (or Hebrew) Bible. The original patriarch, Abraham (originally called "Abram"—strange how so many people in the Bible have two names), allegedly lived sometime between 1800 and 1500 BC; he was the traditional father of not only Judaism and thus Christianity but, centuries later, of Islam as well. Thus, one sometimes reads that Judaism, Christianity, and Islam are all viewed as the "Abrahamic" religions.

According to the Bible, Abraham was the father of two sons: Isaac and Ishmael. Ishmael was in turn the forefather of the Arabic people, and eventually—many centuries hence—of the Islamic prophet Muhammad. Isaac in turn also had two sons: Esau and Jacob. Esau's lineage included the Edomites—the people of present-day Iraq and Syria (the Edomites later came to encompass 'Europeans'). And Jacob, later called "Israel," gave rise to the Jews, via his 12 (!) sons (by four different women)[1], who founded "the 12 tribes of Israel." See Figure 1.

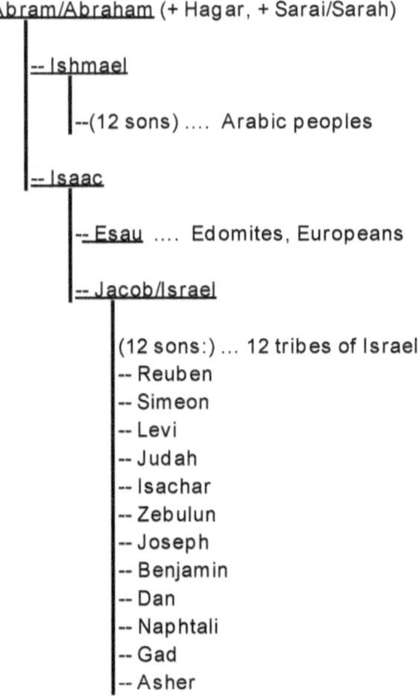

Figure 1. Abraham family tree

Now of course, all this is certainly mythology; it is an attempt by the Jews of the pre-Christian era to account for both their own origins and that of the people around them. We won't begrudge them that. But even so, the stories told—by Jews to their fellow Jews—are instructive; they tell us much about the Jewish worldview and the Jewish mindset.

The next major figure, Moses, allegedly lived around 1300 BC; but again, given that we have no real evidence of his existence, he is almost certainly another mythological figure. In any case, sometime later, the so-called "Five Books of Moses" began to take shape, at first as an oral tradition, and only written down much later, perhaps in the 400s BC.[2] These five books, as we know, would eventually form the *Pentateuch* (or

---

[1] See Genesis 35:23-26.
[2] Possibly much later. Russell Gmirkin (2006) argues that these five books were likely written in Alexandria circa 270 BC.

Torah)—the beginning of the OT. They are Genesis, Exodus, Leviticus, Numbers, and Deuteronomy.

Unlike Abraham and Moses, we are fairly confident that an actual people called "Israel" existed at this time, thanks to the discovery of the Merneptah Stele—an engraved stone created around 1200 BC. It is the earliest known reference. The stele includes this line: "Israel is laid waste and his seed is not." This sentence has some interesting implications that I will discuss later on. A second reference to Israel, and to the "House of David," comes with the recent discovery of the Tel Dan Stele, dating to around 850 BC. This has similar consequences.

After the first five OT books appeared in oral form, beginning (say) 1000 BC, thereafter followed the remaining 30-odd books of the OT. These books were written in Hebrew, but a Greek translation—called the Septuagint—was begun sometime after 200 BC, completed circa 50 BC. The Dead Sea Scrolls, which date to the first century BC, contain fragments from every book of the Hebrew OT, and thus are our earliest proof that the complete document existed by that time.

What's in a Name: Hebrew, Israelite, or Jew?

This is a good point to take a short detour to explain some very relevant terminology. Much confusion exists around three apparently-interchangeable terms: *Hebrew*, *Israelite*, and *Jew*. In the book of Genesis (14:13), Abraham/Abram is first referred to as "the Hebrew"—a term of ambiguous origin and no clear meaning. Regardless, Abraham was the original "Hebrew," and this designation came to be attached to his son Isaac (but not Ishmael) and to Isaac's son Jacob (but not Esau) and to Jacob's 12 sons and their descendants—all of whom would henceforth be "Hebrews".[3]

The term 'Israel,' as I noted above, had been in existence since at least 1200 BC. In Hebrew language, 'Israel' means 'he who strives with God,' and thus is a term of honor. It first appears in the Bible in Genesis (32:28), when Jacob is renamed Israel. Thereafter, Jacob and his 12 sons (and all their heirs) are called Israelites.

But what about 'Jew'? We see above that one of Jacob's 12 sons was Judah—or in Hebrew, *Yehudah*. Judah was Jacob/Israel's 4th son,

---

[3] Jacob's son Joseph is explicitly called a Hebrew at Genesis 39:14 and 39:17.

but as it turns out, the first three (Reuben, Simeon, and Levi) ended up in his disfavor, and so Judah takes a leading role. Speaking to his sons, Jacob says:

> Judah, your brothers shall praise you; your hand shall be on the neck of your enemies… Judah is a lion's cub… The scepter shall not depart from Judah, nor the ruler's staff from between his feet, until he comes to whom it belongs [or, 'until Shiloh comes'], and to him shall be the obedience of the peoples [nations, Gentiles]. (Gen 49:10)

In any case, as the 12 tribes and their descendants became established in Palestine, the 10 northern-most tribes became known as 'Israel' and the southern-most two, as 'Judah.' At some point, the 'man of Judah' or 'descendant of Judah' became a *Yehudi*—a Jew.

After the Babylonian exile and return (597 to 538 BC), the 12 tribes became known collectively as both 'Israel' and 'men of Judah' or *Yehudim*. We see a variation on this term appear on a coin minted around 120 BC, with the word *Hayehudim* ("of Judah" or "of the Jews"). *Yehudi*, or plural *Yehudim*, appear several times in the OT; typically this is translated into English as 'Jew' or 'Jews', although sometimes as 'man of Judah'. The first appearance is in 2 Kings (16:6 and 25:25), and then several times later in Ezra, Nehemiah, Esther, Jeremiah, Daniel (twice), and Zecharia (8:23). 'Jew' is not in the first five books (Pentateuch) like 'Hebrew' and 'Israel' are, which suggests that it is not quite as ancient within Jewish culture; but still, its presence throughout the remainder of the OT shows its importance to the Jewish authors, who, of course, were writing strictly to a Jewish audience. When Jews were writing to their fellow Jews, they had no compunction about using the word 'Jew.'

As the OT spread into Greek and (later) Latin culture, *Yehudi* became translated as *Ioudaios* and *Iudaeus*, respectively. The Latin term lost its 'd' when moving into the region of modern-day France, and the people there created a contracted version, *giu*. This then worked its way into Old English around the year 1000, where it took a variety of forms: *Gyu, Giu, Iew, Iuu,* and so on. By the late 1300s, Chaucer was using the word *Iewes*. And by the late 1500s, playwrights like Marlowe and Shakespeare were writing, simply, 'Jews.'

The bottom line: The terms 'Hebrew,' 'Israelite,' and 'Yehudi' (Jew) have a long history in Jewish culture, with all three in common use by 400 BC, at the latest. Further, in a functional sense, *they all refer to the same people*: 'Hebrew' refers to anyone in the Abraham / Isaac / Jacob line; and 'Israelite' and 'Jew' to anyone of the 12 returned tribes. *But these were all the same people.* Over the centuries, their insularity and inbreeding (and eugenics!)[4] led to their developing unique physical and mental characteristics—some negative, some positive. Notably, all three terms continued to be used in the New Testament, often at the same time (see, for example 2 Cor 11:22-24), and again, *all referring to the same people*. Functionally, then, the terms are interchangeable.

For present purposes, we are therefore correct in using the term 'Jew' to apply to "the people of the 12 tribes"—a distinct and readily identifiable ethnicity in the Middle East, with a distinct genetic profile, from at least 500 BC onward.[5] And to the point: our man Jesus, if he existed, was almost certainly a Jew. But this requires further discussion.

Back to the Facts

If we are to accept the standard view, then, the OT was originally an oral tradition of unknown origins, perhaps dating back to 1000 BC. It was sustained orally for several centuries, eventually becoming written down sometime between 500 and 300 BC. Lacking any original texts, we have no way of knowing how much change or editing occurred over that time. We also have no factual information on any of the alleged authors. In essence, all we know of the OT is that it was spoken, modified, evolved, and debated over hundreds of years by unknown individuals. It first appears in physical form with the Dead Sea Scrolls, dating from around 50 BC. Anything prior to that date is more or less speculation.

---

[4] The wisest ('smartest') and most-learned men were encouraged or allowed to father the most children, often with multiple wives. Over time, this led to a notable rise in average intelligence among Jews, which persists today.

[5] I can't elaborate here, but modern genetics has generally confirmed this conclusion. Modern-day Ashkenazi, Sephardic, and Mizrahi Jews all have a significant Middle Eastern genetic heritage. Harry Osterer (2012) argues that all major Jewish groups share a common M-E origin.

Dating of the OT texts is one thing; accuracy is another matter altogether. First of all, the earliest dates cited above are purely conjectural. Furthermore, archeologists have discovered evidence in recent years that refutes many of the historical claims of the OT. For example, Israeli archeologist Ze'ev Herzog has shown the increasing discrepancies between archeological data and the biblical stories.[6] Efforts in the 1900s to confirm the OT yielded a plentitude of new information, but this "began to undermine the historical credibility of the biblical descriptions instead of reinforcing them." Scholars were confronted with "an increasingly large number of anomalies," among these are, first, "no evidence has been unearthed that can sustain the chronology" of the Patriarchal age. Second, of the Exodus, "the many Egyptian documents that we have make no mention of the Israelites' presence in Egypt, and are also silent about the events of the Exodus".[7] Third, the alleged conquest of Canaan (Palestine) by the Israelites in the 1200s BC is refuted by archeological digs at Jericho and Ai that found no existing cities at that time. Even the famed monotheism of the early Jews is undermined by inscriptions from the 700s BC that refer to a pair of gods, "Yahweh and his consort, Asherah."

An overall picture thus comes into view: There was a Jewish people called "Israel," and perhaps "Hebrews," in the region of Palestine from at least the 1200s BC who engaged in a number of conflicts with the surrounding peoples, including the Egyptians. They recorded their own history in the books of the OT, but with substantial amounts of embellishment and speculation, such that many claims are unsubstantiated by modern research. And from the texts themselves, we know that this people

---

[6] The following quotations are from his article "Deconstructing the walls of Jericho," *Ha'aretz Magazine*, 29 October 1999.

[7] "Most historians today agree that, at best, the stay in Egypt and the Exodus events occurred among a few families, and that their private story was expanded and 'nationalized' to fit the needs of theological ideology." There is one later Egyptian documentation of such an event, by the high priest Manetho from the third century BC, which comes to a similar conclusion. As recounted by Lindemann, "the Jews had been driven out of Egypt because they, a band of destitute and undesirable immigrants who had intermarried with the slave population, were afflicted with various contagious diseases." The Jews were thus expelled "for reasons of public hygiene." In sum, "the account in Exodus was an absurd falsification of actual events, an attempt to cover up the embarrassing and ignoble origin of the Jews" (Lindemann 1997: 28).

viewed themselves as specifically chosen or blessed by their god, Yahweh or Jehovah. As a result, they viewed all non-Jews—the Gentiles, or goyim—as pagan non-believers, to be treated with contempt.[8]

Enter the Roman Empire

In the wake of the death of Alexander the Great in 323 BC, his great empire fragmented. One large piece fell to the Macedonian general Seleucus in 312 BC, who promptly began his own expansion, now known as the Seleucid Empire. This empire included present-day Palestine and the Jewish tribes who lived there. The Jews were naturally unhappy with foreign rule and continually opposed Seleucus' government. Eventually, in 165 BC, a Jewish group, the Maccabees, led a successful revolt against him, reestablishing Jewish rule over Palestine. The resulting Hasmonean dynasty was formed in 141 BC and reigned for some 80 years.

Farther to the west, however, was growing another and greater empire, that of the Romans. They were rapidly expanding to the east, and in the year 63 BC they incorporated the territory of Palestine. Suddenly the Jews were once more subject to foreign rule. And it was, at first, a rather ignominious rule; Roman general Pompey forcibly entered the great Jewish temple in Jerusalem, desecrating it; non-Jews were never allowed inside. A few years later, in 55 BC, the general Crassus plundered the temple treasury, hauling the booty back to Rome. And within a couple years of taking power, the Romans were deporting Jews and selling them as slaves.[9]

We must keep in mind that the Jews had a long history of foreign occupation. In past centuries they lived under the Persians, the Babylonians, Alexander the Great, and Seleucus, to name the major figures. All this time, they apparently adapted to their foreign rulers, even as they continued to periodically resist and revolt. Even with the Romans, and despite the actions of Pompey and Crassus, things went relatively well—at first. At least from 60 BC, Julius Caesar displayed a kind of "gratitude"

---

[8] Recall this passage: "For you [Jews] are a people holy to the LORD your God; the LORD your God has chosen you out of all the peoples on earth to be his people, his treasured possession" (Deut 7:6). I will elaborate in chapter four.
[9] Mass deportations occurred in 61, 55, 52, and 4 BC. See Fairchild (1999: 519).

toward his new Jewish conscripts. When Marc Antony came to power in 42 BC, he too was relatively beneficent toward them; he supported the Jewish king Herod I ("the Great") as the local ruler.[10] Augustus (later, Octavian) initiated the true Roman Empire in 27 BC, and his general Marcus Agrippa was favorably disposed toward the Jews, even through his visit to Jerusalem in 15 BC. But things quickly went downhill from there.

First of all, Herod was seen as an increasingly compliant, even supplicating king who regularly deferred to Rome. Jewish riots began to break out in 7 BC, and a few years later, in 3 BC, he was replaced by his son, Herod Archelaus. It was also in 3 BC that, allegedly, one Jesus of Nazareth was born, allegedly in the remote village of Bethlehem, allegedly with a mysterious "star" showing the very location.

Into the "Christian era," events accelerated. Around 5 or 6 AD, the Romans made Judea a formal Roman province, now under direct control from Rome; King Herod would be a mere puppet leader. Perhaps as a result, it was at this time that the militant Jewish "Zealot" movement was formed, becoming a so-called fourth sect of Judaism.[11] They advocated violent resistance toward Romans, Greeks, and especially fellow Jews who collaborated with the foreigners. Notably, there are reasons to believe that both Jesus and Paul were Zealots.[12] Of particular note was a violent subset of the Zealots known as the Sicarii, or 'dagger men'; they took it upon themselves to knife to death Romans or compliant Jews.

It was also at this time that a future Jewish "tentmaker" was born in the city of Tarsus (present-day Turkey)—a child by the name of Saul, later to become Paul: Saint Paul, creator of the Christian church as we know it today.

Pressure on the Jews increased in the first decades of the Christian era. At least from the year 14 AD, Emperor Tiberius was negatively disposed toward the Jews. Five years later, in 19 AD, he expelled the Jews

---

[10] Even if Cleopatra would have preferred that Antony "destroy" Herod; see Grant (1973: 70).

[11] The others being Pharisees, Sadducees, and Essenes.

[12] I discuss the evidence for Paul below. For details on Jesus as a zealot, see Brandon (1967) or Aslan (2013). I provide a critique of Aslan's book in Appendix B.

from Rome for aggressive proselytizing and for criminal activity.[13] In that same year, a high-ranking Roman official, Sejanus, deported 4,000 Italian Jews to Sardinia as punishment, presumably for similar reasons. And he continued to pressure them; in 30 AD, reports Philo, Sejanus made efforts to "destroy the Jewish nation".[14] That same year of 30 AD was, on most readings, the very year that Jesus of Nazareth was crucified. Jesus' punishment was ordered by the current Roman procurator, Pontius Pilate, who governed Palestine from 26 to 36 AD, and was known for his aggressive treatment of the Jews.

But things grew even worse for them after Pilate's removal from power and the ascension of Emperor Caligula in Rome in the year 37. Hayim Ben-Sasson writes, "The reign of Caligula (37-41 AD) witnessed the first open break between the Jews and the Empire. ... [R]elations deteriorated seriously during [this time]".[15] Hence, Jewish opposition, and repression, accelerated. In 38, the governor of Alexandria, A. A. Flaccus, took harsh action to restrict Jewish power and influence in that city. According to Philo, he also initiated violent pogroms that resulted in many fatalities.[16] But it seems that they had it coming; as Michael Grant (1973: 134) observes, from the standpoint of Rome, "the Jews of Alexandria were troublemakers on a worldwide scale." And indeed, just three years later, Emperor Claudius issued his third edict, *Letter to the Alexandrians*, in which he accused those Jews of "fomenting a general plague which infests the whole world." This is a striking passage; it suggests that Jews all over the Middle East had succeeded in stirring up dangerous agitation toward the empire. It also marks the first known occurrence in history of a "biological" epithet used against the Jews. By the year 49, Claudius had to undertake yet another expulsion of Jews from Rome.[17]

---

[13] According to Suetonius (circa 120 AD): "[Tiberius] abolished foreign cults at Rome, particularly the Egyptian and Jewish... Jews of military age were removed to unhealthy regions [and] the others of the same race were expelled from the city" (*Twelve Caesars*, III.36).

[14] According to Philo (*In Flac* I.1). See also Eusebius, *Ecc Hist* II.5.

[15] *A History of the Jewish People* (1976), pp. 254-255.

[16] *In Flac* IX.65-71.

[17] "Because the Jews at Rome caused continuous disturbances at the instigation of Chrestus [apparently Jesus Christ], he expelled them from the city." Suetonius, *Twelve Caesars* (V.25).

All this set the stage for the first major Jewish revolt, in the year 66. Also called the First Jewish-Roman War (there were three), this event was a major turning point in history. It eventually drew in some 75,000 Roman troops, who battled against perhaps 50,000 Jewish militants and thousands of other partisans. The war lasted for four years, ending in Roman victory and the destruction of the Jewish Temple in Jerusalem in the year 70. It remains in ruins to this day; only the western wall ("Wailing Wall") still exists.

There would be two more Jewish wars: in 115-117 (the Kitos War), and in 132-135 (the Bar Kokhba Revolt). Thousands died in each, but both ended in Roman victory.

"We Are Among Jews"

Returning specifically to Christianity, I must note a central fact of the entire religion: *The Bible is an entirely Jewish document.* Front to back, cover to cover, A to Z, Old Testament and New—the Bible is an entirely Jewish document. The morality, the theology, the social attitudes, the worldview…all thoroughly Jewish. The Old Testament obviously so; it was written by Jews, about Jews, and for Jews. The same holds with the New Testament, although with a slight twist: it was written by Jews, about Jews, *but for non-Jews.* This twist is crucial to the whole Jesus story.

So let's now look specifically at the New Testament (NT) and the beginnings of the Christian church. Grant (1973: 114) correctly notes that "the earliest church of these years was wholly Jewish." Lüdemann (2001: 4) emphasizes that "it is certain that Jesus was active exclusively in the Jewish sphere." Both men may well have had Nietzsche in mind, who said, "The first thing to be remembered, if we do not wish to lose the scent here, is that we are among Jews".[18] That is, all the characters are Jews, and all the writers—as far as we can determine—were Jews.

Let me start with Jesus. Virtually everything that we know about Jesus' life and teachings comes ultimately from the four Gospels: Mark, Matthew, Luke, and John. Paul is no help here; his 13 epistles (letters) contain almost no factual information about Jesus at all. The other NT letters are likewise useless. So we are stuck with the Gospels. The immediate

---

[18] *Antichrist*, sec. 44 (Ludovici, trans.).

problem is that the Gospels are very unreliable when it comes to factual, historical information. They seem to be a mixed bag—some fact, some fiction, and a lot of story-telling. The hard part is separating the truth from the falsehood.

If we temporarily set aside the various miracle stories, let's assume for now that the rest is factual information. What do we then know about Jesus? The first fact, above all, is that he was Jewish. If the Gospels tell us anything of certainty, it's that *Jesus was a Jew*. In fact, he was a Jew from birth, because both his father Joseph (not God!) and his mother Mary were Jews. Joseph, we read, was "of the house of David" (Luke 1:27), and the Gospel of Matthew opens with a lengthy genealogy leading to him from Abraham, Isaac, Jacob, and Judah. Mary was a blood relative of Elizabeth, of the tribe of Levi (Luke 1:5, 36). Both parents attended Passover every year (Luke 2:41) and both "performed everything according to the [Jewish] law of the Lord" (Luke 2:39). This is significant because Jewishness (in the orthodox view) is matrilineal; if you are born of a Jewish woman, you are a Jew.

Jesus himself is repeatedly called 'Rabbi'—or *ραββί*, in the original Greek of the New Testament.[19] In fact, this seems to be the earliest occurrence in print of the word 'Rabbi'; Jesus, perhaps, was the very *first* Rabbi. He celebrated Passover (John 2:13). He was circumcised (Luke 2:21). The Gospel of Matthew opens with these words: "The book of the genealogy of Jesus Christ, son of David, son of Abraham." Paul certainly thought he was a Jew. In Romans (9:5), he says that his kinsmen, "by race," "are Israelites," and furthermore, "of their race, according to the flesh, is the Christ." And in Galatians (4:4), Paul says that "God sent forth his Son, born of a woman [Mary], born under the [Jewish] law."

Outside the Gospels, we read in Hebrews that "it is evident that our Lord was descended from Judah" (7:14). And there are more signs: Jesus regularly attended the local synagogue (Luke 4:16). He himself told the people that he came "to fulfill the [Jewish] law and the [Jewish] prophets" (Matt 5:17) and called on his followers to "keep the [10] commandments" (Matt 19:17). He even claimed to be the Messiah, the Jewish savior (John 4:26). And of course everyone thought of him as "king of the Jews" (Matt 2:2; John 19:3).

---

[19] Mark 9:5, 11:21, 14:45; Matt 23:7, 26:25; John 1:38, 49; 3:2; 4:31.

Jesus, then, was actually *doubly-Jewish*: he was an *ethnic Jew*, by birth ("of the flesh," as Paul says) and he was a *religious Jew*, based on his beliefs and practices. And the same was true of Joseph and Mary.

At this point, we tend to see one of two reactions: (1) "You're lying! Jesus can't be a Jew! He's the original Christian!" or (2) "Of course Jesus was a Jew; everyone knows that." A very strange situation, actually.

Let me take the second view first. It is true that many theologians and scholars have long accepted that Jesus was born a Jew, and thus, at least, was ethnically (genetically) Jewish. And many of these also accept that his life and teachings were generally in accord with Judaism. Many books have been published with that explicit theme, often focusing on Jesus as a Rabbi; here are some recent examples:

- *Rabbi Jesus*, by Bruce Chilton (2000)
- *Short Stories by Jesus: The Enigmatic Parables of a Controversial Rabbi*, by Amy-Jill Levine (2014)
- *Sitting at the Feet of Rabbi Jesus*, by Ann Spangler (2009)
- *Reading the Bible with Rabbi Jesus*, by Lois Tverberg (2017)
- *The Forgotten Jesus: How Western Christians should Follow an Eastern Rabbi*, by Robby Gallaty (2017)
- *What every Christian needs to know about the Jewishness of Jesus: A New Way of Seeing the Most Influential Rabbi in History*, by Evan Moffic (2016)
- *The Jewish Gospels: The Story of the Jewish Christ*, by Daniel Boyarin (2012)
- *Jesus the Rabbi Prophet: A New Light on the Gospel Message*, by Jacques Baldet (2005)
- *The Wisdom & Wit of Rabbi Jesus*, by William E. Phipps (1993)
- *A Marginal Jew: Rethinking the Historical Jesus*, by J. Meier (1991)
- *The Historical Jesus: The Life of a Mediterranean Jewish Peasant*, by John Crossan (1991).
- *Rabbi J*, by Johannes Lehmann (1971)

Interestingly, more than half of these authors are themselves Jews. It seems that Jewish scholars are anxious to play up Jesus' Jewish origins, far more than conventional Christian scholars—many of whom would prefer to forget it. Perhaps the former want to "claim" the Son of God for themselves, whereas the latter are likely worried about the "bad optics" of Jesus the Jew.

The other response—"You're lying!"—generally comes from people who are ignorant of the details of the Bible, or who are surreptitious anti-Semites who can't abide the notion that their personal savior might be a Jew. Their anger is almost always directed at the writer (i.e., me!) rather than at themselves (for not knowing such a fundamental fact) or at their priest or pastor, who could be blamed for misleading his flock.

But in a sense, the confusion is understandable, given the ambiguity regarding what it means to be a Jew. Jewishness refers to two distinct qualities: *ethnicity* and *religion*. There are ethnic Jews and there are religious Jews, and the two are independent. Ethnicity is a matter of genetics; you are born with it, and it cannot change. Ethnic Jews are Jews for life, and they pass Jewishness along to their offspring. This is an indisputable fact of modern genetics.

Religion, though, is entirely different. One's religion is a matter of choice; it can change from day to day. The Jewish religion—Judaism—can be adopted by anyone: an ethnic Jew or a Gentile. Anyone of any race can, in principle, become a religious Jew. But anyone can also leave Judaism at any time, and it obviously does not get passed along to one's offspring.

Jesus (the man) was born to ethnically Jewish parents, and thus he was ethnically a Jew—for life. All his physical characteristics, including such things as height, facial appearance, eye color, hair color, and so on, would have been consistent with all other ethnic Jews of that place and time. As for religion, from the passages above, we see that he also was raised with, and practiced, Judaism. On both counts, then, Jesus was a Jew. It is true that, in some ways, Jesus allegedly departs from orthodox Judaism; but this issue gets entangled with the hoax thesis, so I will set that aspect aside for now.

What about the 12 disciples (later, 12 apostles)? We know so little about any of them that it's hard to be conclusive, but it seems certain that all 12 were Jews. The mere fact that there were 12 seems to mirror the "twelve tribes of Israel" (Matt 19:28). When Jesus takes the 12 to Jerusalem, he predicts that he himself will be turned over "to the Gentiles" (Matt 20:19), that is, to the non-Jews; Jesus would not speak this way unless his disciples were all Jews. Furthermore, as I noted above, they frequently called him 'Rabbi,' a term that only Jews would use. Clearly, "we are among Jews."

While I am on the topic, let me ask: Who, exactly, were the 12 disciples? That is, what were their names? This is an important question; these 12 men were the closest to Jesus and were his most fervent believers. They spent time with him, spoke to him, and listened to him speak. The reader is invited to take a moment and draw up a list, to see how many he can recall. In my experience, few people can name more than two or three, and many pick wrong names like Paul, Luke, or Mark. And there is a good reason for this: *The Bible itself is confused about their names*. Since we are addressing now "just the facts," let's see what the facts are—that is, what each of the Gospels has to say (or not say) about *the most important men in Jesus' life*, his disciples. Consider Figure 2:

Mark: (3:16)	Matthew: (10:2)	Luke: (6:14)	John: (various)
Simon ('Peter')	Simon ('Peter')	Simon ('Peter')	Simon Peter
Andrew	Andrew	Andrew	Andrew
James (son of Zebedee)	James (son of Zebedee)	James	"son #1 of Zebedee"
John (son of Z.; 'Boanerges')	John (son of Zebedee)	John	"son #2 of Zebedee"
Philip	Philip	Philip	Philip
Bartholomew	Bartholomew	Bartholomew	
Thomas	Thomas	Thomas	Thomas ('twin')
Matthew ('Levi')	Matthew	Matthew ('Levi', tax collector)	
James #2 (son of Alphaeus)	James #2 (son of Alphaeus)	James #2 (son of Alphaeus)	
Thaddeus	Thaddeus		
Simon #2 (the Cananaean)	Simon #2 (the Cananaean)	Simon #2 ('zealot')	
Judas Iscariot	Judas Iscariot	Judas Iscariot	Judas Iscariot
		Judas #2 (son of James)	Judas #2 ("not Iscariot")
			Nathanael

Figure 2: The 12 Disciples (Apostles), by Gospel

I have listed the sources in the order of writing (earliest to latest), according to most authorities: Mark (70 AD), Matthew and Luke (85 AD), and John (95 AD).[20]

---

[20] I will have much more to say on this chronology in Chapter 3. Also, I note here that the book of Acts also has a listing of the 12 disciples (1:13). But given that Acts was almost certainly written by the same author as Luke, and at the same time, it is unsurprising that the Acts list matches almost exactly Luke (except for Judas Iscariot, who, in Acts, was dead by suicide, and replaced by Matthias; apparently, it was *mandatory* to have "12 apostles"—likely to match the "12 tribes" of Israel.)

Note, first, that Jesus' own brother, James, was not among the 12. Either Jesus did not consider him trustworthy, or James was not that impressed with his miracle-working brother—an interesting fact.

Secondly, we see a fair discrepancy as we move across the list, left to right. The first-written gospel, Mark, has a clear list of 12 names. Three of the disciples have two names (Simon, John, and Matthew), which is confusing. Worse, we see in this list *two* 'Simons' and *two* 'James'—strange, but true. I would guess that not one in a million Christians know that the 12 include two doubles.

Third, "John" is evidently not the Gospel-writer John, otherwise that would be clear in the John Gospel. And "Matthew" is not the Gospel-writer Matthew, or that would have been clear from his gospel. Apparently we are dealing, yet again, with doubles: two Johns and two Matthews.

The next two gospels, Matthew and Luke, were apparently written about the same time (both around 85 AD). Presumably, they both knew about the Gospel of Mark—how could they not? It had been around for some 15 years at that point. Matthew follows Mark exactly, though dropping two of the 'second names.' Luke, however, introduces a few changes: (1) Thaddeus disappears, (2) Simon the Cananaean is now Simon the Zealot, and (3) a new name, Judas #2, suddenly appears. Some have speculated that Judas #2 was "really" Thaddeus—but why? Did Thaddeus have an unknown second name? Did Luke know something that Mark and Matthew did not? A mystery.

But now look at John, and we see that it is a total mess. Now we have only nine names, not 12, and they are never neatly mentioned together, as elsewhere. Five names vanish, and yet another new one—Nathanael—is introduced, for the first and only time. This situation is inexplicable, especially if we consider that John was the last-written of the gospels; John presumably knew exactly what was in the other three, and yet he knowingly (or unknowingly?) deviated significantly, on this most-important of topics. No one has ever come up with a convincing explanation for this. It is, frankly, a huge embarrassment for Christianity. It is another clue that "something is up."

We are left with the question of Why: Why did Luke deviate from Mark? (We'll give him a pass on Matthew, which may have been written almost simultaneously.) Why did John deviate dramatically from Mark, Luke, and Matthew? There are only two possible explanations: (1) they didn't know about those earlier gospels, or (2) they knew, but didn't care. Option (1) seems impossible; Christianity was a small movement among Jews at that point, and all surely must have known of each other and of any significant writings. Option (2), though, is bizarre: Why would Luke and John knowingly and deliberately give different information than their predecessors? Were they "correcting errors"? But the Gospels are said to be infallible, the literal Word of God. Were they intentionally creating confusion? If so, why? More riddles.

Paul and the Gospels

In our focus here on the facts, it seems that the next person we know with some certainty is Paul. Paul is a major figure in our story, the key to understanding what happened at that time. I note, first of all, and despite what many people think, that Paul was *not* one of the 12 disciples. He never knew Jesus personally. He was not even a Christian until the year 33, some three years after the crucifixion. His life story is instructive.

Born as Saul in Tarsus (modern-day Turkey) around the year 6 AD, Paul was a Pharisee, an elite, orthodox Jew, "a Hebrew born of Hebrews" (Phil 3:5). He also may have been a Zealot, advocating violent resistance to Rome. Speaking in Acts (22:3), Paul says "I am a Jew, born in Tarsus of Cilicia." He continues: "I was a zealot for God..." (CJB, DLNT) or "I was zealous for God..."—the translations vary. Elsewhere he says, "I was more of a zealot for the traditions handed down by my forefathers than most Jews my age..." (Gal 1:14). There is a subtle difference between him saying "I was a zealot..." and "I was a Zealot..."; the text is not clear, and interpretations differ. But it seems clear that he was an ardent Jewish nationalist opposed to Roman rule, as was the case with most elite Jews of the time.[21]

Saul was not only anti-Roman; he was anti-*Christian*. As a younger man, he "laid waste to the church" (Acts 8:3) and imprisoned its followers. He was even complicit in murder: He consented to the stoning death of the Christian Stephen (Acts 8:1). Even after the crucifixion in the year 30, Saul was "still breathing threats and murder against the disciples of the Lord" (Acts 9:1). At one point he admitted directly that "I persecuted

---

[21] For details of the case for Paul as a Zealot, see Fairchild (1999).

this Way [of Jesus] to the death" (Acts 22:4). This suggests that there was a prominent "Jesus movement" underway at an early point, which is not too surprising if Jesus was a particularly charismatic rabbi.

But Paul had an epiphany in the year 33. On his way to Damascus (now, Syria), Saul allegedly saw an intense bright light in the sky and then heard a voice, "Saul, Saul, why do you persecute me?"[22] It was the risen Jesus, informing him that he was now to be a "chosen instrument" to "carry [Jesus'] name before the Gentiles and kings and the sons of Israel" (Acts 9:15)—in other words, to build the Christian church. So he changed his name from the Jewish 'Saul' to the Gentile 'Paul' (Acts 13:9) and began his work.

For the next 20 years we have no recorded documentation of any kind by Paul. The Book of Acts, which was anonymously written sometime in the 90s,[23] claims that Paul undertook his so-called first journey to Cyprus and parts of present-day Turkey, but the dates are utterly unclear. Acts simply uses phrases like "for a long time" or "no little time," but, oddly, gives no precise dates. We presume it was in the late 40s and lasted perhaps two years.

Starting around the year 50, we do have, apparently, some actual concrete evidence: the first letters by Paul himself. Of the 13 Pauline epistles, the earliest two are Galatians and 1 Thessalonians, both now dated to about the year 50 or 51. This was also the time that he began his second journey, which ran through present-day Turkey, into northern Greece, through Athens, and then back to Jerusalem. Paul's remaining letters appear to date between the mid-50s and the mid-60s.

At some point Paul was imprisoned in Rome, probably around the year 60, and lived there under house arrest for two years. Oddly, this is where his story ends. Acts simply stops at those two years (28:30). It says nothing of what happened afterward, and nothing of Paul's death. This is doubly odd because Acts was written at least 20 years after Paul died; it's almost as if the author ("Luke") deliberately chose not to finish Paul's life story; perhaps it was of no use—or worse, contradictory—to the emerging narrative. Much later, in the 100s and 200s, various writings appeared that claim Paul was beheaded or crucified, possibly in the

---

[22] This phrase is repeated three times in Acts: 9:4, 22:7, 26:14.

[23] As stated above, most scholars assume that Acts was written by the same author as Luke, at about the same time.

late 60s or the year 70. But these accounts are so far removed from the actual events that they have little credibility.

If Paul was dead by the year 70, then he just missed the destruction of the Temple that dealt a shattering blow to the Jewish community. But something else happened around that time, something equally significant: the appearance of the first Gospel, Mark. It's an astonishing fact that, in all of Paul's letters, nothing indicates any knowledge of any of the four Gospels. Surely, in 13 letters, Paul would have wanted to quote his savior or to cite a fact from his biography.[24] But we find nothing like this; no quotes from Jesus, no facts about his past, no virgin birth, no miracle stories. All these are found only in the Gospels. So why didn't Paul ever cite the Gospels? The conclusion is obvious: *They did not yet exist*. And indeed, this is what modern scholarship confirms.

Mark, as mentioned, seems to have been written around the year 70, nearly four decades after the crucifixion. It was the first text to mention any details about Jesus' life, to record his sayings, and to document his alleged miracles. The next two Gospels, Matthew and Luke, were written in the mid-80s. They largely repeated, but also embellished and supplemented, many of the same stories.[25] And John was not written until the mid-90s—a full 60 years after the death of Jesus. These late dates raise many problems for the conventional Jesus story, as I will explain.[26]

In the foregoing, I have presented many dates; the key dates are depicted on the timeline in Figure 3.

The other major problem with the Gospels is authorship. Formally they are anonymous. Mark is "the Gospel according to Mark." It's written in third-person grammar, like a textbook, rather than as the personal account of a specific man. The same is true of Matthew. Luke is different; it's a first-person essay directed to a generic person, "Theophilus,"

---

[24] With perhaps one exception: in 1 Cor 11:24, Paul quotes Jesus referring to the bread as his body, and the wine as his blood. Apart from this, it remains true that there are no quotations of Jesus by Paul.

[25] Mark, Matthew, and Luke are called the 'synoptic' Gospels because of their considerable overlap. They have much in common but also many notable differences.

[26] A few scholars argue for much earlier dates for the Gospels. Pitre (2016), for example, places the first three Gospels well within Paul's lifetime, that is, prior to 62 AD. But he is out of the mainstream.

which simply means "beloved of God".[27] The fourth Gospel, John, returns to the third-person style of Mark and Matthew.

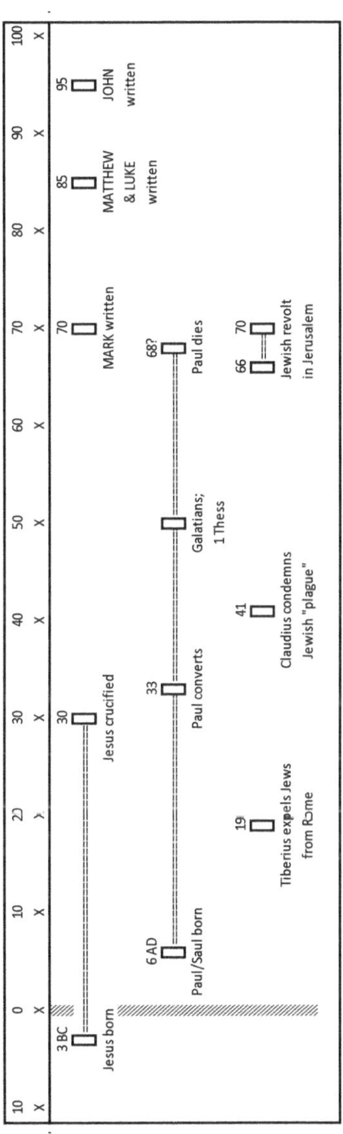

Figure 3: Timeline of Key Events (0 to 100 AD)

---

[27] Acts is the same, which provides strong evidence of common authorship.

Many people assume that each Gospel was written by its namesake, i.e. Mark by someone named Mark, Luke by Luke, etc. But even if true, we have absolutely no information on who these individuals actually were. Some like to believe that "Matthew" was the apostle named Matthew, and that "John" was apostle John, but as I noted above, this is sheer speculation. "Mark," we are told, was a friend of apostle Peter. A "Luke" is mentioned by Paul as his friend (Col 4:14; Phil 1:24), but we have no way of knowing if this is the (later) Gospel author. It's significant that all we get are generic first names, and no biographical details at all.

In any case, it's almost certain that all the Gospel writers, whoever they were, were Jews. All four contain numerous references to the OT, something that would only be expected of elite and educated Jews. Matthew has the most references—something like 43 direct citations. Mark and Luke have about 20 each, John around 15. But if we include indirect references, parallel wording, and other allusions, the numbers triple or quadruple.

Matthew is clearly and heavily Jewish, the "most Jewish" of the Gospels. No scholars dispute this. Mark has been challenged by some writers, calling him, if not a Gentile, then "a heavily Hellenized" Jew— but still a Jew nonetheless. The confusion seems to arise because he was writing to and for Gentiles; this is an important fact, as I will explain. But it doesn't change the Jewish authorship.

Luke, though, is claimed by some to be a Gentile work. But this doesn't hold up to critical analysis. First, Paul himself claims that the word of God was given to the Jews (Rom 3:2) and therefore the Gospel, as the word of God, must have been written by a Jew. Second, the claim that 'Luke' is a Gentile name is irrelevant; other Jews, notably Paul, changed their names upon conversion to the cause. Third, Luke is never cited as a Gentile, and his alleged companion, Paul, is never condemned for fraternizing with such a Gentile. Luke furthermore had detailed knowledge of Jewish religious customs, as we see in (1:8-20); Gentiles would not know this. Finally, he claims intimate knowledge of the Virgin Mary, including what is "in her heart" (2:19)—something that a non-Jew would be unlikely to know. By all accounts, Luke too was a Jew.

But what about the final Gospel, John? This appears to be the most anti-Jewish—some would say, the most anti-Semitic—of the four. This could not possibly have been written by a Jew, true? Not quite. We need to observe an important point here. The nascent Christian movement, occurring entirely within the Jewish community, found substantial internal dissent. Orthodox Jews did not believe that their Messiah had come in the form of this "Jesus," and they strongly resisted any claims to the contrary. In a sense, they wanted to "kill" the Jesus story (we can see where this is leading!). Paul and his small band of Jewish Christians thus had to combat the anti-Christian sentiments of the majority of Jews, particularly the Jewish elite of the day. John, then, reads much more naturally as an account of intra-Jewish squabbling rather than as a Gentile attacking "the Jews."

John is, indeed, heavily critical of the Jews. They "sought to kill" Jesus (7:1). In his Gospel we read of Jesus' own harsh words:

> You [Jews] are of your father the devil… He was a murderer from the beginning, and has nothing to do with the truth, because there is no truth in him. When he lies, he speaks according to his own nature, for he is a liar and the father of lies.[28] (8:44)

But this and other strong language does not indicate a Gentile-written anti-Semitism. There is a compelling argument to be made that this is best seen, as mentioned, as Jewish in-fighting. As James Dunn says, "John, in his own perspective at least, is still fighting a factional battle within Judaism rather than launching his arrows from without, still a Jew who believed that Jesus was the Messiah, Son of God, rather than an anti-semite".[29] John was targeting the Jewish elite, his main adversaries. Michael Coogan agrees:

> Although its scathing portrayal of "the Jews" has opened it to charges of anti-Semitism, a careful reading of the Gospel reveals "the Jews" to be a class designation, not a religious or ethnic grouping; rather than denoting adherents to Judaism

---

[28] Such talk is mirrored in the later Book of Revelation ("to John"), where we read of the Jews and their "synagogue of Satan" (2:9, 3:9).

[29] Dunn (1992: 201).

in general, the term primarily refers to the hereditary Temple religious authorities.[30]

And Delbert Burkett offers this commentary:

> John once appeared to be a Hellenistic Gospel, full of non-Jewish ideas. Now, however, scholars have come to recognize that it arose among a community of Jewish Christians. … Several passages in the Gospel indicate that it arose among Jewish Christians who were being expelled from the synagogue. These [Jews] came into conflict with the larger Jewish community because of their high esteem for Jesus and their rejection of the traditional institutions of Judaism.[31]

Even if the Gospels underwent later modification by Gentiles, as Price and others suggest, this does not change their essentially Jewish nature.

The remainder of the NT also seems very likely to have had Jewish authors. The lengthy Hebrews—which is claimed by some to have been written by Paul—is addressed to Jews and contains at least 36 direct references to the OT. James is addressed to "the twelve tribes in the Dispersion," and so is 1 Peter. It's clear that Gentiles would not be lecturing to Jews about God. The other short letters are ambiguous but contain nothing to indicate Gentile authorship.

At some point, of course, Gentiles did join the church and start writing about it. The earliest Church Fathers were probably Jews, including Clement of Rome (died ca. 100) and Ignatius of Antioch (d. 110). But the second generation of Fathers, which would include Quadratus (d. 129), Aristides of Athens (d. 135), Polycarp (d. 155), and Papias (d. 155), likely were not. Certainly by the time of figures like Marcion, Justin Martyr, Irenaeus, Tertullian, and Origen—in other words, mid-second century to mid-third century—we are dealing strictly with Gentiles.

As an aside, I note here that, by the late 300s, the intra-Jewish squabbling recorded in the Gospels had indeed transformed into true anti-Semitism, by Christian Gentiles directed toward the Jews. Thus we

---

[30] Coogan (2007: 147)
[31] Burkett (2002: 215-216).

witness the harsh statements by the likes of Gregory of Nyssa (335-395), who said:

> [Jews are] murderers of the Lord, murderers of prophets, rebels and full of hatred against God… leaven of the Pharisees, Sanhedrin of demons, accursed, utterly vile, quick to abuse, enemies of all that is good.

Another prominent figure, John Chrysostom (347-407), wrote:

> [The synagogue is] a brothel… It is a den of robbers and a lodging for wild beasts… [T]he Jews themselves are demons.

And then we have St. Jerome (345-420), who said:

> [The synagogue is] a den of vice, the Devil's refuge, Satan's fortress, a place to deprave the soul.

Remarkably harsh words from these "men of God." But we need to recall the theological context in which they were living, and we should note that many Christian parishioners had had run-ins with local Jews, either as moneylenders, merchants, or landlords. Such animosity is unlikely to derive strictly from a reading of the Bible; there had to be many negative, real-world experiences in order to issue such scathing condemnations.

To wrap up this chapter: Paul now appears as a religious fanatic and ardent Jewish nationalist, initially willing to resort to violence and even kill the early (Jewish) Christians. After his miraculous conversion in the year 33 AD, his attention turns to the (Gentile) masses as he seeks to promulgate his new theology. But if Paul was, at any time, a Zealot or even sympathetic with that movement, this means that he strongly opposed Roman rule (like virtually all elite Jews) and was willing to do anything, even commit further murder, to undermine them; that surely did not change, even after his "conversion." Paul knew nothing of "the four Gospels," because they did not exist in his lifetime. The Gospel writers themselves were all Jews, as likely were the anonymous authors of the remainder of the NT. The Gospels as documents were likely written between 70 (Mark) and the mid-90s (John).

With this factual background in place, we can now examine precisely why the traditional Jesus story is not true. Then we will be one step closer to my central argument: namely, that since the biblical Jesus story is false, it was evidently constructed by Paul and his fellow Jews in order to sway the gullible Gentile masses to their side and away from Rome.

CHAPTER 3

WHY THE JESUS STORY IS FALSE

The Bible makes a number of ordinary and extraordinary claims regarding Jesus. The most dramatic of these qualify as miracles: a star appeared in the sky and led men to his birthplace; he was born of a virgin; he walked on water; he fed thousands with a few fish; he healed some two-dozen people; he raised at least three people from the dead; and he himself was bodily resurrected. Such events are the prime basis for believing that he was a divine man, a Son of God, even a god himself. They are the ultimate justification for accepting Jesus as our 'savior' and thus as worthy of a new religion. Without them, he was just another spiritual teacher, one among thousands.

Extraordinary claims require extraordinary justification. At a minimum, they require *some* justification. At a bare minimum, they require *any* justification. In the case of Jesus, unfortunately, we have *no justification*. In other words, we have no evidence for anything like these miracles occurring at all, let alone by a Jesus of Nazareth. In fact we have no evidence that a historical Jesus even existed, until decades after his death. We have no bodies, no tombs, no physical remains, no letters, no engravings—nothing that counts as evidence. *We have no evidence.*[1]

In addition to this, we have documented dates for the various writings of Paul, of the Gospels, and others who commented on the Christians. But these spell big trouble for the standard view. In no sense do these dates align with what we would expect for the appearance of God incarnate. They are not merely 'puzzling'; they strongly suggest that there are drastic errors in their portrayal of events.

So we have two major categories of problems. I will call these (1) the Problem of the Evidence, and (2) the Problem of the Chronology. The first considers that which we do *not* have, and the second that which we *do*. Let me examine each of these problems in turn.

---

[1] Amazingly, researchers may in fact have found at least some of Jesus,' and his mother Mary's, bodily remains; see the discussion below on the Talpiot Tomb.

(1) The Problem of the Evidence

Miracles are funny things. First, they seem to be, by and large, things of the past—the *distant* past. We just don't have miracles anymore. Of course, there are "miraculous" recoveries from illness and disease, and the "miraculous" finding of lost children. But these have entirely natural explanations. Their alleged miraculous nature can never be proven. Rather, I'm referring to the grand and glorious kind of miracles: parting of seas, voices booming out from the sky, the raising of the dead, large-scale physical transformations, storms ceasing upon command. Such things would be very impressive indeed. Yet, for some reason, they just don't seem to happen anymore.

For that matter, we have obvious reasons to doubt that they ever happened at all. Prominent Jesus scholar Gerd Lüdemann grew up as a believing Christian but later came to doubt much of the conventional story, and especially the miracles. Regarding the "miracle stories," he says,

> Today it is generally recognized that numerous words and actions were attributed to Jesus only after his death. ... Today, no one seriously accepts that Jesus in fact walked on the sea, stilled a storm, multiplied bread, turned water into wine and raised the dead. Rather, these actions were invented for Jesus only after his death or his supposed resurrection in order to heighten his importance. (2001: 1)

We would like to know *who* added those words and deeds to Jesus' story, *when*, and *why*.

A second fact about miracles is that, in many cases, they are somewhat like rainbows: they appear, and then they vanish without a trace. Or at least, over the course of time, all possible evidence of them vanishes. It's very easy to posit miracles in the past when all traces of evidence are gone.

Take, for example, the Virgin Mary. How could we demonstrate that she was a virgin when she gave birth to Jesus? We have no hope of proving such a thing, one way or the other. Even if we had her full bodily remains, we could not prove or disprove her virginity. This situation is, of course, very convenient for those promoting the conventional story; it is very useful to be able to make claims that can never possibly be refuted.

Unfortunately, most of the 'Jesus miracles' are of this sort; there is no conceivable evidence that could prove or disprove them. People risen from the dead eventually (I presume!) die again anyway. People divinely healed don't, presumably, have 'miracle scars' or other traces of their miraculous recovery. Physical remains are all but non-existent. In fact, this could almost serve as a definition of a miracle: *that which leaves no evidence*.

The best we can hope for in such cases is *corroboration*: that is, of someone else—an independent, unbiased (or even biased!) observer—acting as a witness. This is not *proof*, but it is at least a kind of substantiating evidence. Each of the 'Jesus miracles' had at least one witness—someone who, in theory, could have written, spoken, or otherwise recorded what he or she had seen. Some of the miracles had many witnesses; some, thousands. There were many, many opportunities for documentation of the miracles. And yet, nothing exists.

Let's take a look at a few of the specific miracles, in order to better understand the problem of the evidence.

Apart from the virgin birth (or rather, virgin conception), the very first Jesus miracle was the Star of Bethlehem. We know the story: a star appears "in the east" and guides three wise men to the manger where baby Jesus lay. This simple story is rife with problems. The first is a kind of chronological problem: Paul never mentions the star, or Bethlehem, or anything about Jesus' birth. The first Gospel, Mark, does not mention the star or the birth; instead, it starts right in with the adult Jesus. The star does not appear in Luke, and it does not appear in John. The *only* place it appears is in the Gospel of Matthew (2:1)—written some 85 years after the alleged event. This fact alone argues against its veracity.

Periodically over the centuries, astronomers and scientists have speculated that some kind of unusual natural event may have given rise to the 'star' story. Meteors, comets, supernova, and planetary conjunctions (two planets so close as to appear as one object) have all been proposed. But if a miraculous star, or luminous body, did appear in the heavens, as an actual celestial event, someone else would have documented it. Ancient astronomers have been doing similar things for millennia. Eclipses have been documented as far back as 2,000 or 3,000 BC. Halley's Comet was documented in China in 240 BC, and again by the

Babylonians in 164 BC. The Chinese documented a supernova in 185 AD, but nothing around the year 0.

There were, however, two plausible candidates. One was a "broom star"—likely a comet—that the Chinese recorded in the year 5 BC, which is quite close to our presumed year of 3 BC. Comets, however, were traditionally a sign of impending doom, not the birth of a savior. The other event was a conjunction of Jupiter and Venus in the summer of 3 BC that persisted, off and on, for nearly a year. But two planets side-by-side, while interesting, could hardly have been an earth-shaking cosmic event.

Furthermore, we have the embarrassingly obvious fact that one cannot "follow" a star, certainly not to any specific point on Earth. Stars, or any celestial object, move throughout the night as the Earth rotates. Your star that is first in "the east" will soon be, perhaps, over your head, and then later to "the west." To follow this star would be to walk in circles. And even if someone were to take a "snapshot" view of a star and move in that direction, that of course could not direct you to any specific place. At best you are simply walking in a straight line. The story makes no sense. Perhaps, as some have said, the entire star incident was a "pious fiction." No harm there, surely—unless it was just the first of many.

The Miracle Men

Let's move now to the specific miracles performed by Jesus. Depending on how we count them, there are something like 36 specific miracles claimed of him—all recorded in the four Gospels. By Gospel, the numbers are:

> Mark: 19 miracles
> Matthew: 22 miracles
> Luke: 21 miracles
> John: 8 miracles

(Note that many overlap, with different Gospels recording the same miracle.)

We can break down the 36 miracles into three categories: raisings from the dead (3), healings (24), and natural events (9). These are all listed in Appendix A.

We note some interesting trends. Mark, for example, has only one raising of the dead—Jairus' daughter. Matthew repeats this. So does Luke, but he adds another: the widow's son. John, for some reason, ignores both of these but comes up with a new one, the famous Lazarus tale. Strange how the most famous raising-of-the-dead story appears not until the very last Gospel, some 60 years after the alleged event.

Mark recounts 13 miracle healings (which include exorcisms). Matthew repeats 11 of these, and then adds four new ones. Luke covers 12 of the Mark/Matthew miracles, but then adds another four of his own. John, inexplicably, ignores *all* the previous healing miracles, but then describes three brand new ones.

It is a similar story with the nature miracles. Mark has five. Matthew repeats these, and then adds one of his own. Luke cover two of the previous ones, then adds a new one. John includes two old miracles, but then adds two new.

What are we to make of this? Did the miracle stories just not quite make the rounds back then? Especially, we recall, since all these documents were written 40 years or more after the crucifixion. Did the writers, perhaps, feel a need to increase the miracles over time, to make the Jesus story just a bit better? Or to take ordinary events and make them extraordinary?

Amazingly, it's not only Jesus who performs miracles. I think many would be surprised to learn that Paul, Peter, and in fact all the apostles have done them. Paul's are documented in Acts. There we read that he makes a man blind (13:11), heals the sick (14:10, 28:8), and even raises the dead! (20:9-12). Paul generally performed "extraordinary miracles" (19:11), and indeed was viewed as "a god" (28:6)—at least by Luke, the presumed author of Acts.

For his part, Peter walked on water (Mt 14:30), healed the sick (Acts 3:7, 9:34), and *also* raised the dead (9:40). Apostle Philip healed the sick (8:7). Figure 4 summarizes the "Apostle miracles."

| | | Citation | |
		Acts	**Gospels**
Paul	causes blindness	13:11	
	heals sick	14:10, 28:8	
	"miracles"	19:11	
	raises the dead!	20:9-12	
	is "a god"	28:6	
Peter	walks on water		Mt 14:30
	heals sick	3:7, 9:34	
	raises the dead!	9:40	
Stephen	signs & wonders	6:8	
Philip	heals sick	8:7	
All	signs & wonders	2:43, 5:12	2 Cor 12:12
	cast out demons		Mk 6:13
	heal sick		Mk 6:13
	signs		Mk 16:14-20
	raise the dead!		Mt 10:8
"the 70"	heal sick		Lk 10:9

Figure 4: Apostle miracles

Generally speaking, all the apostles performed "signs and wonders" (2:43, 5:12), and in Matthew we read that Jesus specifically directed his apostles to "heal the sick, raise the dead, cleanse lepers, cast out demons" (10:8). Quite a task that Jesus has laid at their feet.

Vanishing Evidence

But let me return to the question of evidence. Most of Jesus' miracles were conducted in front of only a small number of people—in some cases, just one. Still, each witness then had an opportunity to tell his story, to write it down, or to engrave something in stone. Imagine the interest today, for example, in finding Lazarus' tombstone: "Here lies Lazarus. Died age 40, raised from the dead by Jesus Christ, died again aged 78"—or something similar. That's not proof, but it would be a compelling bit of evidence. But nothing like that exists.

"But the people back then were simple farmers and fishermen, largely uneducated; they didn't know how to write," says the Christian. Perhaps, but *someone* did know how to write back then, many did, and it wouldn't have been impossible to relate a miracle to a known and trusted writer. But again, not one person did so.

Some of the miracles had many witnesses, the prime example being the 'fishes and loaves' story. Not many people realize that there were, in fact, *two* such incidents. Mark (6:30-44) tells us, first, that Jesus fed "five thousand men" with "five loaves, and two fish." Then a bit later, Mark (8:1-13) informs us that he fed "about four thousand people" with "seven loaves…and a few small fish".[2] Therefore we have 9,000 witnesses to a miracle. Surely some of those people, perhaps many, would have somehow documented the event. Even if they were illiterate peasants, they still knew rabbis or other men who could write. And according to John, they *did* tell such men. He writes that the Pharisees were worried by all the miracles: "What are we to do? For this man performs many signs. If we let him go on thus, every one will believe in him, and the Romans will come and destroy both our holy place and our nation" (Jn 11:47-48).[3] This is revealing: the masses knew about the miracles, the elite Jews knew about them, and surely the local Romans had heard rumors, at least. And yet, no one documented anything.

The point bears repeating. During Jesus' entire lifetime, from, say 3 BC to 30 AD, not one person—not a Christian, not a Jew, not a Roman, not a Greek—wrote *anything* about the miracles, what Jesus said, or what his followers did. *No one wrote anything*. It is as if nothing extraordinary happened at all.

This would be all but impossible if the Jesus story were true. Consider the situation of Pontius Pilate. Here he is, governor of Palestine, located some 1,400 miles from Rome as the crow flies. He has his hands full already with rebellious Jews. He is struggling to keep order, when appears…*the Son of God*, a Jew, who is working all sorts of miracles. Undoubtedly he would be writing furiously back to Rome, asking for help, advice, extra centurions, you name it. The Romans were excellent

---

[2] The two incidents are repeated in Matthew (14:13 and 15:32). Luke and John only record the first feeding, for some reason.

[3] This was after John had documented all eight of his listed miracles.

record-keepers; surely any such astonishing letters would have survived. And yet we have not one. Pilate, at least, knew of nothing extraordinary.

At the same time there lived a famous Jewish philosopher, Philo. He was born around 20 BC, and thus was an adult at the time of the Bethlehem star. He lived well past the crucifixion, dying about the year 50 AD. He would have been the ideal man to record everything about a Jewish miracle-worker and savior.[4] He wrote about 40 individual essays, which now fill seven volumes. Yet he says not one word about Jesus or the Christian movement.

It gets worse. For the next 20 years after the crucifixion, *we still have no evidence*. From the years 30 to 50 AD, not one thing has survived that documents Jesus or his miracles: not a letter, not a book, not an engraving, nothing. Nothing by Jews, nothing by Christians, nothing by Romans—*nothing*. This is utterly inexplicable, if the Jesus story is true. On the other hand, if Jesus were simply a minor insurrectionist who was executed one day, it's not at all surprising that nothing remains. In fact, it's exactly what we would expect.[5]

And yet, it's worse still. We know that, from the year 50, we have a few letters by Paul. These letters are finished when Paul dies by the year 70. Now, of course, his letters cannot count as evidence, because it is exactly his accounts of Jesus that we are trying to validate. Apart from Paul's letters, from the years 50 to 70, *we still have no evidence*. Nothing by other Christians, nothing by Jews, nothing by Romans—nothing.

And still it gets worse. The Gospels appeared between 70 and the mid-90s. But they, too, cannot count as evidence because it is precisely these documents that need confirmation. Apart from the four Gospels, from 70 to the mid-90s, *we still have no corroborating evidence*.

In sum: for the entire period of the early Christian era—that is, from say 3 BC to the mid-90s AD—we have no corroborating evidence from anyone who was not a party to the new religion. Not a shred of anything exists: documents, letters, stone carvings…nothing at all. It is hard to

---

[4] He did live in Alexandria, not Palestine. But by his own account, he visited Jerusalem at least once, and surely had connections and contacts in that famous city.

[5] In fact, we may actually have some of Jesus' physical remains! See discussion below.

overstate the importance of this problem. This fact alone argues for a huge inconsistency with the Biblical account.

When confronted with this damning situation, Christian apologists typically have two excuses. First: "All evidence was lost." Of course this is theoretically possible, but it is extremely hard to believe. A body of material, consisting of surely hundreds or thousands (including copies) of contemporaneous documents citing the miracles of Jesus, some written by friends, some by enemies, some by neutral bystanders, all lost to history. This, despite having countless historians, researchers, journalists, and others searching hard for two thousand years. This is all but impossible.

The second excuse: "All documents of the time were repressed or destroyed, either by the Jews or the Romans." Is it possible that both the Jews and the Romans—*all* of them—were so shocked by the appearance of the Son of God that they both deemed it an unspeakable secret of some kind, never to be written or spoken about? And to have all remaining evidence utterly destroyed? The Jews, perhaps, had something to fear in this Jesus, but they were not so scared that they couldn't push for his execution. And once he had arisen, did they then realize the magnitude of their crime, and vow to say or write nothing? Perhaps.

But the Romans, particularly those back in the imperial capital of Rome, would not have been so intimidated. They didn't believe the superstitions of the Jews, and surely would have placed no weight on any alleged miracles or resurrection. Any panicked letters from Pilate would have been given calm and pragmatic replies. Even Pilate would not have been overly-impressed. Once Jesus of Nazareth was executed, he was done and gone forever. The sheer fact of his crucifixion proved to all Romans that he was no miracle man, no Son of God. There likely would have been a few final 'case closed' letters to Rome, and that was that. Certainly no mass suppression or destruction of evidence. The Romans had no reason to do so.

And it wouldn't have only been government officials doing the writing. Many important intellectuals of the day would certainly have been in a position to document the coming of God. Men such as Petronius, Seneca, Martial, and Quintilian all lived in the immediate aftermath of the crucifixion and would have been ideally situated to write about Jesus' extraordinary life. So too with Philo, the Jewish philosopher, as I noted above. And yet not one of these men wrote a single word about him.

And apart from Romans and Jews, there were many neutral parties who might have commented: Phoenicians, Persians, Egyptians, Greeks—all had no vested interest in the Christian story and thus could have easily written about the alleged miracles. But not one of them did.

I must conclude, then, that neither the 'lost' excuse nor the 'repression' excuse holds any water. It is simply not possible for such a monumental event to have occurred and yet not a shred of documentation from that time remains. The only reasonable conclusion is that no such miracles occurred.

(2) The Problem of the Chronology

Given the above, one could be excused for thinking that there is no corroborating evidence at all for an early Christian movement. But of course, that's not true. There is evidence, along with fairly well-accepted dates. The problem for Christians is that it's not at all what we would expect. Rather than helping, the evidence that we do possess is actually detrimental to their cause. The actual evidence points more strongly toward a 'hoax' explanation.

Recall that the very first documented bits of evidence are the letters by Paul. They date from around 50 AD to his death in the late 60s. Next comes the Gospels: Mark (ca. 70 AD), Matthew and Luke (ca. 85), and John (ca. 95). Paul's dates are to be expected, given that he was the founder of the movement. It does seem strange that his first 20 years are lost, with no letters or other documentation at all. Perhaps most of his early work was local, not requiring letters. Or perhaps he was so unknown that no one felt an urge to save his correspondence. But when his new church began to go global around the year 50, then we should rightly expect to see some documentation—and we do. The Pauline chronology poses no real concerns for us, other than that the letters appear two or three decades after crucifixion.

The Gospels, however, are very problematic for Christians. Consider this obvious question: Why did it take someone nearly 40 years to write down what Jesus had said? Wouldn't that have been the *first* thing someone would have done, once it was clear that he was resurrected from the dead? What about his 11 surviving disciples/apostles (not including Judas, of course)? Each one of them should have been furiously documenting every word, every sound that they could recall from their savior's lips. There should have been 11 well-written, complete, and consistent gospels within a year of Jesus' death. Instead we have—nothing. The 11 men, now apostles, more or less vanish from the face of the Earth. No letters, no books, no engravings, no tombstones, no life histories—nothing.[6]

Then Paul comes along, and he too gives us nothing on the life of Jesus. No—we must wait 40 years after Jesus' death for Mark to document his life history and teachings; forty years after death, and 70 years after birth. By all accounts, Mark never knew or met Jesus. Therefore he got all his information second-, third-, or fourth-hand. If the information was written down, it is lost. If it was not written down, then it was sustained orally, and this is a notoriously unreliable method of transmission. One can easily imagine tales of a charismatic rabbi becoming, after his death, a divine rabbi, then one 'beloved-of-God,' then god-like, then even God himself, as the stories got passed along. In essence, we have no way of determining how accurate Mark is, and good reason to think it is highly altered, perhaps centering around a core of rather ordinary information about a rather ordinary Jesus of Nazareth. The other Gospels, being later in time, are even less likely to be reliable.

But it gets worse. The dates that we have for the four Gospels, cited above, are conjectures based on much later manuscripts and fragments. It's not as if we have an "original Mark" from the year 70, or an "original Luke" from 85. Not even close. The oldest existing portion of Mark is the Chester Beatty fragment P^{45}, which includes about half of the Gospel. It dates to about the year 250. We have no idea how many changes, transcription errors, or other modifications may have occurred in those intervening 180 years. The oldest full copy of Mark comes in the Vatican Codex, which is even later, dating to around 350. So half of Mark underwent unknown changes for 180 years, and the other half for 280 years. And yet we are expected to have complete confidence in this document as the literal word of God.

The oldest fragment of any Gospel comes with Rylands P^{52}, a mere scrap of papyrus that contains a few words from John. It supposedly dates to 125, but this is based strictly on handwriting analysis and not

---

[6] Acts contains a few references to Peter and John, but little of verifiable content.

carbon dating or other physical techniques. The earliest Matthew fragment, P^{104}, again containing just a few words, dates to 175. The oldest
Luke fragment, P^{75}, to around 200. We can see that we have no access to
any of the original Gospels, and all underwent unknown modifications
for decades or centuries.

Enter Josephus

The dating of the Gospels represents a kind of 'internal' chronology
problem. But there is also an external one. It relates to the question of
corroborating evidence from outside the sphere of the church. Above I
showed that, for nearly the entire first century, all we have are Paul's
letters and the four Gospels. And since these documents are the very ones
in question, they cannot serve as their own confirmation. We need something independent, and that's what we do not have.

But then along comes Josephus. Born around the year 37, he became a learned member of the Jewish elite, and like all such elite, he was
a member of the resistance to Rome. He fought in the first Jewish-
Roman war and was captured in 67. Emperor Vespasian decided to free
him in 69 to serve as a high-level slave and translator. In exchange for a
modest freedom, Josephus willingly sided with the Romans, changing his
name to Flavius Josephus. In time he wrote two major books: *The Jewish
War* (ca. 75) and *Antiquities of the Jews* (ca. 93).[7] The former told the
story of the first Jewish war, and the latter gave a history of the Jewish
people.

As an elite, educated Jew living in Palestine just after the crucifixion, Josephus was perfectly situated to comment on Jesus. He would
have known all the stories and legends inside and out. As a writer, he
certainly would have recorded these events in his books.

So, what did he write? His first book, *The Jewish War*, contains
nothing on Jesus or the Christians. Granted that the topic was the war and
not religion, but even so, it would have been difficult to avoid mention,
had he heard about Jesus. The most reasonable conclusion is that, as of
the year 75, he had heard nothing. His void on Christianity is inexplicable

---

[7] A third important work, *Contra Apion*, was composed near the end of his life,
around 100.

if the Jesus story is true, but it's exactly as expected if the early Christian movement, now post-Paul, had barely begun.

By 93, though, things change. Now, for the first time in history, we find independent, non-Christian confirmation of an actually existing Christian movement. In *Antiquities*, Josephus writes one paragraph, and then one additional sentence, on the Christians. Here is the first passage, known as the 'Testimonium Flavium':

> About this time there lived Jesus, a wise man, if indeed one ought to call him a man. For he was one who performed surprising deeds and was a teacher of such people as accept the truth gladly. He won over many Jews and many of the Greeks. He was the Christ. And when, upon the accusation of the principal men among us, Pilate had condemned him to a cross, those who had first come to love him did not cease. He appeared to them spending a third day restored to life, for the prophets of God had foretold these things and a thousand other marvels about him. And the tribe of the Christians, so called after him, has still to this day not disappeared. (Bk 18, Ch 3, 3)

A fascinating passage, to be sure. Here we have all the basics of the Christian story in a nutshell. And yet even here, there are problems. Almost no one accepts that this passage was originally written by Josephus. Rather, the literary analysts have determined that words were added or modified at a later date. But the experts cannot agree on what was changed, when, or by whom. "He was the Christ" seems an obvious interpolation (insertion), but it is very likely that other edits occurred as well.

Unfortunately, like most ancient documents, we have no "original." What we have are copies of copies from much later dates. In this case, the oldest copy of this critical passage comes from the Christian apologist Eusebius, from roughly the year 324. We can only imagine what changed in the intervening 230 years.[8]

Josephus' second passage includes this line: "Albinus...assembled the Sanhedrin of judges, and brought before them the brother of Jesus,

---

[8] The earliest full copy of the book dates to the 1000s.

who was called Christ, whose name was James, and some others" (Bk 20, Ch 9, 1). But nothing more here on Jesus. The reference to a brother James is consistent with Paul's letter to the Galatians: "But I saw none of the other apostles except James, the Lord's brother" (Gal 1:19).[9]

I'll not debate the authenticity of these passages here. For my purposes, it doesn't really matter. It is not at all surprising that, by the 90s AD, there would be a visible Christian movement. But by all accounts, it was small and insignificant, based on the scant space that Josephus allows to the topic (assuming that at least some of those words are actually his; there is a fair chance that none of those were authentic). Of course, it doesn't prove that any of the reported things actually happened; all it shows is that someone *believed* that it happened.

The Roman Perspective

Josephus is important because he is the first non-Christian to confirm that a Christian movement existed, at least by the late first century AD. But what about the Romans? I already noted that Pontius Pilate evidently wrote nothing about Jesus, nor did any other early Roman commentator. Eventually, though, the Romans did get around to mentioning the new religion, including three important writers: Tacitus, Pliny the Younger, and Suetonius. All three briefly commented on the Christians, at about the same time.

Tacitus was born in the year 58 to an aristocratic family. Between 98 and 105 AD he wrote four books, including the highly important work *Histories*. As it happens, not one of them so much as mentions Jesus or the Christians.

But his final work, *Annals*, which dates circa 115 AD, does include two sentences on them. In section 44 of Book 15, we read the following:

> Consequently, to get rid of the report, Nero fastened the
> guilt and inflicted the most exquisite tortures on a class hat-
> ed for their abominations, called Christians by the popu-
> lace. Christus, from whom the name had its origin, suffered

---

[9] Mark (6:3) also mentions a brother James, along with brothers Joses, Judas, and Simon.

> the extreme penalty during the reign of Tiberius at the hands of one of our procurators, Pontius Pilatus, and a most mischievous superstition, thus checked for the moment, again broke out not only in Judaea, the first source of the evil, but even in Rome, where all things hideous and shameful from every part of the world find their centre and become popular.

Nero, it seems, was anxious to blame someone for the Great Roman Fire of 64 AD. Apparently he placed it on a "hated" group, the Christians, "a most mischievous superstition." The passage is likely authentic but yet odd in that we have no other reference to Christians in Rome at the time of Nero, or of Nero actually blaming them for anything. Perhaps Tacitus is recording what he heard or read elsewhere, and was unable to actually confirm it himself.

But this is not relevant here. What matters is the stunning fact that it took until the year 115—80 years after the crucifixion, nearly 120 years after the miracle birth—for the first Roman to document the Christians. And even then, he grants them all of two sentences.

A second Roman reference—and the third non-Christian—comes from Pliny the Younger. Like Tacitus, Pliny was an educated and highly literate aristocrat. By the year 110, at around age 50, he had assumed the position of imperial governor of a province in the north of present-day Turkey. In a letter to Emperor Trajan, from about the same time as Tacitus' *Annals*, he writes an extended critique of the Christian movement. Over the course of about five paragraphs, Pliny explains his need to repress the Christians, including executing the non-citizens and shipping citizens to Rome for punishment. Christianity is described as a "depraved, excessive superstition," and Pliny is worried that the "contagion of this superstition" is spreading. But still, he thinks it "possible to check and cure it." The full passage is reproduced in Appendix C.

Pliny's suggestions aside, what we find here is a fascinating account of a growing but troublesome new religion. The Romans were generally tolerant of other religions, and thus we must conclude that there was something uniquely problematic about this group. It may perhaps have been their Jewish origins, or the fact that they embodied particularly repellent values. We lack the details here to determine the cause of the enmity.

The third mention—consisting of just two isolated sentences in his book *The Twelve Caesars*—is by the writer and civil servant Suetonius, which I mentioned in passing in a note in Chapter 2. The first sentence is this:

> Because the Jews at Rome caused continuous disturbances
> at the instigation of Chrestus, he [Claudius] expelled them
> from the city. (V.25)

The name 'Chrestus' has been the source of much speculation over the centuries; was it a misspelling of 'Christ,' as commonly assumed? Or an entirely different, and unknown, person?

The second sentence comes later, in the chapter on Nero, and recalls (or copies?) Tacitus:

> Punishments were also inflicted on the Christians [during
> Nero's reign], a sect professing a new and mischievous re-
> ligious belief... (VI.16)

One wonders what, exactly, was the "new and mischievous" belief of the Christians. In any case, the common threads among all three commentaries are (a) the early Christians were Jews, (b) they were superstitious, (c) they were troublemakers, and (d) they had to be punished. It seems clear that the early Christians were not simple apostles of love. Something else was going on with this group that the Romans found truly galling and, indeed, a kind of threat to the social or moral order.

Again, it may be helpful to show a simple timeline of these events. See Figure 5 below. We see here, graphically, how far-removed are the corroborating sources: the one (questionable) mention in Josephus in 93, and the Roman citations in 115 and 120. I emphasize that these are the only independent and thus unbiased sources that we have, prior to the year 120, to confirm even the mere existence of a Christian movement or a person named Jesus.

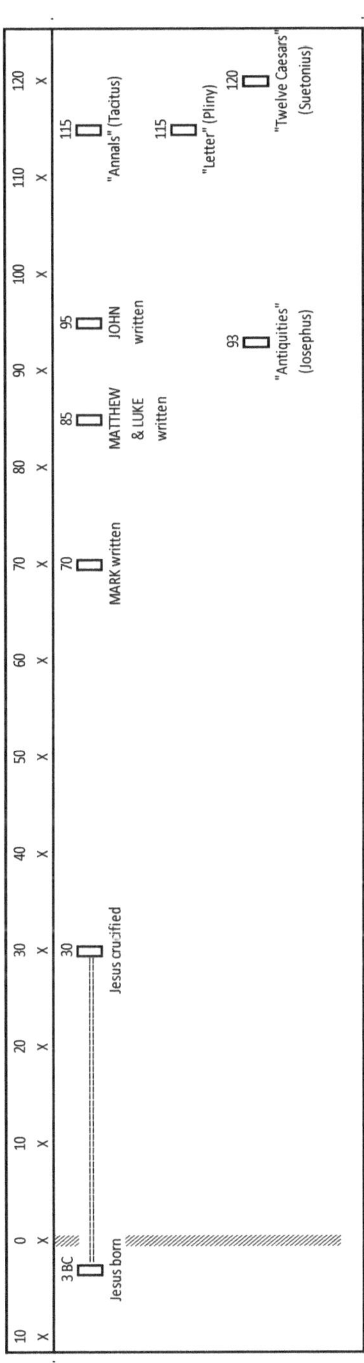

Figure 5: Evidentiary timeline

The Talpiot Tomb

An interesting archeological discovery was made in 1980 in the Talpiot district of Jerusalem. A sealed tomb, roughly the size of a typical modern coffin, was uncovered, and inside were found 10 ossuaries—small boxes containing human bones. Six of the ossuaries had inscriptions on them which were barely legible, yet intriguing. One seemed to say, *Yeshua bar Yehosef* ("Jeshua [Jesus], son of Joseph"). But of course, there were many with the names Jesus and Joseph back then, so this alone proves nothing.

But there were five other names found in the tomb, including *Yoseh* (Joses), *Mariamene Mara* (Miriam 'the Lady'), *Yehuda bar Yeshua* (Judah, son of Jesus[!]), *Maria* (Maria/Mary), and *Matya* (Matthew). These are fairly astonishing; they suggest that perhaps we have the bones of Jesus and his mother Mary. It implies furthermore that Jesus had a son, Judah, who is otherwise totally unknown to history. And if Jesus had a son, then he had a female partner or even wife, who could well be the Mariamene, who some have identified with Mary Magdalene of the Bible. Hence, there is a chance that we have here the physical remains, not only of Jesus, but of several key members in his family, including the Virgin Mary, and Jesus' own previously-unknown son! It is a remarkable find, without doubt.

This whole story is well-documented by James Tabor and Simca Jacobovici in their 2012 book *The Jesus Discovery*. As added evidence in support of this being the actual Jesus of Nazareth, the authors note that 'Joses' is a rare nickname for 'Joseph,' and was rarely found in the ancient world. And yet we read in Mark (6:3) that one of Jesus' brothers was in fact named Joses.

And then we have the 'Mariamene Mara.' The normal ancient form of 'Maria/Mary' is 'Mariame.' The added 'ne' is highly unusual, and apparently represents a term of endearment or special affection. The 'Mariamene' variant is very rare in ancient Christian literature, but appears twice (in Hippolytus and the *Acts of Philip*), both, remarkably, referring explicitly to Mary Magdalene. And the 'Mara' is, according to the authors, an honorific title, something like 'Lord' or, in this case, 'Lady' or perhaps 'Dame.'

What are we to make of all this? Potentially, it is the greatest archeological find in history. But unsurprisingly, the Christian orthodoxy is unimpressed. They are almost uniformly opposed to the 'Jesus tomb' thesis. Tabor and Jacobovici discuss five common objections by the experts: (1) The names are common and thus nothing exceptional; (2) the real Jesus had no wife or children; (3) Jesus was too poor to afford an ossuary and family tomb; (4) Jesus would have been buried in Nazareth, not Jerusalem; and (5) Jesus was bodily resurrected and therefore cannot have left any physical remains, such as bones.[10]

Their replies, in brief: (1) The individual names are fairly common, but this particular combination, which matches so closely to the NT, is extremely improbable; (2) Paul and the Gospel writers either did not know about the wife and child, or more likely, did know but suppressed the facts—in other words, more lying!; (3) a wealthy supporter, perhaps Joseph of Arimathea, provided for the tomb; (4) Jewish law forbid transporting corpses, and so most Jews were buried where they died; and (5) the resurrection was spiritual, not physical. Importantly, all this allows the authors to maintain a kind of compatibility with traditional Christianity. They do not attempt to overthrow the orthodox view, and they do not pinpoint any hoaxers or liars.

More to the point, this entire account meshes perfectly with my Hoax thesis. On my view, Jesus, as an ordinary mortal rabbi, would likely have had a wife and child by the age of 33. But if Paul and friends had decided that they were going to portray him as a celibate divine savior in order to both demonstrate his "purity" and, more importantly, to serve as a model to his Gentile followers—as I elaborate in Chapter 6—then they certainly did not want to acknowledge a Jesus spouse or Jesus child. And since they were largely making things up along the way, it was no problem to erase a child, or to relegate a female partner like Mary Magdalene to an ancillary role.

Most importantly, the mere fact that have (apparently) the *bones* of Jesus shows that he was not bodily resurrected, and that he died and was buried like all other Jews of the time. This is just as I have proposed. And nothing written on the ossuaries suggests that he was a miracle man, Son of God, or any such thing—just as I have proposed. Of course, we do not know if this is, in fact, the true Jesus ossuary, and there seems to be little appetite to find out—naturally, since all parties have little reason to over-

---

[10] See Tabor and Jacobovici (2012: 123).

throw the traditional story and thus to finger some fraudsters like Paul and the Gospel writers. The question remains open. But it is striking that all the archeological evidence that has come to light so far tends to support something like a Jesus Hoax theory, rather than a miracle-man, Son-of-God story.

In this chapter I hope to have shown that the utter lack of expected evidence is damning for the biblical Jesus, and what evidence we do have is equally damning in its own way. As it stands, there is nothing to be said for the Christian side of the story. It's a lose-lose proposition. Therefore, the only reasonable conclusion is that the traditional Jesus story must be false.

And yet, *something* happened. We know for certain that by the mid-90s or early 100s at the latest, that Christians were becoming noticed and causing trouble for the Empire. We are fairly sure that Paul lived and wrote between the mid-30s and late-60s, and that the Gospels first appeared between 70 and 95. The issue now before us is to reconstruct the details regarding what may have actually happened.

But we still have a bit more preparatory work to do. We know that the first Christians were all Jews, from Jesus and Mary down to the apostles and Gospel writers. We know that the Jews had been under pressure from Rome since the occupation began in 63 BC. What we have yet to examine is *why* the Jews were so antagonistic to Rome, the depth of their hatred, and the extent to which some of them, at least, were willing to go to drive out the Romans. Jewish attitudes toward others, and the attitudes of others toward them, need to be made clear so that we can better understand the milieu in which Paul and his band of followers were able to construct such a monumental Jesus hoax.

CHAPTER 4

ONE AGAINST ALL

In the early years of Christianity, Jews were front and center. As I have already shown, the entire early Christian movement and the entire Bible itself were thoroughly and completely Jewish. We have seen how the traditional Jesus story cannot be true, due to the lack of contemporaneous evidence and the many internal and external chronology problems.

Let us now examine, first, how the Jews viewed themselves and others. Then we will take a look at how others—mostly Greeks and Romans—viewed them. An understanding of these attitudes, on both sides, is critical to a proper perspective of the origins of Christianity. Without such knowledge, we can never come to correct and rational conclusions about the nature of this new "religion of love." Hence, this whole topic merits a detailed discussion in the present chapter.

To properly understand the context for Christianity, we need to understand Jewish attitudes. Fortunately for us, Jewish attitudes are clearly documented in the Bible. We can see there, simply by reading the OT text, how they felt about themselves and the other nations—the non-Jews, the Gentiles.

In my analysis, I find two interrelated Jewish characteristics to be central to this whole discussion: (1) the striving for "dominion" or world domination; and (2) misanthropy—a dislike or hatred of Gentile humanity. Both are well-documented in the Old Testament; they are as striking as they are consequential. They have far-reaching implications to the present day, well beyond the bounds of Christianity.

Jewish Attitudes #1: Dominion

Let me begin with the dominion aspect. It is well-known that, at the beginning of the Bible, in the Book of Genesis, we find surprising and telling passages about dominion and control of the Earth. In fact, the first relevant passage occurs at the beginning of Genesis—in fact, on the very first page of the Bible. At Gen 1:26, we read the following:

> Then God said, "Let Us make man in Our image, according to Our likeness; let them have *dominion* over the fish of the sea, over the birds of the air, and over the cattle, over all the earth and over every creeping thing that creeps on the earth." … Then God blessed them [Adam and Eve], and God said to them, "Be fruitful and multiply; *fill the earth and subdue it; have dominion* over the fish of the sea, over the birds of the air, and over every living thing that moves on the earth." (1:26-28)

The passage is clear and explicit, but despite this, some have argued over the precise meaning of 'dominion.' On the positive side, some see it as a call for humanity to be stewards and caretakers of the Earth; on the negative side, to expropriate and utilize every living thing for human purposes. But regardless of whether it is a 'good' dominion or a 'bad' dominion, dominion it is. God has directed humans—or at least, his chosen—to dominate and subdue the Earth.

A few pages later in Genesis, after the great Flood, God speaks to Noah:

> So God blessed Noah and his sons, and said to them: "Be fruitful and multiply, and fill the earth. *And the fear of you and the dread of you* shall be on every beast of the earth, on every bird of the air, on all that move on the earth, and on all the fish of the sea. They are given into your hand. Every moving thing that lives shall be food for you. I have given you all things, even as the green herbs." (9:1-3)

So much for 'good' dominion. Everything is for *us*; everything is our *food*. God gave *everything to us*—or at least, to his chosen.

Just a page later, and Abram/Abraham comes into view. He is clearly God's favorite. God says to him, "To your descendants I will give this land [of Canaan/Palestine]" (Gen 12:7)—or at least, to his *chosen* descendants. Then at Genesis 17:5, God renames Abram as Abraham. God then makes him a promise:

> I will establish my covenant between me and you and your
> descendants after you, throughout their generations for an
> everlasting covenant… And I will give to you, and to your
> descendants after you, the land of your sojourning, all the
> land of Canaan, for an everlasting possession. (17:7-8)

As a sign (God needs proof?) of our commitment, he demands that Abraham's male descendants be circumcised; any who are not circumcised shall be "cut off from his people," and will earn God's disfavor. God elaborates:

> You are to undergo circumcision, and it will be the sign of
> the covenant between me and you. For the generations to
> come every male among you who is eight days old must be
> circumcised… Whether born in your household or bought
> with your money, they must be circumcised. My covenant
> in your flesh is to be an everlasting covenant. Any uncir-
> cumcised male, who has not been circumcised in the flesh,
> will be cut off from his people; he has broken my covenant.
> (Gen 17:11-14)

So now it is clear who are the blessed and chosen: the circumcised. They are the ones promised great things; they are the ones granted dominion over the Earth.[1] A few chapters later, the whole dominion concept becomes much clearer. In Chapter 27, Isaac is speaking to his son Jacob/Israel:

> May God give you of the dew of heaven, and of the fatness
> of the Earth… Let peoples serve you, and nations bow
> down to you. (Gen 27:28-28)

The "nations" refers to the non-Jews—the Gentiles, or in less polite terms, the goyim. They will serve you, Jacob/Israel; they will bow down to you; such is the nature of your God-given dominion.

---

[1] The practice of circumcision seems to have arisen in Egypt circa 6,000 BC, but it eventually became the defining physical feature of the Jews. It was such a clear marker that we have reports of Romans forcing Judaean men to strip naked, in order to determine if they were Jewish.

Moses Takes the Stage

Next we move to the Book of Exodus, where we read of the many travails of Moses. After Moses and his people leave Egypt and reach Sinai, God speaks to him, explaining the special nature of the Israelites:

> You [Jews] shall be my own possession among all peoples;
> for all the earth is mine, and you shall be to me a kingdom
> of priests and a holy nation. (Ex 19:5-6)

God owns the Earth, and the Jewish priests will be his representatives, his "holy nation" here in this world. Some chapters later, Moses speaks to God, confirming the "special status" of the Jews: "we are distinct...from all other people that are upon the face of the earth" (Ex 33:16).

Moving into the fifth and final "Book of Moses," Deuteronomy, we finally get very explicit explanations regarding Jewish dominion. There, God declares:

> I will put the dread and fear of you upon the peoples that
> are under the whole heaven, [the Gentiles] shall tremble
> and be in anguish because of you. (Deut 2:25)

Jewish dominion is to be something dreadful, something fearful. Jewish rule will cause great anguish among the Gentiles. God further promises the Jews "houses full of all good things, which you did not fill, and cisterns hewn out, which you did not hew, and vineyards and olive trees, which you did not plant" (Deut 6:11). These "good things" come from the Gentiles, the goyim, who will kneel before the fearful Jewish dominators.

Then a few chapters later, we read the fateful words:

> [Moses recalls the words of God]: "For you are a people
> holy to the Lord your God; the Lord your God has *chosen*
> *you* to be a people for his own possession, out of all the
> peoples that are on the face of the earth." (Deut 7:6, repeated at 14:2)

If there is any opposition, the God of the Jews will step in and exert his divine wrath:

> Moreover, the Lord your God will send the hornet among them [the Gentiles] until even the survivors who hide from you have perished. Do not be terrified by them, for the Lord your God, who is among you, is a great and awesome God. The Lord your God will drive out those [Gentile] nations before you, little by little. You will not be allowed to eliminate them all at once, or the wild animals will multiply around you. But the Lord your God will deliver them over to you, throwing them into great confusion until they are destroyed. He will give their kings into your hand, and you will wipe out their names from under heaven. No one will be able to stand up against you; you will destroy them. The images of their gods you are to burn in the fire. (Deut 7:20-25)

In sum, says Moses to his Hebrews, "you shall rule over many nations" (Deut 15:6).[2] And indeed, "they shall be afraid of you" (Deut 28:10). Such is the nature of Jewish dominion. Clearly it is not "man" who is to dominate, but "Jewish man," the Hebrew, the Israelite.

The Torah is not the only place in the OT where we learn the ugly truth about Jewish dominion. The Book of Isaiah is especially blunt in this regard. There we read such passages as the following:

- "Those who strive against you shall be as nothing and shall perish" (41:11).

- "Kings shall be your foster fathers… With their faces to the ground, they shall bow down to you, and lick the dust of your feet" (49:23).

- "The wealth of the nations shall come to you" (60:5).

---

[2] Notably, rule through *loan-interest*: "you shall lend to many nations, but you shall not borrow." This has fascinating implications in the present day.

- "Foreigners shall build up your walls, and their kings shall minister to you… that men may bring you the wealth of the nations" (60:10-11).

- "You shall suck the milk of nations" (60:16).

- "Gentiles shall stand and feed your flocks, foreigners shall be your plowmen and vinedressers… you shall eat the wealth of the nations" (61:5-6).

A nice future, if you happen to be a Jew; not so nice, if you are among the other 99.8% of humanity.

Apart from these several passages in Isaiah, there are scattered references to world domination and control throughout the rest of the OT. For example:

- "What is man that You are mindful of him, and the son of man that You visit him? For You have made him a little lower than the angels, and You have crowned him with glory and honor. You have made him to have *dominion* over the works of Your hands; You have put all things under his feet, all sheep and oxen — Even the beasts of the field, the birds of the air, and the fish of the sea that pass through the paths of the seas." (Psalms 8:4-8)

- The Lord says to my lord: "Sit at my right hand until I make your enemies a footstool for your feet." The Lord will extend your mighty scepter from Zion, saying, "Rule in the midst of your enemies!" (Psalms 110:1-2)

- This is what the Lord Almighty says: "In those days, ten people from all languages and nations will take firm hold of one Jew by the hem of his robe and say, 'Let us go with you, because we have heard that God is with you'." (Zechariah 8:23)

I began this chapter with a discussion of the dominion question, and now the Jewish intention is clear: Jews hope and believe that they will "rule the world," and that God gave them the mandate to do so. This is repeatedly expressed in the essential books of the Pentateuch, Isaiah, and elsewhere in the OT. But we can see already that this automatically leads to a superiority complex and thus to a necessary diminishment of the non-Jews. If the Jews are special and different, if they are chosen and blessed, then everyone else is, of necessity, not chosen and not blessed. If Jews are first class humans in the eyes of God, then everyone else is second-class at best. It's one thing to be a ruler over others, but it is something altogether different if you rule with an iron fist. And if one thing is clear, it is that Jews are to rule with an iron fist. Gentiles will live in "fear," "dread," and "anguish." Jews will seize the products of the goyim's hard labor. And if the Gentile kings will "lick the Jews' feet," what can the rest of us expect? It is starkly, brutally transparent: on the OT view, the goyim are lowly, contemptible creatures, fit only for serving their Jewish overlords.

Jewish Attitudes #2: Misanthropy

Such a view has a name: *misanthropy*, or hatred of (non-Jewish) humanity. It was unprecedented in the ancient world, and in fact, the Hebrews seem to have all but invented the concept. Misanthropy is a common thread woven throughout the Old Testament; Jews are special, better, different, 'chosen,' and the Gentiles are something far less. One could call it Jewish Supremacism—the idea that Jews are, and ought to be, superior to all other people. This would be considered reprehensible for any other ethnicity—especially Whites—but here, since it is in the [Jewish] Bible, it passes without comment. And conveniently, the Jews have a ready excuse: *It's not our idea, it was ordained by God. What can we do?* Anyone who accepts that as a valid explanation is beyond hope.

Now of course, we have to be clear that all this is really the Jewish view of themselves. No one believes that God literally came to Abraham or Moses and said those things. These religious documents are a reflection of how the Jews viewed, and continue to view, themselves. They saw themselves as special, different, 'select,' and thus they put these ideas into the mouth of their God, Yahweh. Certainly, no one would deny a people pride in themselves. But these extreme statements go far beyond normal bounds. They indicate a kind of self-absorption, a self-glorification, perhaps a narcissism, perhaps a conceit. To be chosen by the creator of the universe, and to be granted right to rule, ruthlessly, over all other nations, bespeaks a kind of megalomania that is unprecedented in history.

"But what about the Ten Commandments?" says the apologist.[3] "Honor your parents? Do not kill? Do not steal? Do not lie? Do not covet? Where is the supremacy in all that? Where is the misanthropy?" The person who tries to make this argument forgets the first rule of the OT: *It was written by Jews, about Jews, and for Jews.* "Do not kill" means "don't kill a fellow Jew"; Gentiles are exempt from this rule. "Do not steal" means "…from a fellow Jew." "Do not lie" means "…to a fellow Jew." Commandments 9 and 10 are explicit in that they say "do not bear false witness *against your neighbor*" and "do not covet *your neighbor's* house, wife, etc." The Jews' "neighbor" is, naturally, his fellow Jew. Nietzsche understood this clearly: "'the neighbor'—really, the coreligionist, the Jew".[4]

The 10 Commandments are *not* meant for Gentiles; they are *rules for Jews.* The entire OT was not meant for Gentiles, *only for Jews.* Once seen in this light, it changes everything.

Misanthropy: The Testimonies

Clearly, when other people began to encounter these ideas and the attitudes that derived from them, one would expect a backlash. And there was. Hence we find a consistent thread of opinions from non-Jewish observers, for centuries, who were repelled by such arrogance and misanthropy.

The first sign of trouble comes with the very first mention of a people called "Israel." As I mentioned above, archeologists have discovered a large engraved stone, the Merneptah Stele, from around the year 1200 BC that references that nation. The one relevant line is this: "Israel is laid waste and his seed is not." Evidently there existed a people (or person) called 'Israel' at that time; they got into some kind of conflict with the people who carved the stone; and Israel was badly defeated. It is hard to infer much more, but clearly this is an inauspicious start to the Jewish people.

A second ancient, and also negative, reference comes from another stone, the Tel Dan Stele. Carved around 850 BC, this engraving records a

---

[3] See Exodus 20:1-17.
[4] *Antichrist*, sec. 33.

King Hazael boasting of his victory over the kings of Israel and the "House of David." It seems that Israel had invaded his father's country in the past, and Hazael was now exacting revenge. The details are hazy, but it's clear that Israel was once again a belligerent people, and once again paid a price.

Next we shift to the Bible itself, and the story of the Exodus. Early in that book we read that the Jews are still in Egypt, having travelled there at the end of Genesis. An unnamed new pharaoh arises, and he has an issue with the Jews. "Behold," he says, "the people of Israel are too many and too mighty for us. Come, let us deal shrewdly with them, lest they multiply, and, if war befall us, they join our enemies and fight against us…" (Ex 1:10). In general, "the Egyptians were in dread of the people of Israel" (1:12). Eventually the pharaoh drives Moses and the Jews out of Egypt and into Palestine, where they establish the Kingdom of David by 1000 BC.

It should be clear that, even back then, that mass expulsions were an extraordinary event, not to be undertaken lightly. There was evidently something about the Jews—perhaps their arrogance, perhaps their deceit, perhaps, as the pharaoh said, their disloyalty to their host nation—that caused this action. Below I will cite a few later and illuminating commentaries on this particular event.

Another revealing incident occurred in the year 410 BC, in the southern Egyptian city of Elephantine. A Jewish community and temple existed there since about 650 BC, and in 525 BC the Persian king Cambyses invaded and incorporated the territory into his empire. Pragmatic people that they were, the Jews quickly allied themselves with the new ruler, but this had the negative effect of placing them on the side of the foreign invaders and against the indigenous Egyptians. Peter Schafer writes, "the Jews are the supporters of the hated foreign rule and do not join…in the struggle against the oppressors".[5] It was furthermore *only* the Jews who were targeted: "[A]lthough members of different ethnic origin were stationed at Elephantine, it is solely the Jews against whom the Egyptian priests direct their animosity".[6] Despite official directive to support the Jewish community, local Persian commander Vidranga

---

[5] (1997: 134).
[6] Ibid: 135.

found them objectionable and indeed intolerable; he soon sided *with the Egyptian rebels*, against the Jews. Vidranga pillaged and destroyed the Jewish temple in 410 BC. Once again, where the Jews settled amongst other peoples, they seem to have made enemies.

The first outsiders to explicitly comment on the Jews were the Greeks. Through sea-faring trade and imperial expansion they came into contact with many groups of the eastern Mediterranean, including Egyptians, Phoenicians, Syrians, and Jews. The earliest direct references come from Aristotle's leading pupil, Theophrastus, circa 300 BC. He had a concern about one of their customs: "the Syrians, of whom the Jews (*Ioudaioi*) constitute a part, also now sacrifice live victims... They were the first to institute sacrifices both of other living beings and of themselves".[7] The Greeks, he added, would have "recoiled from the entire business." The victims—animal and human—were not eaten, but burnt as "whole offerings" to their God, and were "quickly destroyed." The philosopher was clearly repelled by this Jewish tradition.[8]

Hecateus of Abdera, working at about the same time as Theophrastus, wrote a text: *On the Jews*. Two fragments survive, one by Josephus and the other by Diodorus. Generally speaking, both fragments (and likely the book itself) are sympathetic to the Jews, and thus it's striking that the latter includes this observation on the story of the Exodus: "as a consequence of having been driven out [of Egypt], Moses introduced a way of life which was to a certain extent misanthropic and hostile to foreigners".[9] Here is a remarkable early passage, by a sympathetic author, explicitly criticizing Jewish misanthropy. Above I cited this as one of two central characteristics of the Jews, and we see it here, in writing, in 300 BC already. It is unlikely that Hecateus knew about the OT, but he clearly knew about the Jewish reputation for misanthropic behavior.

It was around that time that the Macedonian general Ptolemy I came to rule Egypt. His military, for various reasons, could not conscript Egyptian citizens, and so a mercenary army was necessary. Ptolemy had a ready supply at hand in the Jews. Gabba relates that the king employed

---

[7] In Stern (1974: 10).

[8] Some have argued that Theophrastus was incorrect in his statement about human sacrifice. Perhaps so; but that was clearly his belief, right or wrong. Perhaps certain Greeks had *false* negative perceptions, but still, they were negative.

[9] In Gabba (1984: 629).

30,000 Jews, chosen from among his many prisoners of war. "Well paid and highly trustworthy, they served to keep the native population at bay, and the natives apparently retaliated against them from time to time"—a situation that recalls the previous events in Elephantine.[10] This, in addition to the cultural and religious quirks, was another basis for indigenous animosity towards Jews. But again, this incident is revealing. It's understandable to want to get out of prison, but one must wonder at the evident readiness of the Jews to side with their enemies, for pay, and to do so enthusiastically, with little compunction.

But there is still a lingering question here: Why were the Jews driven out of Egypt? Egyptian high priest Manetho (ca. 250 BC) tells of a group of "lepers and other polluted persons," 80,000 in number, who were exiled from Egypt and found residence in Judea. There they established Jerusalem and built a large temple. Manetho comments that the Jews kept to themselves, as it was their law "to interact with none save those of their own confederacy." As the story continues, the Jews ("Solymites") marshaled allies from amongst other 'polluted' persons, returned to Egypt, and temporarily conquered a large territory. When in power they treated the natives "impiously and savagely," "set[ting] towns and villages on fire, pillaging the temples and mutilating images of the gods without restraint," and roasting the animals held sacred by the locals.[11] This is a very different version than we read in the Jewish Bible.

Into the Roman Era

The Seleucid king Antiochus IV Epiphanes ruled over the territory of Judea in the early second century BC. Internal Jewish disputes elevated to a general insurrection, which angered him. His army invaded Jerusalem in 168 BC, killing many Jews and plundering their great (second) temple. Greek philosopher Posidonius adds that, upon seizing the temple, Epiphanes freed a Greek citizen who was being held captive, only to be fattened up for sacrifice, and eaten. This was allegedly an annual ritual. He further remarks that the Jews worshipped the head of an ass, having placed one of solid gold in their temple.

---

[10] (1984: 635).
[11] In Stern (1974: 82-83).

The decline of the Seleucids coincided with Roman ascent. Rome was still technically a republic in the second century BC, but its power and influence were rapidly growing. Jews were attracted to the seat of power, and travelled to Rome in significant numbers. As before, they grew to be hated. By 139 BC, the Roman praetor Hispalus found it necessary to expel them from the city: "The same Hispalus banished the Jews from Rome, who were attempting to hand over their own rites to the Romans, and he cast down their private alters from public places".[12] In even this short passage, one senses a Roman Jewry who were disproportionately prominent, obtrusive, even 'pushy.'

Perhaps in part because of this incident, and in light of the Maccabean revolt some 30 years earlier, the Seleucid king Antiochus VII Sidetes was advised in 134 BC to exterminate the Jews. Referring to the account by Posidonius, Gabba explains that the king was called on

> to destroy the Jews, for they alone among all peoples refused all relations with other races, and saw everyone as their enemy; their forbears, impious and cursed by the gods, had been driven out of Egypt. The counselors [cited] the Jews' hatred of all mankind, sanctioned by their very laws, which forbade them to share their table with a Gentile or give any sign of benevolence.[13]

Needless to say, Sidetes did not heed his counselors' advice. Still, it is remarkable that Gabba can admit that "they alone, among all peoples" viewed everyone as enemies. Jewish misanthropy was unique and exceptional.

Two or three decades after Posidonius, around the year 75 BC, prominent speaker and teacher Apollonius Molon wrote the first book to explicitly confront the Hebrew tribe, *Against the Jews*. From his early years in Caria and Rhodes he would likely have had direct contact with them, and thus was able to write from personal experience. Molon referred to Moses as a "charlatan" and "imposter," viewing the Jews as "the very vilest of mankind".[14] Josephus adds the following:

---

[12] Valerius Maximus, *Facta et Dicta* (1.3.3).
[13] (1984: 645).
[14] In Stern (1974: 155-156).

> [Molon] has scattered [his accusations] here and there all
> over his work, reviling us in one place as atheists and mis-
> anthropes, in another reproaching us as cowards, whereas
> elsewhere, on the contrary, he accuses us of temerity and
> reckless madness. He adds that we are the most witless of
> all barbarians, and are consequently the only people who
> have contributed no useful invention to civilization.[15]

The Jews are 'atheists' in the sense that they reject the Roman gods. The
'misanthrope' charge recurs here. But the complaints of cowardice, vil-
lainy, and recklessness are new, as is the statement that the Jews have
contributed nothing of value to civilization. The rhetoric is clearly heat-
ing up.

In 63 BC, as we know, Roman general Pompey took Palestine.
Thus it's unsurprising that we find a quick succession of anti-Jewish
comments by notable Romans. Four are of interest, beginning with Cicero. In the year 59 BC, Cicero gave a speech, now titled *Pro Flacco*, that
offered a defense of L. V. Flaccus, a Roman propraetor in Asia. Flaccus
was charged with embezzling Jewish gold destined for Jerusalem. Strikingly, Cicero begins by noting the power and influence of the Jews:

> You know what a big crowd it is, how they stick together,
> how influential they are in informal assemblies. So I will
> speak in a low voice so that only the jurors may hear; for
> those are not wanting who would incite them against me
> and against every respectable man.[16]

It is rather shocking that Cicero, speaking near the height of Roman power,
should voice this concern—if even as a mock concern.

He continues on, noting that the senate had a long-standing policy
of restricting gold exports, and that Flaccus was only enforcing this rule,
not withholding the gold for himself. Here was his downfall: "But to resist this barbaric superstition (*barbarae superstitioni*) was an act of firm-
ness, to defy the crowd of Jews (*Iudaeorum*) when sometimes in our

---

[15] In Stern (1974: 155). See also *Contra Apionem*, II.148.
[16] In Stern (1974: 197).

assemblies they were hot with passion…" All the gold is accounted for, Cicero hastens to add. The whole trial "is just an attempt to fix odium on him" (recalling present-day attempts to smear 'anti-Semites'). The Jewish religion is "at variance with the glory of our empire, the dignity of our name, the customs of our ancestors." That the gods stand opposed to this tribe "is shown by the fact that it has been conquered, let out for taxes, made a slave."

Ten years later Diodorus Siculus wrote his *Historical Library*. Among other things, it again recounts the Exodus:

> [T]he ancestors of the Jews had been driven out of all Egypt as men who were impious and detested by the gods. For by way of purging the country of all persons who had white or leprous marks on their bodies had been assembled and driven across the border, as being under a curse; the refugees had occupied the territory round about Jerusalem, and having organized the nation of Jews had made their hatred of mankind into a tradition… (34, 1)

The *Library* then includes a retelling of Antiochus Epiphanes' takeover of the Jewish temple in 168—the same event found in the earlier work of Posidonius. But this is no mere duplication; it demonstrates an acceptance and endorsement of that account. Here, though, it is Antiochus Epiphanes, not his successor Sidetes, that was urged "to wipe out completely the race of Jews, since they alone of all nations avoided dealings with any other people and looked upon all men as their enemies".[17] Again we see the idea that the Jews, "alone of all nations," exhibited misanthropic behavior—and this, in an original source from 50 BC.

Upon entering the temple, Antiochus finds a statue of a bearded man on an ass—Moses, the one "who had ordained for the Jews their misanthropic and lawless customs." Antiochus' advisors were "shocked by such hatred directed against all mankind," and therefore "strongly urged [him] to make an end of the race completely." In his magnanimity, he declined.

---

[17] HL 34, 1. Also see Stern (1974: 183).

The great lyric poet Horace wrote his *Satires* in 35 BC, exploring Epicurean philosophy and the meaning of happiness. At one point, though, he makes a passing comment on the apparently notorious proselytizing ability of the Roman Jews—in particular their tenaciousness in winning over others. Horace is in the midst of attempting to persuade the reader of his point of view: "and if you do not wish to yield, then a great band of poets will come to my aid…and, just like the Jews, we will compel you to concede to our crowd" (I.4.143). Their power must have been legendary, or he would not have made such an allusion.

The last commentator of the pre-Christian era was Lysimachus. Writing circa 20 BC, he offers another variation on the Exodus story, placing it in the reign of the pharaoh Bocchoris (or Bakenranef) of 720 BC. On his version, the Jews, "afflicted with leprosy, scurvy, and other maladies," sought refuge in Egyptian temples. The oracles advised Bocchoris to cleanse the temples, to banish the impious and impure, and "to pack the lepers into sheets of lead and sink them in the ocean"—which he did. The exiled ones, led by Moses, were instructed to "show goodwill to no man," to offer "the worst advice" to others, and to overthrow any temples or sanctuaries they might come upon. Arriving in Judea, "they maltreated the population, and plundered and set fire to the [local] temples." They then built a town called Hierosolyma (Jerusalem), and referred to themselves as Hierosolymites.[18] If indeed they persecuted the indigenous population, one can see in this a distant predecessor to the current Israeli atrocities in Palestine.

But I must emphasize here the exceptional nature of the charge of misanthropy, especially in light of its importance for the Christian story. It has recurred several times already—in Hecateus, Posidonius, Molon, Diodorus, and now Lysimachus. This is striking because the Romans were notably tolerant of other sects and religions, owing in part to their polytheistic worldview. A society of many gods implicitly recognizes religious diversity; if there are many such godly beings, who can claim complete knowledge of the divine realm? Monotheism, by contrast, claims exclusive and absolute knowledge; it has *one God* and *one truth*. Therefore, other religions with other god(s) are necessarily false. Thus, it

---

[18] In Stern (1974: 384-385).

is reasonable to assume that the Jews, as the first monotheists of the Middle East, did not reciprocate Roman tolerance.

This in fact seems to have been a general rule throughout history: religious intolerance derives from the monotheistic fundamentalists (Jews, Christians, Muslims), not the polytheists or religious pluralists. In the case of the Jews, though, monotheistic arrogance was combined with racial distinctness and other cultural characteristics, resulting in a deeply-embedded misanthropic streak, one that likely sanctioned abusive and brutal treatment of Gentiles.

And lest we think that this was merely some age-old custom, long since overcome, we need only listen to the words of present-day orthodox Jews. Consider a recent statement by leading orthodox Rabbi, Yosef, who said, "Goyim [non-Jews] were born only to serve us. Without that, they have no place in the world—only to serve the people of Israel. They will work, they will plow, they will reap. We will sit like an effendi and eat" (*Jerusalem Post*, 18 Oct 2010). It would be difficult to find a cruder statement of Jewish misanthropy. It is persistent, it is entrenched, and it is widespread.

Romans of the Christian Era

This brings us directly to our period of interest: the Christian Era. We are nearly ready to start piecing together a picture of what likely *really* happened back then, based on all available evidence. But before doing so, let me follow this thread a bit further, well into the Christian Era, to better flesh out this sketch of ancient views of Jews and (now) Christians.

The turn of the millennium was significant on several counts. Rome had formally become an empire under Augustus, as of 27 BC. Jesus of Nazareth was (allegedly) born in 3 BC. Jewish philosopher Philo was active at this time, as was perhaps the most infamous 'anti-Semite' of that age, Apion. Apion's notoriety derives not so much from his accusations—which, for the most part, were preexisting ones—but instead for his renown amongst the upper classes of Alexandrian society, and because Josephus elected to title one of his own books *Against Apion*. A sample of the criticisms laid by Apion in his book *Against the Jews* includes:

- the leprosy-ridden Exodus story;
- an etymology of the Jewish term 'Sabbath' that derives from 'tumors of the groin';
- numerous tales of Jewish foolishness or naiveté;
- well-deserved mistreatment by Cleopatra (withholding of corn during a regional famine, and various conflicts with the Jewish king Herod);
- Jews' failure to erect statues of the emperors;
- tendency "to show no goodwill to a single alien, above all to Greeks" (misanthropy);
- unjust laws;
- sedition (against Rome);
- "erroneous" religious practices;
- failure to produce any geniuses in the arts or crafts;
- not eating pork;
- circumcision.

Again, little in the way of original criticisms, but apparently sufficiently influential to warrant a refutation by Josephus.

Additionally, there were solid, objective reasons for the Roman public to be wary in that first century. With the Roman incorporation of Judea in 63 BC, Jews flocked to the imperial capitol in ever-greater numbers. Once again, the authorities took action. Emperor Tiberius expelled them in the year 19 AD:

> He abolished foreign cults, especially the Egyptian and Jewish rites, compelling all who were addicted to such superstitions to burn their religious vestments… Jews [and] others of the same race were expelled from the city, and threatened with slavery if they defied the order.[19]

The expulsion did not succeed. Eleven years later, as we recall from Chapter Two, Sejanus found reason to oppose them again.

---

[19] As recorded by Suetonius, *The Twelve Caesars*, III, 36. See also Stern (1980: 112-113).

Back in Rome, anti-Jewish actions continued. In 49, Claudius once again had to expel them. In a fascinating line from Suetonius circa the year 120, we find mention of one 'Chrestus' (Latin: *Chresto*) as the leader of the rabble; this would be perhaps the fourth non-Jewish reference to Jesus. "Because the Jews at Rome caused continuous disturbances at the instigation of Chrestus, [Claudius] expelled them from the city".[20] This is an important observation that, even at that late date, the Romans still identified Christianity with the Jews.

Despite all this, the beleaguered tribe still earned no sympathy. The great philosopher Seneca commented on them in his work *On Superstition*, circa 60. He was appalled not only by their 'superstitious' religious beliefs, but more pragmatically with their astonishing influence in Rome and around the known world, despite repeated pogroms and banishments. Seneca first derides the Jews as lazy because they dedicate every seventh day to God: "their practice [of the Sabbath] is inexpedient, because by introducing one day of rest in every seven they lose in idleness almost a seventh of their life…"[21] "Meanwhile," he adds,

> the customs of this accursed race (*sceleratissima gens*) have gained such influence that they are now received throughout all the world. The vanquished have given laws to their victors.

Seneca is clearly indignant at their reach.

Then came the historic Jewish revolt in Judea, during the years 66 to 70, culminating in a crushing Roman victory. The Romans were surely gratified; to their mind, the Jews received their just deserts.

Tacitus and the Second Century AD

The second century of the Christian era saw a continued string of critical comments, for the most part reiterations of past complaints that were evidently still valid. Quintilian (circa 100) observed that, just as cities can bring together and exacerbate the problem of social undesirables, so too

---

[20] *Twelve Caesars*, V, 25. See also Stern (1980: 113).
[21] In Stern (1974: 431).

Moses knit together scattered individuals into a single Jewish tribe: "founders of cities are detested [when] concentrating a race which is a curse (*perniciosam*) to others, as for example the founder of the Jewish superstition".[22] Additionally, Damocritus' book *Peri Ioudaion* (On the Jews) remarked that "they used to worship an asinine golden head, and that every seventh year they caught a foreigner and sacrificed him"[23]—in contrast to the story by Posidonius in which the sacrifice was an annual event.

This brings us once again to Tacitus. In the previous chapter I quoted his early remarks on Christianity—the first, in fact, by any Roman commentator. There I cited his late work *Annals*, but here it is his other main work, *Histories*, that is relevant. In Book V, Tacitus recounts historical events from the year 70 AD. Roman general Titus had been sent to subjugate Judea once and for all. He found allies in the indigenous Palestinians, "who hated the Jews with all that hatred that is common among neighbors" (5.1). The enmities of that region are deep-seated.

Tacitus then breaks off the narrative to give an account of the origin of the Jews—that "race of men hateful to the gods" (*genus hominum invisium deis*). He offers two or three variations, apparently siding with Manetho. The religion of Moses, he adds, is diametrically opposed to that of the Romans: "The Jews regard as profane all that we hold sacred; on the other hand, they permit all that we abhor." He continues:

> Whatever their origin, these rites are maintained by their antiquity: the other customs of the Jews are base and abominable (*sinistra foeda*), and owe their persistence to their depravity. For the worst rascals among other peoples…always kept sending tribute and contributions to Jerusalem, thereby increasing the wealth of the Jews; again, the Jews are extremely loyal toward one another, and always ready to show compassion, but toward every other people they feel only hate and enmity (*hostile odium*).

"As a race," he adds, "they are prone to lust," and have "adopted circumcision to distinguish themselves from other peoples" (5.5). Tacitus notes

---

[22] In Stern (1974: 513).
[23] In Stern (1974: 531).

their abstract monotheism, suggesting that this is yet another cause of friction. He closes the section with the comment that "the ways of the Jews are preposterous (*absurdus*) and mean (*sordidus*)."

In besieging Jerusalem, and consequently the mighty Jewish temple, Titus had the Jews trapped. There was thought of sparing the temple, but Titus opposed this option. For him, "the destruction of this temple [was] a prime necessity in order to wipe out more completely the religion of the Jews and the Christians." These two religions, "although hostile to each other, nevertheless sprang from the same sources; the Christians had grown out of the Jews: if the root were destroyed, the stock would easily perish".[24] The passage closes by noting that 600,000 Jews were killed in the war.

Such are his comments on the "obnoxious and superstitious race" (*gens superstitioni obnoxia*; 5.13)—a group who are the "most despised" (*despectissima*) of subjects and "the basest of peoples" (*taeterrimam gentum*; 5.8).

The second Jewish war, in 115, gave further cause for critique. Cassius Dio describes the Jewish brutality graphically in his *Roman History*:

> Meanwhile the Jews in the region of Cyrene had put a certain Andreas at their head, and were destroying both the Romans and the Greeks. They would eat the flesh of their victims, make belts for themselves of their entrails, anoint themselves with their blood, and wear their skins for clothing; many they sawed in two, from the head downwards; others they gave to wild beasts, and still others they forced to fight as gladiators. (Bk 68.32)

The third and final Jewish uprising occurred just a few years later, in 132. The reasons for this were many, but two stand out: the construction of a Roman city on the ruins of Jerusalem, and Emperor Hadrian's banning of circumcision: "At this time the Jews began war, because they were forbidden to practice genital mutilation (*mutilare genitalia*)".[25]

---

[24] These last two quotations are from a supplemental work now called *Fragments of the Histories*. Its date is uncertain.
[25] *Historiae Augustae*, 14. See also Stern (1980: 619).

Dio describes the conflict in detail. "Jews everywhere were showing signs of hostility to the Romans, partly by secret and partly overt acts".[26] They were able to bribe others to join in the uprising: "many outside nations, too, were joining them through eagerness for gain, and the whole earth, one might almost say, was being stirred up over the matter." For those today who argue that Jews were perennially the cause of wars, this would provide some early evidence. Hadrian sent one of his best generals, Severus, to put down the insurgency. Through a slow war of attrition, "he was able…to crush, exhaust, and exterminate them. Very few of them in fact survived."

Two final figures close out the second century. Famed astronomer Ptolemy was also a bit of an astrologer, and took to using the stars to explain earthly conditions. In his *Apotelesmatica* of 150 AD, Ptolemy observes that the tribes of Palestine, including Idumaea, Syria, Judea, and Phoenicia, have some common characteristics.

> These people…are more gifted in trade and exchange; they are more unscrupulous, despicable cowards, treacherous, servile, and in general fickle, on account of the stars mentioned. [The Judaeans in particular] are in general bold, godless, and scheming. (II, 3)[27]

Given the four centuries of conflict with the people of that region, Ptolemy can hardly be blamed for viewing them as cursed by the heavens.

Finally we have Celsus, a Greek philosopher who composed a text, *The True Word*, sometime around 178. The piece is striking as an extended and scathing critique of the increasingly prominent Christian sect. Celsus' main target is clearly Christianity, but in the process, he makes a number of remarks on the Jews—all negative. Beginning with Moses, the Jews "were deluded by clumsy deceits into thinking that there was only one God" (I.23). They were "addicted to sorcery" and thus "fell into error through ignorance and were deceived." Celsus mocks "the race of Jews and Christians," comparing them all "to a cluster of bats or ants coming out of a nest, or frogs holding council round a marsh, or worms

---

[26] *Roman History* 69.13.
[27] See also Stern (1980: 165).

assembling in some filthy corner, disagreeing with each other about which of them are the worse sinners" (IV.23). "The Jews," he adds, "were runaway slaves who escaped from Egypt; they never did anything important, nor have they ever been of any significance or prominence." Fate has been justifiably harsh to them, and they are "suffering the penalty of their arrogance" (V.41).

Judeo-Christian theology, says Celsus, is a mish-mash of mythology and absurdity. "The God of the Jews is accursed" because he created, or allowed, evil in the world—a classic statement of the Problem of Evil.[28] The cosmogony of Genesis is ridiculous, as is the creation story of mankind; "Moses wrote these stories because he understood nothing... [He] put together utter trash" (VI.49). In the long run Jewry is doomed—"they will presently perish" (VI.80).

Cherry-Picking? The Hunt for Contradictory Evidence

So what can we conclude from this brief overview of some 600 years of the ancient world? To say that the Jews were disliked is an understatement. The critiques come from all around the Mediterranean region, and from a wide variety of cultural perspectives. And of the comments that express an opinion (as opposed to mere statement of fact), they are virtually all negative. I note here that it's not a case of 'cherry-picking' the worst comments and ignoring the good ones. The remarks are nearly all negative; positive opinions on the Jews or early Christians are few and far between.[29]

A reasonable conclusion is that there is something about the Jewish culture that inspires widespread disgust and hatred. As the saying goes, "When one person hates you, it's probably them; when everyone hates you, it's probably you." Arrogance, insularity, superstition, self-absorption, and misanthropy surely all play a part. Monotheism is also a likely contributor, though indirectly.

The vast, negative commentary on Jews throughout the ancient world is accepted as fact by nearly all researchers, both Jewish and Gentile.

---

[28] Recall my brief discussion in chapter one.

[29] One need only peruse the 3-volume work by M. Stern, *Greek and Latin Authors on Jews and Judaism*, to see a complete list of all ancient commentaries, and to then determine the percentage of positive and negative remarks.

Jewish scholars tend to view this as a result of the widespread contagion of some anti-Semitic 'virus,' or as a sign of some inexplicable form of mental illness; never do they attribute such views to Jewish actions or behavior. Gentile scholars tend to dismiss this history with a slightly embarrassed wave of the hand and a quick sweeping under the rug; John Crossan (1991: 418), for instance, briefly addresses "what Jews were saying about Gentiles and Gentiles about Jews" in ancient times and he notes, "it is not always nice reading—in either direction." Enough said, for Mr. Crossan; no need to get into that sticky wicket.

But still, the question remains: Are all ancient commentaries negative, or are there some—or perhaps just as many, or maybe even more— positive ones? In my research, I have found only one academic scholar who even attempted to make the claim that ancient commentators had nice things to say about Jews: Louis Feldman, a now-deceased orthodox Jewish academic who taught at Yeshiva University in New York. His lifelong work is summarized in his book *Jew and Gentile in the Ancient World* (1993), and which attempts to defend the idea that "Judaism elicited strongly positive and not merely unfavorable responses from the non-Jewish population" of antiquity.[30] But does he succeed? A look at his book shows a substantial amount of preliminary and peripheral discussion, such that only one chapter—Chapter 7: "Attractions of the Jews: The cardinal virtues"—contains relevant and specific quotations. Let me, therefore, briefly run through his strongest claims from that chapter, in order to determine if my above quotations need to be balanced by philosemitic views.

Feldman's chapter centers on the four classic virtues of antiquity: wisdom, courage, temperance, and justice. These can be found, explicitly, in Plato's *Republic*, circa 375 BC. He then throws in a fifth virtue, piety. He proceeds to run through a list of ancient quotations defending the five virtues in the Jews; half of the chapter is dedicated to 'wisdom', and half to the remaining four. But more importantly, Feldman includes quotations issued by ancient Jews (mostly, Josephus) as well as by the non-Jews—but it is precisely the non-Jewish view that is in question here. Jewish opinions are all but worthless. It is no surprise that ancient Jews had good things to say about their fellow Jews. And yet Feldman

---

[30] For his earlier efforts, see Feldman (1958; 1988; 1991).

treats these equally to the others. Thus, for present purposes, we can essentially dismiss half of his chapter as unremarkable and irrelevant.[31]

So let's look at the half that remains and pull out the strongest positive claims, starting with 'wisdom.' Feldman begins with the assertion that the great philosopher Pythagoras was an "admirer" (p. 201) of the Jews. But his only evidence is from the writings of the Jew Josephus, working some 600 years later. Josephus cites an obscure but real philosopher, Hermippus of Smyrna, who allegedly said that Pythagoras "introduced many points of Jewish law into his philosophy." This quotation is found nowhere else, and we know for certain that Josephus takes great pains—and even fabrications—to construct a rosy history of his Jewish people.[32] Thus the passage, which is only implicitly positive, cannot be trusted. This is typical of Feldman's "evidence" for Jewish virtues.

The next compliment, such as it is, comes from Theophrastus—the same man cited above in his critique of Jewish human sacrifice. In the same passage, Theophrastus refers to the Jews as "philosophers by race" (or "by birth"), which Feldman takes as a positive remark. He then cites a Christian Father, Clement of Alexandria (circa 200 AD), who claimed that the wisdom of Greek philosophy could also be found in the Hindus and the Jews.[33] But this again is dubious because the Christian Fathers had a strong incentive to find "wisdom" in the Jewish Old Testament and to devalue the "pagan" wisdom of the Greeks. And this is not to mention that Greek philosophy was put down on paper in the 400s and 500s BC, whereas the OT is not known to be documented before 270 BC; if anything, it is far more likely that the Jews drew from the Greeks than vice versa.[34] In sum, neither Jewish nor Christian sources can be trusted to provide accurate and unbiased claims about Jews.

Moving to Hecateus—again, cited above—Feldman cites a passage in which Hecateus refers to Jewish priest Ezechias as "an able speaker";

---

[31] Seven of 14 sections in the chapter are dedicated to quotations by Jews.

[32] In his *Against Apion* (I.176-183), Josephus invents an entirely fictious meeting between Aristotle and a "learned Jew," simply in order to impute a Jewish influence on the great philosopher.

[33] *Stromata*, book I, chapter 15.

[34] This is the precise contention of Russell Gmirkin; see his book *Berossus and Genesis, Manetho and Exodus.*

this Feldman sees as "a great compliment." Hardly; and even so, does this really provide any insight about the Jewish people?

Other of Feldman's "complimentors" are utterly obscure and likely fictious people. He cites pseudo-Lucanus, pseudo-Longinus, and pseudo-Ecphantus (p. 204), all who are claimed to "paraphrase Genesis" in their writings; again, this is what passes for laudatory remarks about Jews. Next we have the (real) Roman historian Pompeius Trogus, who "pays enormous tribute" to the biblical Joseph, calling him an "extraordinary talent" and "shrewd." Joseph, we might recall, allegedly conned his way into power in Egypt, exploited the masses, and accrued vast wealth in the process; we can call this "talent" and "shrewdness" if we like, but it certainly is no compliment.

Another criticism of the Jews, cited above, is that they have contributed nothing useful to society—with the implication that they are mere leeches, drawing off the creative powers of non-Jews. But even here, Feldman finds a silver lining. Rather than denying that the Jews have done nothing of importance, he turns it into a virtue: "lack of inventiveness" is "a laudatory trait in Herodotus"—the Greek historian who supposedly said of the ancient Egyptians that (according to Feldman) "no change had taken place in their nature, manners, or customs".[35] So he distorts the words of Herodotus to benefit the Jews. Feldman then adds that Plutarch wrote of the Spartans' outlook: "Foreigners inevitably bring with them into a country foreign notions, novel ideas lead to novel choices, and these in turn are bound to cause the development of a number of feelings and inclinations which clash with the euphony [harmony], as it were, of the existing political system".[36] An interesting quote, but again, nothing that can transform Jewish non-inventiveness into a virtue. Feldman, it seems, is a master of turning historical lemons into philosemitic lemonade.

Feldman continues on, in similar fashion, for several pages:

---

[35] In reality, Herodotus said "nothing in Egypt was altered at these times [the past 11,000 years]—nothing growing in the earth or living in the river was any different, and there was no change in the course of diseases or in the ways people died" (II.142). How this translates into a Jewish virtue is a mystery.
[36] *Greek Lives*, Lycurgus, 27.

- Comments by Emperor Hadrian that all synagogue chiefs were also astrologers "might very well be regarded as a compliment" (p 214).

- One Vettius Valens referred to "the first Jew, Abraham" [?] as "most wonderful"—though of course, Abraham was the precursor of several peoples, not only Jews, as we have seen.

- Pausanias referred to "a Hebrew Sibyl named Sabbe, who is said to have given oracles," and simply to name her as a Hebrew, says Feldman, "adds to her praise."

- The Greek philosopher Numenius (circa 200 AD) asserted a connection between Plato and Moses, and wrote "What is Plato but Moses speaking in Attic Greek?" This, says Feldman, is "a great tribute paid to the Jews" (p. 215). But it wrongly assumes that (a) Moses was an actual person, (b) an actual connection exists between the two, and (c) Moses' ideas preceded Plato's. And as before, the source for this is the highly dubious *Stromata* of Clement, the Christian Father.

- Diogenes Laertius says that "some unspecified writers trace the Jews back to the same origins [i.e. the Magi]. This is a great tribute because the Magi were revered as wise men par excellence" (pp. 215-216). Unspecified writers?

- The anti-Semite Apion first criticized Jews as blind, lame, and diseased, and yet elsewhere he accepts that, in their Exodus, they traveled the harsh journey to Judea in only six days. Therefore, says Feldman, Apion "is actually complimenting the strength and courage of the Israelites" (p. 221). Again, lemons into lemonade; can anyone really see this as complimentary?

- By a similar distorted logic, Feldman turns that great critic of the Jews, Tacitus, into an admirer: Of the siege against Jerusalem, Tacitus stated that the Jews were fanatical fighters, showing "equal stubbornness on the part of men and women... [T]hey were more fearful of life than death." This "contempt for death" (Feldman) is turned into a virtue because certain Stoics had argued that death is nothing to fear.

- But "the greatest tribute…to the high ethical standards of the Jews," says Feldman, "is paid by Emperor Severus," circa 230 AD, who occasionally recalled sayings "from certain Jews or Christians." Severus allegedly expressed a version of the Golden Rule: "What you do not wish done to yourself, do not do to another" (p. 227). Feldman attributes this rule to Hillel the Elder, a Jewish scholar who lived around the time of Jesus; and therefore, it is yet another "compliment." But Feldman forgets (or ignores) that the "Golden Rule" actually dates back to Plato; if anything, Severus was praising Plato, not the Jews.[37]

"In sum," says Feldman, optimistically, "intelligent observers in antiquity would have found much to admire in Judaism—and in particular, in the great figures of the Bible as paragons of the cardinal virtues so dear to the ancients" (p. 232). *Would* have, *might* have…but did not. Obviously, one is bound to find a handful of marginally complimentary remarks, but that in no sense outweighs or offsets the overwhelmingly negative assessment by a large number of major critics. The reader is invited to read through Feldman's Chapter 7, and indeed his entire book; one finds almost exclusively such 'stretched,' implied, or imputed remarks as I have shown above. And this, I emphasize, is the *sole* researcher to claim positive remarks in ancient times.[38]

Thus, I think it is clear that the Jews had few if any friends in the ancient world. Their religion instructed them to despise others (the Gentiles), and others in turn despised them. But the originating source was the Jews themselves: their religion, their worldview, their values. They believed that God promised them dominion over the Earth. They were

---

[37] Plato: "no one should touch my property or tamper with it…; and if I am sensible, I shall treat the property of others with the same respect" (*Laws*, XI, 913a).
[38] The entire book can be found here: https://library.mibckerala.org/lms_frame/ eBook/Jew and Gentile, in the Ancient - Louis H. Feldman.pdf

willing to use and exploit non-Jews for their own purposes. And they were willing to kill, and to die, to achieve their ends.

This situation feeds directly into the circumstances of the Roman occupation and Paul's reaction. The preceding analysis suggests that Paul was interested in nothing other than saving 'Israel,' the Jewish people. We have seen a few textual clues indicating that he was willing even to commit murder in order to further his ends. Surely he hated the Romans with a vengeance, and yet he also could see the futility of confronting them directly. The violent Zealot movement would surely be crushed, as would any Jewish uprising. Something much more subtle and clever, something more intellectual, perhaps even spiritual, would be required to undermine their position of power.

In the next chapter I will lay out my vision of the truth—of what I believe actually happened back in those murky days of the ancient Middle East.

CHAPTER 5

RECONSTRUCTING THE TRUTH

"They say they are Jews, but they are liars."
Revelation (3:9)

"Pay no attention to those Jewish myths…"
Titus (1:14)

We now have the background in place to begin to reconstruct the likely truth of what happened during the early years of Christianity. Again, I'll not claim certainty here; no one can do that. But I think the ensemble of facts points to a clear scenario, one in which Paul and his band of fellow Jews constructed a Jesus hoax in order to weaken Roman rule and ultimately lead to its demise. It took a few centuries, but in the end, amazingly, it worked.

As an invading force in Palestine, the Romans were numerically a small minority, but they had access to limitless power. The Jews were also a small minority but had been able, prior to Rome, to acquire and hold power over the Palestinians. (The Hasmonean Dynasty held a territory roughly equal to present-day Israel, although it included the entire West Bank and a small portion of present-day Syria.) For their power, Rome required at least the tacit consent of the masses—and by and large, they achieved this. The Romans came, not as bloodthirsty slaughterers, but as bringers of civilization. They only fought if they encountered resistance. Their aim was not to kill masses of people, but to expand the Empire. As proof of this, they generally allowed the people in newly-acquired territories to govern themselves, as long as they recognized the ultimate authority of the emperor. In some cases, the Romans granted citizenship to those in conquered realms. The general public held no predetermined antipathy to the Empire, and in fact may have welcomed it if they disliked their previous rulers—as was likely the case in Palestine prior to Rome.[1] Rome brought many benefits and few drawbacks; taxes always had to be paid, no matter who was in charge. And in any case, there were clear advantages to being a member of the greatest power on Earth.

Paul, as we have seen, was likely sympathetic to the violent Zealot movement that was militantly opposed to the Romans and anyone collaborating with them. Paul even sanctioned murder to achieve his ends. As a teen, he likely remembered Tiberius' expulsion of the Jews from Rome in 19 AD, and he certainly would have known of Sejanus' attempt to "destroy" the Jews in the year 30. He likely was aware of Apion's anti-Jewish tract that was circulating in educated society. All the while, Jews were actively and passively fighting against Roman rule. He would have seen his fellow Zealots rounded up and executed, some by the highly visible form of crucifixion, a punishment reserved for rebels, insurgents, and other criminals against the State. All in all, it would have been a highly depressing situation.

Many Jews were resolved to live and let live with the Romans. Herod Antipater ("Antipas"), nominal 'king' of the Jews between 6 and 40 AD, was one such collaborationist. He feared incurring the wrath of the Empire and urged his fellow elites to tamp down any insurrectionist activity. Most of them evidently heeded his advice. It surely didn't take much of an argument; any sober-minded individual could see that militant resistance was futile.

Thus it was that, in the early 30s AD, Paul, as a (say) 28-year-old young man, came to contemplate his options. He hated the Romans, and detested the common Palestinians who were happily acquiescing to foreign rule. Like all Jews, he felt entitled to dominate the known world; seeing the Romans take this role must have been galling in the extreme.

Paul must have thus despised the entire Roman project—a civilizational force that began with the innovations of ancient Greece. The Greeks, as he knew, founded the Western worldview, an outlook that emphasized reason and rationality, empirical study of nature, and logic. The Greeks embraced life and sought to live it to its fullest. Any afterlife was sheer speculation for them, and so they placed all value on this life, their *real* life, rather than live for some unknown future. Like the Jews,

---

[1] Recall the comments by Tacitus in Chapter Four, in which he observes the animosity between Palestinians and Jews.

the Greeks viewed themselves as superior to their 'barbarian' neighbors, but this was by dint of their accomplishments in life rather than some divine blessing. The Greek value system, now absorbed into the mighty Roman Empire, was visible for the world to see. Its success was transparent to all.

How could Paul oppose such a thing? Militant action was virtually suicidal. Political machinations, which might have worked with a regional power, were hopeless here. The Empire was too big, and Rome too far away, for anyone living in Palestine to have a direct impact. The Jews themselves were divided; some were willing to fight but most were resigned to sit it out, however long it might be. The Jews were, after all, famous for always taking the long-term view of things.

Then one day, perhaps while on his way to Damascus, young Paul had an idea: What if he could work on the masses—the poor, misguided, superstitious masses—to steer them away from Rome and toward the Jewish side? The local power of Rome rested on them, as a foundation, but they were like a shifting sandbar; if they could be 'eroded,' then perhaps the mighty Roman superstructure might begin to wobble and crack—at least in Palestine. If the masses could be subtly moved toward the Jews, or even simply morally degraded somehow—or best of all, *both at once*—then they would be of little use to Rome. The Romans might then eventually just give up and go away. And under the circumstances, that would certainly count as victory.

But how? This must have seemed an impossible task. Only a god, only a new religion could perform such a trick. And then it came, like a flash from the blue, "a light brighter than the sun" (Acts 26:13)—an epiphany, a wondrous idea, Paul's great innovation.

We can imagine him thinking to himself…

> *Jesus! He was that popular young rabbi from Nazareth that drew such large crowds of ordinary Jews. They loved and adored him. But he couldn't keep his mouth shut! He would constantly talk about the need for the Jewish people to "rise up" against the Romans. Eventually—what was it, three years ago?—he got fingered by the Romans and was crucified along with two of his friends.*

As I recall, he also had a penchant for speaking in esoteric terms, about a new kingdom of God that was coming soon, and about the evil, sinful nature of those devils, the pagan Romans. "Fight the devils," he would say, and then your salvation is at hand.

People said that this Jesus was utterly divine. What if...he actually was God? A god in human form, as Homer and others wrote about? Or maybe, like the Egyptian pharaohs, a "son" of God? If that was the case, then the Romans crucified God! Why, that would make them the Devil incarnate.

What a great story. But what proof could we offer for it? Wait—didn't his followers say that he arose from the dead to continue his ministry? There were some stories about how they stole his body from his grave only to claim a miraculous resurrection. No one really believed it. But...what if it were true? Or at least, true enough? That could be our proof.

And who's going to know, anyway? That was three years ago and most people have already forgotten about him by now. But more importantly, the Gentile masses never heard about him at all. For them, his story would be brand new. And they're the ones we need to reach.

But what message could our "Jesus" take to the masses? We need to build sympathy to our side, of course, and to counter the Roman ideology. We need them to be pro-Jewish, but not make them Jews—no, that would never work. We need something new, a "third way" between Judaism and paganism.

Maybe, as a start, we could get them to worship our God, Jehovah, and not that ridiculous Roman pantheon. We need to convince them that God loves them, and that he sent his son to Earth to "save" them. Sure it's ridiculous, but those superstitious, ignorant peasants will swallow almost anything. I think it could work...

Or so we can imagine.

It is not a terribly farfetched or complicated story. A god-man comes to Earth, preaches loves for the masses, and promises to "save" them. He gets unjustly killed by the evil ones. He then rises up from the dead, proving to his followers that they, too, will be risen up and bask in eternal life if they follow him and his God. Those who don't believe, or who side with the devils, will suffer God's eternal damnation—notably, Paul never directly uses the word 'hell,' but the idea is there. This carrot-and-stick approach, Paul knows, is perfect for manipulating the superstitious masses.

This, in fact, is all we read in Paul's letters. No complicated theology, no lengthy life history of Jesus, not even any miracle stories—just a god in human form who preaches love for all, and who was resurrected after death. Furthermore, the god-man is a Jew—that's perfect. His "father" is Jehovah, the Jewish God—that's also perfect. The story focuses on the afterlife, and thus is able to keep the masses in perpetual suspension, in a state of "hope," for which they will expend their entire lives. The story also invites, even welcomes, suffering; all the better when it comes time to sacrifice for the cause. The whole outlook is thus simultaneously pro-Jewish and anti-Roman—an ideal situation.

But Paul needed one more thing: a message of resistance. It couldn't be explicit; that would be too obvious, would never draw in the masses, and would probably get him executed. It had to be more subtle. No explicit mention of Rome at all; just "evil," "Satan," "the worldly powers." That would suffice.

With these concepts in hand, Paul set off to build his church.

Of Men and Myths

Before proceeding further, let me elaborate on a few of the above points. Some Christ mythicists have emphasized the mythological similarities between the traditional Jesus and other, more ancient god stories. Doherty, Price, and Thompson, among others, have argued that the many parallels with older mythologies suggest that Paul or the Gospel writers (or others) simply stole from more ancient traditions when they constructed the life of Jesus. I think this is true, although it's probably less complicated than the mythicists suggest. All that matters for present purpose is the fact that there were preexisting ideas in circulation, for centuries, which would have made it easy for Paul to construct his limited Jesus story.

Let me just mention two sources here. First, consider the 14th-century BC pharaoh known as Akhenaten. Famous as the husband of Nefertiti and the father of King Tut, Akhenaten was almost certainly the first true philosopher-king. As a young man and absolute ruler of Egypt, he demonstrated a remarkable capacity for deep metaphysical thought. His primary accomplishment was the displacement of the ancient Egyptian pantheon for a single god, Aten—the sun. As such, he created the first monotheism in world history. It may well have been the root source of ideas that ultimately became Judaism and Christianity.

Very little of Akhenaten's writings remain, and much of his philosophy is obscure, but what little we have shows some intriguing parallels to the Jesus story and Christian theology generally. In particular, Akhenaten himself seems to take on a Christ-like aura. In the Longer Hymn, Akhenaten speaks in prayer directly to the Aten. He calls himself "your beloved son" and adds that "no one knows you [Aten] except Akhenaten, your son." And further: "You have revealed yourself to me."

The Aten, as the sun, brings light and life to the world: "You are the light of the Earth." Indeed, "You are life itself, all live through you." Near the end of the poem Akhenaten says, in a very Christ-like fashion, "You raise up the people for the son of your body." At the close, Akhenaten speaks of his beloved queen Nefertiti, stating that she "lives and is rejuvenated forever and ever."

We see similar themes in the Shorter Hymn. Again directly addressing the Aten, Akhenaten says "Your love is great, immense. … [Y]ou fill the Two Lands with your love." Notably, this "rising" god actually, literally, rises! "Every heart acclaims your sight, when you are risen as their lord." Akhenaten calls himself "your holy son" who "performs your praises." In the final stanza, we read: "I am your son who serves you, who exalts your name. Your power, your strength, are firm in my heart." He then reaffirms the monotheism: "You are One." The parallels are truly fascinating.[2]

---

[2] For a fuller account of Akhenaten and his philosophy, see *Son of God, Son of the Sun*, by Savitri Devi (2015).

A second likely source would have been much more well-known: Homer. Consider just the *Iliad*, which was composed sometime around 700 BC. Here we have numerous gods actively intervening in human affairs, somewhat as we see in the OT. As the arch-deity, Zeus plays the role of Jehovah. Homer's universe didn't really have a Satan, but he did have Hades, lord of the underworld. And there wasn't really a hell, but they did have Tartarus, which was the darkest depth of the House of Death.

Of special interest are Homer's many demi-gods—those who are half-human, half-god. Technically, Jesus Christ was a demi-god. Christians like to speak about the "miracle" of immaculate conception, of God impregnating Mary, but that was a very old and well-worn idea. The *Iliad* is filled with such demi-gods, the most famous being Achilles (son of sea goddess Thetis and mortal Peleus). Zeus was notably prolific, having produced nearly a dozen "sons" by mortal women: Aeacus, Amphion, Dardanus, Heracles/Hercules, Iasus, Minos, Perseus, Pirithous, Polydeuces, Rhadamanthys, and Sarpedon. Other gods had sons as well: Aphrodite was the mother of Aeneas, Poseidon fathered Theseus, and Hermes fathered Eudorus, to name three. Sometimes they had demi-god daughters; Helen of Troy was one such person (daughter of Zeus). One gets the impression, in fact, that demi-gods were all over the place in the ancient world; at one point Hera exclaims, "Many who battle round King Priam's mighty walls are sons of the deathless gods" (16.533). As a demi-god himself, Jesus was old news.

There are other relevant themes. For Homer, gods frequently come to earth in human form. In Book 5, war god Ares appears on the battlefield "shaped like the runner Acamas" (5.532), to whip up the troops. Later, in Book 13, the god Poseidon appears "in a prophet's shape" (13.84) to embolden two warriors; specifically, he "takes the build and tireless voice of Calchas" (13.57). Additionally, we find that the dead are occasionally "raised up" by the gods; when the demi-god Sarpedon was killed, Apollo "lifted Prince Sarpedon clear of the weapons, bore him far from the fighting, off and away…" (16.792). We also see Christ-like descriptions; for example, demi-gods "shine" and are a "light" unto the world: "the [mortal] woman bore the god [Hermes] a radiant son, Eudorus…" (16.220). Once again, we find a series of remarkable parallels. Paul and his cabal had plenty of material to draw from.

Jesus Reborn, as Rebel

Paul likely employed these mythological precursors in his construction of Jesus. But as I said, he didn't need any complicated storyline. For his purposes, he only needed Jesus to be God in human form, and to be risen after death—that's it. The life history and teachings are largely irrelevant. We see all this directly in Paul's writings. Take Jesus as God. In Philippians, Paul refers to "Christ Jesus, who, though he was in the form of God…" (2:6). Elsewhere, Jesus "is the image of the invisible God, the first-born of all creation" (Col 15:1). Such talk doesn't recur until the very last Gospel, John.

Even more important for Paul was an emphasis on the resurrection. We see this even from the earliest letters, Galatians and 1 Thessalonians. In the former he refers, at the very beginning, to "Jesus Christ and God the Father, who raised him from the dead" (1:1). In the latter, he writes, "For since we believe that Jesus died and rose again…" (4:14). In Romans we read of "Jesus Christ…designated Son of God in power according to the Spirit of holiness by his resurrection from the dead" (1:4). Later in the same letter Paul says "We were buried therefore with him by baptism into death, so that as Christ was raised from the dead by the glory of the Father, we too might walk in newness of life" (6:4). And again: "Christ Jesus, who died, yes, who was raised from the dead…" (8:34). In 1 Corinthians, Paul offers a more detailed and extended discussion: "Christ died for our sins…, he was buried, that he was raised on the third day in accordance with the [OT] scriptures" (15:3). The importance of this event is then elaborated:

> Now if Christ is preached as raised from the dead, how can some of you say that there is no resurrection of the dead? But if there is no resurrection of the dead, then Christ has not been raised; if Christ has not been raised, then our preaching is in vain and your faith is in vain. We are even found to be misrepresenting God, because we testified of God that he raised Christ, whom he did not raise if it is true that the dead are not raised. For if the dead are not raised, then Christ has not been raised. If Christ has not been raised, your faith is futile and you are still in your sins.

> Then those also who have fallen asleep in Christ have per-
> ished. If for this life only we have hoped in Christ, we are
> of all men most to be pitied. But in fact Christ has been
> raised from the dead, the first fruits of those who have fall-
> en asleep. (15:12-20)

Without a resurrection, all of Paul's grand plans "are in vain." No one
will be convinced of Jesus' divinity, and thus they won't follow him.
Again, even the life and sayings of Jesus were irrelevant for Paul. The
divine resurrection was everything. Nietzsche, as usual, was to the point:

> [Paul] *invented his own history of earliest Christianity.* ... The
> Savior type, the doctrine, the practice, the death, the meaning
> of death, even what came after death—nothing remained un-
> touched, nothing remained even similar to the reality. Paul
> simply transposed the center of gravity of the whole exist-
> ence *after* this existence—in the *lie* of the 'resurrected'
> Jesus. At bottom, he had no use at all for the life of the Sav-
> ior—he needed the death on the cross *and* a little more.[3]

And that's the core of the hoax. Everything else follows naturally.

The Message of Rebellion

With this simple theology in place, Paul was well-situated to interject his
message of resistance to Rome. Throughout his letters we find numerous
references to enslavement, revolution, insurrection, war, the importance
of the disempowered masses, and so on. In the early Galatians we read of
the need for Jesus "to deliver us from the present evil age" (1:4). Later,
the "elemental spirits" seem to be an allusion to the Roman pantheon:

> Formerly, when you did not know God, you were in
> bondage to beings that by nature are no gods; but now that
> you have come to know God, or rather to be known by
> God, how can you turn back again to the weak and beggarly

------

[3] *Antichrist*, sec. 42.

elemental spirits, whose slaves you want to be once more? (4:8-9)

'Be not enslaved to the Roman gods,' he seems to say. And again: "For freedom Christ has set us free; stand fast therefore, and do not submit again to a yoke of slavery" (5:1). The same idea of turning away from the Roman "idols" appears in 1 Thessalonians: "For they themselves report...how you turned to God from idols" (1:9). It will only get worse under the Romans, but thankfully "Jesus...delivers us from the wrath to come" (1:10).

Jesus won't come, however, until there is a *revolution* first. Paul is explicit: "Let no one deceive you in any way; for that day will not come, unless the rebellion comes first, and the man of lawlessness [i.e. the emperor] is revealed, the son of perdition, who...takes his seat in the temple of God, proclaiming himself to be God" (1 Thes 2:3-4). This likely refers to the fact that the Jews were appalled when the emperor insisted on placing his own statue in their temple. Or it could be an allusion to the Jewish quest for world domination and Paul's consequent disgust at the Romans' supervening on God's declaration that the Jews would rule.

The letter to the Romans contains some revealing passages. We learn, first of all, who is the real priority in this whole scheme: "For I am not ashamed of the gospel: it is the power of God for salvation to everyone who has faith, *to the Jew first* and also to the Greek" (1:16). To be saved, the Greek and Gentile must worship Jehovah: "Is God the God of Jews only? Is he not the God of the Gentiles also? Yes, of Gentiles also" (3:29). And indeed, the Gentiles are needed—to save Israel: "A hardening has come upon part of Israel, until the full number of the Gentiles come in, and so all Israel will be saved" (11:25). "For I will not venture to speak of anything except what Christ has wrought through me to win obedience from the Gentiles, by word and deed" (15:18). If all goes according to plan, "then the God of peace will soon crush Satan under your feet" (16:20).

The most passages of interest are found in 1 Corinthians. Paul speaks of a coming "end" in vague terms, but understood as an end of all earthly power—which of course was Rome. When Christ returns, "then comes the end, when he delivers the kingdom to God the Father [i.e. Jehovah], after destroying every rule and every authority and power"

(15:24). And again, "the rulers of this age…are doomed to pass away" (2:6). By "kingdom of God," Paul explicitly intends a concrete ruling authority: "For the kingdom of God does not consist in talk but in power" (4:20). To achieve his ends, Paul is clear that he will do or say anything: to the Jews, he will be a Jew; to the Gentiles, a Gentile; to the weak, he will be weak; indeed, "I have become all things to all men" (9:19-22).

His emphasis on the "the weak" is interesting. Paul needed to reach the lowly Gentile masses, and thus he had to portray them as specially chosen by God. As in society, so too in the human body: "the parts of the body which seem to be weaker are indispensable" (12:22). God himself gives "greater honor to the inferior part" (12:24). This is even more explicit in the anonymous letter of James: "Has not God chosen those who are poor in the world to be rich in faith and heirs to the kingdom…" (Jam 2:5). We of course see this idea later, famously, in Jesus' proclamation that "the meek shall inherit the earth" (Matt 5:5).

But in Paul, the concept is presented with stunning clarity at the outset of 1 Corinthians. He aims directly to undermine the powerful, the wise, the learned—the Romans—in favor of the weak, ignorant, and dispossessed. At (1:19) Paul paraphrases Isaiah: "I will destroy the wisdom of the wise, and the cleverness of the clever I will thwart." Then comes the decisive passage:

> For consider your call, brethren; not many of you were wise according to worldly standards, not many were powerful, not many were of noble birth; but God chose what is foolish in the world to shame the wise, God chose what is weak in the world to shame the strong, God chose what is low and despised in the world, *even things that are not*, to bring to nothing things that are… (1:26-28; italics added)

Here he lays out the essence of the plan. The Romans are the powerful, the noble, the wise and learned; but God did not choose them. He chose *you*, the weak and ignorant masses. God explicitly chose "the foolish," "the low and despised," to form the basis of this new church. And what does Paul mean by "things that are not"? Things that don't really exist? Things that we thought were real, but are not? Like Jesus Christ? Like heaven and hell? Like an afterlife? Is this a subtle admission that he has been lying to his converts? No matter, it's all for a good cause: to bring down the "things that are," namely, the Roman Empire. All in all, a remarkable passage.

It was, in fact, precisely this notion—that Christianity targeted, and appealed to, the lowest of the low within society—that so irritated the Greek philosopher Celsus. Writing in his *True Word* (circa 180 AD), he said that Christian absurdity appeals only to "wool-workers, cobblers, laundry-workers, and the most illiterate and bucolic yokels".[4] Hardly good company—and yet, entirely in keeping with Paul's intent: to appeal to the poor and illiterate masses. Is this really a religion that any thinking person wants to be associated with?

Paul, however, is undeterred. The illiterate masses are his real target audience. Again and again, we see that "the weak" or "the meek" are the key to success. Christ himself is portrayed as meek (2 Cor 10:1), and Jesus himself allegedly told Paul (in a vision) "my power is made perfect in weakness" (2 Cor 12:9). Paul is thereby "content" with his own weakness: "For when I am weak, then I am strong."

The message of rebellion by the "weak" masses is perhaps best summarized in Ephesians:

> Put on the whole armor of God, that you may be able to stand against the wiles of the devil. For we are not contending against flesh and blood, but against the principalities, against the powers, against the world rulers of this present darkness, against the spiritual hosts of wickedness in the heavenly places. Therefore take the whole armor of God, that you may be able to withstand in the evil day, and having done all, to stand. (6:11-13)

Paul goes on to speak cleverly of "the shield of faith," "the helmet of salvation," and "the sword of the Spirit"—nice cover language. No doubt, the real message got through.

Recall that all this was written prior to the first Jewish rebellion of 66-70 AD. War was in the air, but had not yet broken out. The Jews were ready to fight, but the Gentile masses had to be psychologically prepared

---

[4] Cited in Origen's *Contra Celsus* (3.55).

for a coming esoteric "battle with Satan." Thus we see, time and again, a subtle message of conflict, war, insurrection. And where is that famed 'message of love' so endemic to Christianity? Love comes later; now it's time to fight.

The Truth of the Gospels

To recap, I am reconstructing the likely sequence of events based on a total picture and complete analysis of the situation. Paul, outraged at Roman rule over Palestine, devised a clever plan—a new religion, really—based on a real, crucified rabbi by the name of Jesus, whose body had conveniently disappeared. This three-year-dead rabbi now becomes, in Paul's hands, the Son of God, sent here to save humanity, and especially to save the low and despised masses. Paul's objective is to get the masses to worship a dead Jew, to worship the invisible Jewish God, and to adopt intrinsically Jewish values. Lüdemann (2002: 99) noticed this already two decades ago: "Paul taught his Gentile converts two basic things: Jewish monotheism and Jewish ethics." But there was one more component: to turn them away from the power and majesty of Rome. Or better: to *actively resist* the power of Rome, now seen as the Devil incarnate.

Just as Paul's life was ending, war broke out and the great Jewish Temple was destroyed. We can only imagine the distress and outrage of the Jewish community. Their hatred of Rome must have reached atmospheric heights. If the Jews had any illusions about peaceful coexistence, those would have been crushed. Military responses were no longer an option. Perhaps Paul's 'psychological' ploy, the Jesus hoax, would work after all, but it would have to be taken to the next level.

Thus it was that Paul's surviving followers—perhaps Mark, Luke, Matthew, and John, and in his own way, Peter—decided to pick up the game. This band of "little ultra-Jews"[5] needed a more detailed story of Jesus' life; Paul's vague allusions to a real man would no longer suffice. Someone—"Mark"—thus decided to quote Jesus extensively and directly. Unlike Paul's letters, which were targeted at church-builders and, generally, fellow Jews, this "gospel" (Paul's word) would be intended

---

[5] Nietzsche, *Antichrist* (sec. 44). In the original German: *kleine Superlativ-Juden.*

for mass (Gentile) consumption. It had to be impressive—lots of miracles from their miracle-man. It would end up with 19 Jesus miracles wedged into the smallest of the four Gospels.

And there were several other firsts. Here we read, for the first time ever, about the 12 apostles, Jesus as a carpenter, and the concept of hell. Here too Jesus makes a clever "prophecy" that the Jewish temple would be ruined (13:1-2)—an easy call to make, given that the temple was just actually destroyed!

Here we also get the first details of the crucifixion process; interestingly, both the Jews and the Romans come in for blame. Jesus predicts that "the chief [Jewish] priests and scribes" will "condemn him to death," and then "deliver him to the Gentiles [Romans]" who will "kill him" (10:33-34). This is revealing. We have to keep in mind that Paul, Mark, and friends were working against two sets of opponents: the Romans, and their fellow 'non-believing' Jews, mostly the Pharisees and priests who could never accept that this "Jesus" was the Jewish Messiah. In fact, they almost certainly encountered far harsher resistance from their fellow Jews than from anyone else. The Pharisees in truth wanted to "kill" Jesus; they were his internal enemy. But Mark had to finger the Romans as the literal executioners, so that anger would be directed against them. It seems that Mark's anger against his fellow Jews, however, got the better of him; for centuries afterward, Christians would blame the Jews for killing Christ, not realizing that the whole tale was a Jewish construction in the first place. Perhaps there's a kind of justice in that irony after all.

Lastly, hints of rebellion now had to be downplayed by Mark. We now have to be like "mustard seeds," small and inconspicuous, biding our time, all while spreading the kingdom of God. Nevertheless, if push comes to shove, one must be ready to lay down one's life for the cause: "For whoever would save his life will lose it; and whoever loses his life for [Jesus'] sake and the gospel's will save it" (8:35). Don't give up hope, and never forget that "the last [will be] first" (10:31). Chaos is still in the cards: "For nation will rise against nation, and kingdom against kingdom" (13:8). The Jews' ultimate victory is coming soon: "There are some standing here who will not taste death before they see the kingdom of God come with power" (9:1). The end is near.

The Gospel of Mark evidently sufficed for some 15 years. It must have been effective at drawing in Gentiles and building a functioning church. But then perhaps things stalled a bit. Maybe the little Jewish band got impatient. Maybe they splintered over tactical issues. Whatever the reason, sometime around the year 85, two of the group—"Luke" and "Matthew"—decided that they needed to write an even more detailed account of Jesus' life. But evidently the two couldn't agree on a single plan, so they worked apart, drawing from Mark's story while weaving in other new ideas they had jointly invented. Each man went off on his own, drafting his own new gospel.

The new documents had much more detail than Mark; in fact, both were nearly twice as long as their predecessor. They had to keep the same basic story line, of course, but each man added his own embellishments. What was new? The virgin birth in Bethlehem, for one, and the whole manger scene. These now appeared, for the first time ever, some 85 years after the alleged event. We scarcely need to ask how much truth is in them. (I note as an aside that Matthew included the bit about the star, whereas that was apparently an unimportant detail to Luke, since he omitted it completely.) Luke included a vignette about Jesus as a 12-year-old (2:41-51), something utterly lacking in the other three Gospels. The Sermon on the Mount appears for the first time, though Matthew has a much longer version than Luke. In the sermon we find a number of famous sayings, all of which were never seen before: "the meek shall inherit the earth" (Mt 5:5), "you are the light of the world" (Mt 5:14), turn the other cheek (Mt 5:39; Lk 6:29), love thy enemies (Mt 5:44; Lk 6:27), "cannot serve God and mammon" (Mt 6:24), "judge not" (Mt 7:1; Lk 6:37)— all now recorded, for the first time, some 50 years after they supposedly occurred.

Other points were simply elaborations of themes from Mark. The anti-Jewish rhetoric now heats up a bit; the Jews are called "a brood of vipers" (Mt 3:7, 12:34, 23:33) and "lovers of money" (Lk 16:14). Hell becomes more prominent; evidently the prior scare tactics weren't quite working.[6] And there's a greater emphasis on the virtue of suffering.[7]

Finally, revolutionary talk also increases. Mark's passages are carried over into both new gospels, but we now find a number of strikingly

---

[6] See Mt 5:22, 5:30, 10:28, 25:46; and Lk 10:15, 12:5.
[7] See Mt 10:22, 24:9; and Lk 6:22.

explicit lines in each. Followers must now virtually abandon their families for the cause:

- "Brother will deliver up brother to death, and the father his child, and children will rise against parents and have them put to death; and you will be hated by all for my name's sake" (Mt 10:21).

- "And everyone who has left houses or brothers or sisters or father or mother or children or lands, for my name's sake, will receive a hundredfold, and inherit eternal life" (Mt. 19:29).

- "I have come to set a man against his father, and a daughter against her mother… He who loves father or mother more than me is not worthy of me" (Mt 10:35-37).

- "He who is not with me is against me" (Mt 12:30).

- "Henceforth in one house…they will be divided, father against son and son against father, mother against daughter and daughter against mother, mother-in-law against her daughter-in-law, and daughter-in-law against her mother-in-law" (Lk 12:52-53).

- "If anyone comes to me and does not hate his own father and mother and wife and children and brothers and sisters, yes, even his own life, he cannot be my disciple" (Lk 14:26).

These are remarkably cult-like dictates, but perhaps appropriate for the Jewish-led Christian movement, one in which the detested Gentiles are to play their subservient role as dictated in the OT.

Then we have passages of outright militancy. In Matthew, Jesus says, "Do not think that I have come to bring peace on earth; I have not come to bring peace, but a sword" (10:34)—how very un-Christ-like! Luke has Jesus say, "I came to cast fire upon the earth… Do you think that I have come to give peace on earth? No, I tell you, but rather division" (12:49-51). Every man must do his part: "Let him who has no sword sell his cloak and buy one" (Lk 22:36). Jesus becomes downright ruthless: "As for these enemies of mine, who did not want me to reign over them, bring them here and slay them before me" (Lk 19:27). All this is necessary because "the devil" rules all the kingdoms of the world (Lk 4:5-6). But not to worry; if we all stick to the plan, and "this gospel of the kingdom will be preached throughout the whole world," then "the end will come" (Mt 24:14).

And so, sometime around the year 85, two new Gospels were released into the world.

Once again, these apparently sufficed for a good decade or so. But then one more member of the cabal, "John," breaks rank and moves in yet a different direction. He feels the need for an intellectual and esoteric Jesus story, and so constructs a gospel using abstract, almost philosophical terms and concepts. It ends up as mid-length essay, between the short Mark and the longer Matthew/Luke. Miracles are still there, but they are now down-played—just eight appear. We can imagine that John understood that his new, more intellectual audience would likely not be taken in by such nonsense. Also discarded is nearly all rebellious talk. Evidently the intellectual crowd would not be the ones taking up swords.

This fourth Gospel begins with a famously cryptic passage: "In the beginning was the Word, and the Word was with God, and the Word was God" (1:1). I have analyzed this line in detail elsewhere,[8] but in short, "Word" in the original Greek text is *Logos*, which is an ancient and complex philosophical concept meaning 'speech,' 'word,' 'reason,' or 'logic.' The notion that "Logos is God" or "Logos is with God" comes ultimately from the philosopher Heraclitus, circa 450 BC. He believed in a kind of cosmic mind or intelligence, the Logos, that directed all events in the physical realm. This was a perfectly 'weighty' concept for John to equate with the esoteric Jesus, and so he borrowed it with impunity (perhaps via Philo, who also deployed the concept in a similar way).

Correspondingly, John places a renewed emphasis on the idea that Jesus is literally God. Jesus says, "I proceeded and came forth from God" (8:42), and furthermore, "before Abraham was, I am" (8:58). "I and the Father are one," he adds (10:30). And again: "He who has seen me has seen the Father" (14:9). Apparently, Jesus as a demi-god was no longer sufficient; now he had to be a full-blown god, or even God himself.

---

[8] See Skrbina (2015: 19-20).

Also new is an emphasis on the masses as being a sheep-like herd, and Jesus as their head sheep or shepherd. Jesus is "the Lamb of God" (1:29), and later we read an extended passage on Jesus as "the door of the sheep" (10:7), "the good shepherd," one who "lays down his life for the sheep." Near the end of the Gospel, the risen Jesus instructs his disciples to "feed my lambs" and "tend my sheep" (21:15-17). This is all consistent with a de-emphasis on revolution, and with an intent to pacify the intelligentsia.

The Gospel ends, abruptly, with a suitably outrageous final line: "But there are also many other things which Jesus did; were every one of them to be written, I suppose that the world itself could not contain the books that would be written" (21:25). An appropriately absurd closing for the absurd final Gospel.

Thus understood, the whole sweep of events now makes sense. From the Roman invasion to Paul's "vision" at Damascus, to his letters, to the first Jewish-Roman war, to the Gospels—it's all now a coherent and consistent story. Far more coherent, in fact, than a literal tale of a demi-god come to earth to save humanity. But my alternate account has at least one important consequence: "Saint" Paul and his Jewish cabal turn out to be blatant liars. In fact, the epic liars of all recorded history.

Paul, Liar Supreme

Recall my explanation above, regarding how Paul and the Gospel writers had two sets of enemies: the Romans and their fellow elite Jews. In fact, they had a third enemy: *the truth*. Paul and crew knew they were lying to the masses, but they didn't care. The Gentiles were always treated by the Jews with contempt, as I showed in Chapter 4. They could be manipulated, harassed, assaulted, beaten, even killed, if it served Jewish ends. This was not a problem for them. But what they did have to worry about were any dedicated and persistent truth-seekers in the world, who might take the trouble to expose their hoax. The cabal therefore had to oppose any intellectual methodology that might lead to the truth: empiricism, rationality, logic, common sense, 'science.' All these things would henceforth become enemies of the church, allied with the Devil.

As the initiator of the hoax, Paul earns the maximum amount of credit or, if you will, blame. His 'moment at Damascus,' if that's what it was, kicked off the whole series of events. He constructed a simple and elemental lie, based on common ideas in mythology and a kernel of actual truth, in order to manipulate the Gentile masses for the benefit of the Jews. He even *admits* as much: "For I tell you that Christ's life of service was on behalf of the Jews…" (Romans 15:8). It was, quite frankly, a brilliant plan. But to successfully pull it off, Paul must have been a brilliant liar. He had to write down pure fiction as absolute truth. He had to lie to people's faces and pretend to believe it. He had to entice and frighten innocent and simple-minded peasants into believing his outrageous concoction. And he did it. Paul—expert liar, artful liar, master liar.

Not that this is new news. In Chapter 4, I cited numerous ancient sources who criticized Jewish misanthropy, and certainly a willingness to lie is compatible with that complaint. Ptolemy, for example, called the Jews "unscrupulous," "treacherous," "bold," and "scheming." Unfortunately, the label of 'liar' has dogged them for centuries. In the early 1500s, Martin Luther—founder of the Lutheran church—wrote a rather infamous book titled *On the Jews and their Lies*. There he declared that "they have not acquired a perfect mastery of the art of lying; they lie so clumsily and ineptly that anyone who is just a little observant can easily detect it"[9]—a statement that could well be a motto for the present work. I also note the striking irony of a man like Luther who was so opposed to Jewish lies, even as he himself fell for the greatest Jewish lie of all.

In 1798, the great German philosopher Immanuel Kant called the Jews "a nation of deceivers," and in a later lecture he added that "the Jews…are permitted by the Talmud to practice deceit".[10] In his final book, Arthur Schopenhauer made some extended observations on Judeo-Christianity. He wrote, "We see from [Tacitus and Justinus] how much the Jews were at all times and by all nations loathed and despised." This was due in large part, he says, to the fact that the Jewish people were considered *grosse Meister im Lügen*—"great master of lies".[11] Employing his usual blunt but elegant terminology, Nietzsche said this:

---

[9] Luther (2020: 163).
[10] Kant (1798/1978: 33) and (1997: 34), respectively. For a good discussion of lying in the Talmud, see Bischoff (2023).
[11] Schopenhauer (1851/1974, vol 2: 357).

> In Christianity all of Judaism, a several-century-old Jewish preparatory training and technique of the most serious kind, attains its ultimate mastery as the art of lying in a holy manner. The Christian, this *ultima ratio* of the lie, is the Jew once more—even *three times* a Jew.[12]

Similar comments came from express anti-Semites. Hitler called the Jews "artful liars" and a "race of dialectical liars," adding that "existence compels the Jew to lie, and to lie systematically".[13] And Joseph Goebbels, in his personal diary, wrote: "The Jew was also the first to introduce the lie into politics as a weapon. ... He can therefore be regarded not only as the carrier but even the inventor of the lie among human beings".[14]

Finally, a remark by Voltaire seems relevant here. The Jews, he said, "are, all of them, born with a raging fanaticism in their hearts... I would not be in the least bit surprised if these people would not someday become deadly to the human race".[15] If a Jewish lie were to spread throughout the Earth, eventually drawing in more than 2 billion people, becoming the enemy of truth and reason, and causing the deaths of millions of human beings via inquisitions, witch burnings, crusades, and other religious atrocities—well, that could be considered a mortal threat, I think.

This, then, is my "Antagonism Thesis": Paul and his cabal[16] deliberately lied to the masses, with no concern for their true well-being, simply to undermine Roman rule. This little group tempted innocent people with a promise of heaven, and frightened them with the threat of hell. This psychological ploy was part of a long-term plan to weaken and, in a sense, morally corrupt the masses by drawing them away from the potent and successful Greco-Roman worldview and more toward an oriental, Judaic view.

---

[12] *Antichrist*, sec. 44.

[13] *Mein Kampf* (2022; vol 1): ch. 10.4, ch. 2.25, and ch. 11.12, respectively.

[14] Entry dated May 13, 1943. See Goebbels (2019: 216-217).

[15] In Hertzberg (1968: 301).

[16] I have been using 'cabal' throughout the present text. It is, I think, precisely the right word. A cabal is "a small number of persons secretly united to bring about an overturn or usurpation, especially in public affairs." That is a perfect description of Paul and his band.

As we know, it took some time but the new Christian religion did spread, eventually permeating the Roman world. In the year 315, the emperor himself, Constantine, converted to Christianity. In 380, Emperor Theodosius declared it the official state religion. And just 15 years later, in 395, the empire fractured and the classic (western) half utterly collapsed. In the ensuing vacuum, Christianity rose to power—and in Rome itself, of all places. The victory was complete, some 350 years after Paul's grand vision came to him in a flash, "brighter than the sun."

CHAPTER 6

PAUL AS DESTROYER OF GENTILE FAMILIES

There is one other strange aspect of Paul's thinking that is worth examining—something that, on first look, seems bizarre, but upon reflection fits in quite well with my Hoax thesis. It is this: Paul is anti-family; or rather, anti-Gentile-family, to be precise. As is well known, he is an extreme prude regarding sexual relations; he is opposed to sex, all sex, anywhere, *even among the married*. Paul's ideal family, for the Gentiles, is a sexless marriage, and thus a joyless marriage, and worse, a *childless* marriage—in a sense, it is not even a family at all in the traditional sense. And all this, in the name of God and Jesus.

In calling for 'eternal chastity,' even among the married, Paul marks himself as an anti-natalist: someone who *opposes childbearing*. Again, at first blush, this seems crazy. But it fits well with the deep-seated Jewish hatred of the non-Jew; nothing like exterminating future Gentile generations through 'holy chastity.' And it also fits well with the idea that Paul is literally mentally ill—which I will discuss in the next chapter. But is it doubly bizarre for an avowed Christian, someone we would expect to be "pro-life" in every sense of the word; Catholics, after all, are famous for their large families. But strangely, this is not the case. Paul is anti-sex, anti-family, and thus anti-procreation. The story is fascinating, shocking, and virtually unknown—or at least unacknowledged—among Christian scholars.

Let me start with *suffering*. A well-known feature of Paul's thinking is the necessity of suffering: Jesus was condemned and abused, he suffered and died on the cross for our sins, and therefore we, as good Christians, must be prepared to suffer too. Hence, Paul becomes masochistic in the extreme: we welcome suffering, we embrace suffering, we revel in suffering. (Signs of mental illness?) This allows us to "become like Christ," and thus—hopefully—to gain eternal life, as he did. The passages are revealing; consider the following by Paul, in roughly chronological order:

Galatians

•   "I have been crucified with Christ; it is no longer I who live, but Christ who lives in me; and the life I now live in the flesh I live by faith in the Son of God, who loved me and gave himself for me" (2:20). Through suffering, says Paul, we hope for a kind of unity with Jesus.

•   "Far be it from me to glory except in the cross of our Lord Jesus Christ, by which the world has been crucified to me, and I to the world…Henceforth let no man trouble me, for I bear on my body the marks of Jesus" (6:14, 17). Again, Paul claims that he has become 'like Jesus'—physically!

2 Corinthians

•   "For as we share abundantly in Christ's sufferings, so through Christ we share abundantly in comfort too. If we are afflicted, it is for your comfort and salvation; and if we are comforted, it is for your comfort, which you experience when you patiently endure the same sufferings that we suffer. Our hope for you is unshaken; for we know that as you share in our sufferings, you will also share in our comfort" (1:5-7). Again, a call to "share in Jesus' suffering."

Romans

•   "We rejoice in our sufferings, knowing that suffering produces endurance, and endurance produces character, and character produces hope…" (5:3).

•   "[We are] fellow heirs with Christ, *provided* we suffer with him in order that we may also be glorified with him" (8:17).

Philippians

•   "For the sake of Christ, you should not only believe in him but also suffer for his sake" (1:29).

•   "I [Paul] have suffered the loss of all things, and count them as refuse, in order that I may gain Christ… and may share his sufferings, becoming like him in his death; that, if possible, I may attain the resurrection from the dead" (3:8, 10-11). More talk of "becoming like Christ."

Colossians

•   "Now I rejoice in my sufferings for your sake, and in my flesh I complete what is lacking in Christ's afflictions for the sake of his body, that is, the church" (1:24). So, we should suffer for *the church*—the institution, the dogma, that Paul is constructing.

Hebrews:

•   "[Jesus] was made a little lower than the angels [in his human nature], crowned with glory and honor because of the suffering of death... For it was fitting that he [the Father] … should make the pioneer [Christ] of their salvation perfect through suffering. … For because he himself has suffered and been tempted, he is able to help those who are tempted [to sin]" (2:9-10, 18).

•   "Although he was a Son, he learned obedience through what he suffered" (5:7).

2 Timothy

•   "All who desire to live a godly life in Christ Jesus will be persecuted…" (3:12)

Suffering comes in two forms: actual pain (physical or mental), *or*, privation from pleasure. In other words, when we forego pleasures in this world—sensual pleasures, physical pleasures—we accept a sort of pain: the pain of losing something pleasurable that we might have experienced, but did not. Clearly, indulging in worldly pleasures is the opposite to what Paul has in mind, at a minimum; and more, he expects us to get out there and suffer directly, from persecution, 'slings and arrows,' even physical or mental abuse, all for the sake of "the church" and in the hope of "becoming like Christ." And if he could find a way to do it non-fatally, Paul would surely have us *crucify ourselves*—all the better to "become like Christ," of course.

In foregoing pleasures, Paul advocates a kind of asceticism: a voluntary relinquishment of positive experiences, for a "higher" cause. Appropriately, then, sexual desire is the prime urging that must be surrendered by any real ascetic. Celibacy, abstaining from sex, becomes all but a divine commandment. And after all, Jesus himself was celibate—as far as we know.[1]

The strange notion of eternal Christian celibacy is not a new revelation; it was recognized already 200 years ago by the great German philosopher, Arthur Schopenhauer. He wrote:

> The ascetic tendency is certainly unmistakable in genuine and original Christianity… We find, as its principal teaching, the recommendation of genuine and pure celibacy … already expressed in the New Testament.[2]

By "pure and genuine celibacy," he means that, according to their own doctrine, *good Christians should not have sex—ever*. Schopenhauer then dedicates the next several pages to building his case for this "perpetual chastity," which include these lines from an 1832 book by the Catholic author Friedrich Carove:

> By virtue of the Church view…perpetual chastity is called a divine, heavenly, angelic virtue… [Quoting a Catholic periodical,] "In Catholicism, the observance of a perpetual chastity, for God's sake, appears in itself as the highest merit of man." … To both [Paul and the author of Hebrews], virginity was perfection, marriage only a makeshift for the weaker… The self should turn away and refrain from everything that contributes only to its pleasure… We agree with Abbe Zaccaria, who asserts that celibacy…is derived above all from the teaching of Christ and of the Apostle Paul.[3]

Evidence for this astonishing claim must ultimately come from our primary source, the New Testament. Schopenhauer cites two passages from Paul. The first and earliest is 1 Thessalonians (4:3), an oddly cryptic

---

[1] Or perhaps not: the Talpiot tomb (see Chapter 3) includes an ossuary inscribed "Judah, son of Jesus." And Mary Magdalene has long been speculated to be a love-interest. But "officially," Jesus was celibate.

[2] Schopenhauer (1819/1966) vol. 2, p. 616.

[3] Ibid., p. 619-620.

passage. Paul says, "For it is the will of God, for your sanctification, that you abstain from *porneias*." I cite here the Greek original—but what is *porneias*? Among the various English translations we find a range of terms, such as "immorality" (RSV), "sexual immorality" (NKJV), and "fornication" (KJV), all of which suggest illegitimate sex, perhaps unmarried sex, perhaps adultery. But we also find broader terms, like "all sexual vice" (AMPC), "sexual sins" (ERV), "sexual defilement" (TPT), and even "unchastity" (RSV). Paul goes on to say that "each one of you knows how to take a wife in holiness and honor, not in the passion of lust like a heathen." Can he be suggesting that men take wives as "partners in Christ" all while abstaining from the sexual lust of heathens?

The second passage is a lengthy portion from 1 Corinthians 7. Again, it is oddly conflicted. At the start of the chapter, Paul says, bluntly, "It is good for a man not to have sexual relations with a woman" (7:1). But owing to "the temptation to immorality"—presumably meaning sexual intercourse—a man may take a wife. Affirming his own unmarried status, Paul then says "I wish that all were as I myself am. ... To the unmarried and the widows, I say that it is well for them to remain single as I do" (7:7-8). "But if they cannot exercise self-control"—that is, if they are weak—"they should marry." Later in the chapter, Paul returns to the subject: "Are you free from a wife? Do not seek marriage" (7:27). Two lines later he warns, "those who marry will have worldly troubles (!), and I would spare you that."

Paul goes on to state that married people are concerned about worldly matters and about pleasing each other, which distracts from their "undivided devotion to the Lord." A married man may do well, says Paul, "but he who refrains from marriage will do better" (7:38). These are striking words from our "Apostle to the Gentiles." The message seems clear—Paul will accept you if you marry, but he would much prefer that you did not.

And we can cite other Pauline passages. For example, Colossians (3:5): "Put to death, therefore, whatever belongs to your earthly nature: sexual immorality, impurity, lust, evil desires and greed, which is idolatry." Or Galatians (5:16-19): "Do not gratify the desires of the flesh. For the desires of the flesh are against the Spirit... The acts of the flesh are obvious: sexual immorality, impurity and debauchery..." Or 1 Corinthians (6:18): "Flee from sexual immorality [meaning sexual intercourse].

All other sins a person commits are outside the body, but whoever sins sexually, sins against their own body." Or Romans (13:14): "Rather, clothe yourselves with the Lord Jesus Christ, and do not think about how to gratify the desires of the flesh." We might also include the pseudepigraphic Ephesians (5:3): "But among you there must not be even a hint of sexual immorality, or of any kind of impurity, or of greed, because these are improper for God's holy people." This is prudish Puritanism in the extreme. Paul, indeed, seems to strongly prefer that his fellow Christians have no sexual relations at all.

The Gospel writers then continue on in this same theme. We have Matthew (19:10), where the disciples offer to Jesus the idea that "perhaps it is better not to marry." Jesus gives a typically cryptic reply, suggesting that chastity may be best:

> Not everyone can accept this word, but only those to whom it has been given. For there are eunuchs who were born that way, and there are eunuchs who have been made eunuchs by others—and there are those who choose to live like eunuchs for the sake of the kingdom of heaven. The one who can accept this should accept it.

The apparent suggestion here is that we all should 'be like a eunuch,' and not have sex. In Luke (20:34), Jesus addresses the future resurrection of married people: "The people of this age marry and are given in marriage. But those who are considered worthy of taking part in the age to come, and in the resurrection from the dead, will neither marry nor be given in marriage…" Indeed, the unmarried are "equal to angels and are sons of God." It is clear who the preferred people are.

Outside the Gospels and the Pauline Epistles, we have 1 John (2:15): "Do not love the world or the things in the world. … For all that is in the world, the lust of the flesh and the lust of the eyes, is not of the Father but is of the world." Or we could cite 1 Peter (2:11): "Beloved, I urge you as aliens and exiles to abstain from the desires of the flesh that wage war against the soul." And in the late-written Revelations, we read that the Lamb of God will return to Earth only with those "who have not defiled themselves with women, for they are chaste" (14:4).

What should we conclude from all this? It seems that Schopenhauer is right—that perpetual chastity is the prescribed course of action for all good Christians, single or married, young or old. Jesus, Paul, and the Gospel writers all want us to never have sex—ever.

But why? Why would Paul encourage his would-be followers to permanently abstain from sex? Is it just for the "suffering" caused by perpetual frustration? Hardly. Paul did not get this idea from "Jesus" or from God; it was clearly his own invention. He certainly did not get it from the Old Testament, with its many calls to "be fruitful and multiply".[4] The idea itself of a celibate religious group was not unknown to him, as it was characteristic of a number of esoteric cults and secretive groups over the centuries. But Paul wasn't aiming at building some clandestine cult; he wanted a mass movement—of Gentiles. He must have known that it was poor organizational strategy to ask people to commit to chastity. Clearly he had some compelling reason for introducing this component into his new religion.

But is "perpetual chastity" anti-Gentile? Yes—if, by proscribing future children, it erodes Gentile families. This, in fact, is the only practical consequence of Paul's dictate: fewer Gentile children. Seen this way, as a Jewish supremacy strategy to 'defeat' the hated Gentiles, Paul found a way to destroy Gentile families and inhibit the growth of the non-Jewish population.

And it wasn't only Paul, and it wasn't only about sex. Above I gave two chastity quotations from the Gospels of Matthew and Luke. Those same two books also contain, unsurprisingly, a number of broader anti-family passages. In Matthew 10:21, Jesus says, "Brother will betray brother to death, and a father his child; children will rebel against their parents and have them put to death." At Matthew 19:29, Jesus proclaims, "And everyone who has left houses or brothers or sisters or father or mother or wife or children or fields for my sake will receive a hundred times as much, and will inherit eternal life." In the Gospel of Luke (12:52) we read, "From now on, there will be five in one family divided against each other, three against two and two against three." And later (14:26) we find that Jesus says, "If anyone comes to me and does not

---

[4] Genesis 1:28, 9:1, 9:7, 17:20, 28:3, 35:11; Exodus 1:7; Leviticus 26:9; Jeremiah 23:3.

hate father and mother, wife and children, brothers and sisters—yes, even their own life—such a person cannot be my disciple." What is this but a family-destroying message, an admonition to tear apart familial ties, all while staying chaste, simply for the sake of "Jesus"? This is a classic cult-like admonition, thanks to the cult leader, Paul.

In the end, of course, this anti-family stance had to be abandoned, as Schopenhauer himself makes clear. Beginning already with Clement of Alexandria, circa 200 AD—especially in book 3 of his *Stromata*—Gentile Christian Fathers rejected the anti-marriage, anti-family, and anti-child stance of the early Jewish Christians. Clement rails against earlier Fathers like Marcion and Tatian, who held to the literal, anti-natalist reading: "they teach that one should not enter into matrimony and beget children, should not bring further unhappy beings into the world, and produce fresh fodder for death".[5] Writing two centuries later, Augustine too recognized this dilemma in the early Christian Fathers: "They reject marriage and put it on a level with fornication and other vices." By way of modest defense, and with perhaps a touch of comic irony, he adds that, with mass abstention, "the kingdom of God would be realized far more quickly, since the end of the world would be hastened".[6]

Still, it was clear that mass perpetual chastity was not a practical way to build a worldwide religion, and in the end it had to be abandoned or "reinterpreted" by Catholics and Protestants alike. They had to surrender the central aspect of Christian asceticism, its perpetual chastity; but in doing so, they drained away a key element of their own religion. As Schopenhauer says, summing up the situation, "From all this, it seems to me that Catholicism is a disgracefully abused, and Protestantism a degenerate, Christianity".[7]

---

[5] Cited by Schopenhauer (1819/1966), vol. 2, p. 622 note.
[6] Ibid., p. 618 note.
[7] Ibid., p. 626.

CHAPTER 7

TAKING STOCK

For we did not follow cleverly devised myths
when we made known to you the power and
coming of our Lord Jesus Christ...
> — 2 Peter 1:16

God knows that I am not lying.
> — Paul, 2 Cor 11:31

I am speaking the truth in Christ, I am
not lying…
> — Paul, Romans 9:1

In what I am writing to you, before God,
I do not lie!
> — Paul, Galatians 1:20

At this point, I assume that the reader has lots of thoughts bubbling up, and in particular, lots of potential complaints, criticisms, and counter-evidence. Fair enough. I will address as many of those as I can, in due course.

But first, let's take stock by briefly recapping the central facts. The oldest existing physical Bible dates from the year 350 AD; as we move backward in time from there, our confidence in the actual text diminishes significantly—some parts being much more uncertain than others. Expert consensus is that the four Gospels date to the years 70 to 95 AD, and Paul's letters to 50 to 70 AD. The New Testament, like the Old Testament, is a thoroughly Jewish document. Paul, the Gospel authors, Jesus, Joseph, the Virgin Mary, and all twelve apostles were Jews. Many Jews had been in active and passive resistance to Rome from virtually the beginning of the takeover in 63 BC. Between the years zero and 93 AD we have absolutely no independent, corroborating evidence for such things as the Bethlehem star, any of Jesus' 36 miracles, any of the apostles' miracles, any of the Christian-specific events depicted in the New Testament—or even for the sheer existence of a Jesus of Nazareth. Josephus' brief reference in 93—quite possibly a later forgery—is the first independent confirmation of the mere existence of a Christian movement, followed by Tacitus, Pliny, and Suetonius around the year 115.

We further know for certain that the Jews had been in a confrontational and adversarial relationship with their neighbors from the very beginning of recorded history, circa 1200 BC. We know that they viewed themselves as special, different, and superior to the rest of humanity. We know that they believed that they had a God-given right to dominate and rule the world. And we know that these attitudes engendered a reactive hatred toward them by non-Jews that has resurfaced periodically ever since. All these facts are widely accepted by all parties, Christian and non-Christian alike.

Some Possible Explanations

How, then, can we account for the apparent discrepancies and inconsistencies? I have considered various approaches to this situation throughout this book. Let me summarize these, expressed in terms of some possible theories, each with a different response to the many problems that we face. The first is the conventional story:

1) **Biblical Thesis**: Jesus was the miracle-working Son of God who came to earth to save humanity. The Biblical account of his life is largely or entirely correct as written.

On this view, the reason we have no contemporary evidence of Jesus is either (a) it was destroyed by the Romans, or (b) it was accidentally lost to history. Paul's account is true because he had an actual encounter with the spirit of the risen Christ, and because he met personally with some of the apostles. Two of the Gospel writers were apostles (Matthew and John), and the other two were close colleagues of apostles, and thus they can all be trusted. Any discrepancies in the Gospels are due to "different perspectives on the same events," not to errors or mistakes. Paul and his fellow Jews had no malicious intent whatsoever; they were honestly converted to Christianity and selflessly sought to bring the Good Word to all of humanity.

The large majority of Jesus skeptics, those mentioned in Chapter 1, seem to adopt a variation of the Mythicist Thesis:

2) **Mythicist Thesis**: Jesus was an entirely fabricated personage, based on ancient myth-archetypes. His story was created either by Paul, the Gospel writers, or various other later figures, out of whole cloth, for some unspecified reason: perhaps in order to promote a religion and a church that would somehow benefit them personally.

The problems of evidence and chronology all point, they say, to a wholly constructed mythical man, a divine Jesus, that tapped into the human subconscious by calling upon classic archetypes. Paul's (or whoever's) motives are either unknown or, presumably, were a desire for self-glorification and power by placing themselves at the center of a new religion. For this they risked persecution and death.

I have argued for something else:

3) **Antagonism Thesis**: Jesus was a historical person but not the Son of God. His story is a fanciful elaboration of a few grains of truth, created by Paul and his friends, in order to craft an anti-Roman ideology aimed at corrupting and confusing the masses and thus undermining the Empire.

My thesis addresses a key point: *the question of motive*—something that is utterly lacking in the other skeptics. I have shown how the Jews harbored a deep hatred for the Gentile masses and for the Romans in particular, and thus how individuals would have done anything—including lie, and including placing themselves at mortal risk—to benefit the Jewish people. The mythicists and other skeptics have no good account of a motive; the mere quest for personal gain is highly dubious. The low chance of success, combined with a high risk of imprisonment and/or execution, would more than offset any nebulous anticipated advantage. This is the fatal flaw in virtually every Mythicist account.

But there are other possible theses, some less pernicious than a mythicist or antagonist analysis. For example, what if Jesus was merely a historical figure, a mortal rabbi, but his accomplishments became embellished over time, ultimately acquiring legendary and even divine status? And what if someone, upon hearing these amazing stories, then decided—with all good intention—to document them? We can call this the Rumor Thesis:

4) **Rumor Thesis**: Stories of an exceptional but mortal man, a historical Jesus, got exaggerated and embellished over time through oral retellings. After some 40 years, "Mark" heard the stories, innocently believed them, and wrote them down as literal truth. This happened again, after 50 years, separately to "Matthew" and "Luke," and again after 60 years to "John."

This is theoretically possible but highly unlikely. Even in ancient times, people were not idiots. How could a Mark accept, without any apparent evidence or confirmation, such fantastic tales? And accept them so completely that he would write them down as factual truth, as real and actual events? And then how could the same thing happen three more times, to three different individuals? This flies in the face of common sense, not to mention that we have no evidence for such a sequence.

Furthermore, the Rumor Thesis cannot account for Paul. He was too close to actual events to have innocently believed any such stories, which in any case could not likely have become so incredibly exaggerated in just a few years. Paul was a clever man; could he really have fallen so completely for a bogus tale of a crucified Jewish messiah, that he would dedicate his life to spreading the story? It seems highly dubious, to say the least.

Are there other possible theses? Of course. Here's one:

5) **Roman Conspiracy Thesis**: Here, the creators of Christianity were not the Jews, but *the Romans*. And the target audience was not the Gentiles, but *the Jews*. On this thesis, the Romans were terribly worried about the restive Hebrews in Palestine, and thus initiated a process to create a new Judeo-Christian theology, aimed at the Jews, in order to pacify them. This thesis comes in two forms: (a) Josephus (primarily) was conscripted to write the Gospels, and (b) Paul was himself a Roman 'secret agent,' working for Rome, against his fellow Jews.

Thesis (a) is promoted almost solely by one man, Joseph Atwill, in one book, *Caesar's Messiah* (2005). For a man with no ostensible training or skill in research, writing, or theology, and not even a college degree, it is fairly surprising that this one book garners the attention that it does. Atwill agrees that there was a historical Jesus, a rabbi who got crucified, but who worked no miracles and was by no means a son of God. But he then claims that, under the Flavian Dynasty—emperors Vespasian (reign 69 to 79), Titus (79 to 81), and Domitian (81 to 96)—a plan was concocted to employ the Jew Josephus to create a new, pacifistic, pro-Roman theology that would bring the rebellious Jews under control. This is absurd on its face, and thus would require an extensive amount of compelling evidence to be convincing. Suffice to say that Atwill fails to provide such evidence.[1]

There is, however, some actual evidence of Jewish or Christian involvement with the Flavians, which is independently interesting. It involves one Titus Flavius Clemens (born 50 AD), who was a cousin of Emperor Domitian, and Clemens' wife, Flavia Domitilla (b. 60 AD), who was Domitian's niece. Clemens was a minor functionary ('consul') in the Empire, but surely enjoyed a certain prestige, being related to the Flavians. Domitian, though, apparently had little affection for either Clemens or Domitilla, despite the family connections.

In the 15th year of his reign (95 AD), Domitian decided to execute Clemens and banish Domitilla. The reason? "The charge brought against them both was that of atheism, a charge on which many others who drifted into Jewish ways were condemned," according to Cassius Dio.[2] This is a very strange remark; what exactly are the "Jewish ways" to which Dio refers? They were evidently something religious, hence the charge of atheism. Had the couple converted to Judaism? Unlikely. More likely it was Christianity, which, at that time, was still viewed as something Jewish (which of course it was—and still is). It seems likely that the couple had 'converted' to Judeo-Christianity, which was seen as blasphemous and dangerous atheism by the traditional Romans. And evidently, by the 90s

---

[1] Richard Carrier provides a good critique; see his blog entry "Atwell's cranked-up Jesus" (2013).

[2] In his *Roman History* (ca. 230 AD), 67.14. Suetonius briefly comments on the murder: "[Domitian] executed, suddenly and on some trivial pretext, his own cousin, Flavius Clemens" (*Twelve Caesars*, 12.15).

AD, it was viewed as a sufficient threat to warrant death—even to ones' own kin. This is telling, but in no way does it support a Roman conspiracy thesis; in fact, precisely the opposite: if Judeo-Christianity warranted a death penalty from the emperor himself, then it is absurd to think that he, or his family, were behind it.

Thesis (b), that Paul was a secret Roman agent, is attributable mainly to James Valliant and his book (co-written with Warren Fahy) called *Creating Christ: How Roman Emperors Invented Christianity* (2018). But the basic idea was published earlier by Thijs Voskuilen and Rose Mary Sheldon in 2008, with their book *Operation Messiah*. And a related theory is put forth by Henry Davis in his *Creating Christianity: A Weapon of Ancient Rome* (2018).

But as we might suspect, there are a number of serious problems here. First, again, are the qualifications of these writers, which are generally quite dubious. Valliant is a lawyer, Fahy a novelist (!), and Davis seems to be a British undergrad who has yet to earn a degree. Voskuilen apparently has just a BA; only Sheldon has full academic credentials and she has published a number of books with major publishers. Not that these are insurmountable problems, but one should be doubly suspicious of an author with no publishing record and no real training in academic research.

All these books adopt the same general approach: that the Roman elite, primarily the Flavians, decided to enlist a few militant Jews—Paul first, then perhaps James, Peter, and others—to craft a new pacifistic religion that could be promoted amongst the rebellious Jews of Judea. Later, certain unnamed Romans wrote the Gospels in the attempt to flesh out and reinforce the Jesus story. The whole Christian story was a kind of 'psy-op' tactic, cleverly deployed by Rome against the Jews.

There are many problems and unresolved questions with this entire approach, both (a) and (b) versions:

- When and how did the Roman elite contact a Jewish tent-maker like Paul in the first place?
- Did they bribe him? Threaten him?

- By all accounts, Paul was *anti*-Rome, not pro-Rome, and he focused on the Gentiles, not the Jews:
  - Paul declared himself "apostle to the Gentiles," not to the Jews.
  - There are virtually no pro-Roman statements in his letters.
  - Paul was supposedly killed by the Romans.
- Christianity itself is intrinsically anti-Roman:
  - It wants followers to love the Jewish God, not the Roman pantheon.
  - It wants followers to love a Jewish rabbi, Jesus.
  - It opposes wealth and power.
  - It praises the meek.
  - Its focus on the afterlife is opposed to the Greek/Roman focus on the present life.
- Leading Romans eventually converted to Christianity; but why would they believe their own hoax?
- The Gospels say that the Jews killed Jesus—how does this idea pacify Jews?
- Jesus as a crucified Messiah is in direct contrast to orthodox Judaism, which anticipates a powerful and victorious Messiah here on Earth.
- The Book of Revelation is clearly anti-Rome; "Babylon" is an acknowledged codeword for Rome. Which Roman wrote that, and why?
- If Christianity was a Roman strategic lie to pacify the Jews, then it failed miserably: there was the first Jewish War (66-70), then a second (115), and then a third (135).

Apart from all this, there is an intriguing characteristic of the Roman Conspiracy Thesis: it seems contrived to take all attention away from the Jews as guilty parties, and place it on the Romans. I'm not opposed to this, if there is strong evidence for it; but there simply is none, frankly. Thus, the whole thesis comes across as a deflection tactic, to take our eyes away from the Jews as fraudsters and conspirators, and to place it upon the Roman elite—whom popular media love to hate.

On this thesis, the Jews aren't perpetrators, they are *victims*—which fits nicely with their long tradition of victimhood status. And worse: they are *double-victims*: first, of the Roman oppression, and second, of the Roman psy-op called Christianity intended to undermine their morale. This is terribly convenient for the present-day Jewish Lobby, which opposes everyone and everything that might cast any blame upon Jews, any Jews, even long-dead Jews. My Jesus Hoax (Antagonism) Thesis causes them heartburn, but people like Atwill, Valliant, and Sheldon are wonderfully soothing; they nicely deflect all blame and take all attention away from any potential Jewish liars. I'm sure the ADL is quite pleased with their work.

And here is an interesting sixth hypothesis:

6) **Hallucination Thesis**: Paul's "vision" of the risen Christ in or around the year 33 was actually a hallucination or psychotic episode. Paul was not kidding and he was not lying; he really did think he saw something and thought he had a real conversation with Jesus, but it was all in his head. Nevertheless, it was so real and impressive that it became a life-changing event, causing him to go out and build a Christian movement. And he was so fanatically convincing that he persuaded others—and ultimately Mark, Matthew, Luke, and John—to continue on with his vision after he was gone.

Is there any evidence that Paul was mentally ill, or suffered from some severe neurological disorder that might induce hallucinations? Yes. Consider what he himself says about his own condition. Of his "conversion," we read that "suddenly a light from heaven flashed about him... [H]e heard a voice"; when he rose from the ground, "he could see nothing" (Acts 9:3-8). Elsewhere Paul refers to this ecstatic vision as being "caught up to the third heaven" (2 Cor 12:2). To modern medical scientists, this sounds very much like a schizophrenic incident or an epileptic fit, as noted below.

There are other clues. Paul says such things as "I am talking like a madman" (2 Cor 11:23). He admits to having both physical and speech impediments: "For they say [of me], his bodily presence is weak, and his speech is of no account" (2 Cor 10:10). And perhaps most famously: "To keep me from being too elated by the abundance of revelations, a thorn was given me in the flesh, a messenger of Satan, to harass me..." (2 Cor 12:7). There has been much debate about the nature of Paul's "thorn," but to call it "a messenger of Satan" suggests a persistent and severe handicap of some sort, likely psychological in nature—as opposed, say, to a bum knee or bad back.

In Acts we learn that Paul has "visions in the night" (16:9, 18:9) that are clearly more vivid and intense than simple dreams or even nightmares. Later in Acts, as Paul is defending himself in front of King Herod Agrippa II, the Roman procurator, Porcius Festus, allegedly says to him: "Paul, you are mad; your great learning is turning you mad" (26:24).

More clues appear in Romans (7:15-19), where Paul sounds decidedly schizophrenic:

> I do not understand my own actions. For I do not do what I want, but I do the very thing I hate. … [I]t is no longer *I* that do it, but *sin* which dwells within me. For I know that nothing good dwells within me, that is, in my flesh. I can will what is right, but I cannot do it. For I do not do the good I want, but the evil I do not want—this is what I do.

And then there are signs that Paul was a congenital liar, as indicated by his repeated insistence that he is *not lying*: "God…knows that I do not lie" (2 Cor 11:31); "In what I am writing to you…I do not lie!" (Gal 1:20); "I am speaking the truth in Christ, I am not lying…" (Rom 9:1).

The state of Paul's mental health has been examined by modern medical professionals, and in a 2012 study, it was reported that:

> His [Paul's] perceptual experiences, mood variability, grandiose-like symptoms, increased concerns about religious purity, and paranoia-like symptoms could be viewed as resembling psychotic spectrum illness. Psychiatric diagnoses that might encompass his constellation of experiences and manifestations could include paranoid schizophrenia, psychosis NOS, mood disorder-associated psychosis, or schizoaffective disorder.[3]

---

[3] Murray et al (2012).

Other studies—for example, Landsborough (1987)—focus on the likeli-hood of temporal lobe epilepsy. Certainly any modern-day doctor, when faced with a patient matching Paul's characteristics, would find in favor of some form of psychological pathology.

Given that we cannot blame a person with mental illness, we should keep open the possibility that Paul was, at least in part, "mad," and that he suffered from delusions about Jesus and his own role in the world. As we know from experience, madmen can be very lucid and very convinc-ing; he could have been very persuasive, especially in an era that had little knowledge of the nature and causes of such illness.

So where do we stand with these six alternatives? Of the above, I think it's clear that the Biblical Thesis is simply untenable; the problems of evidence and chronology jointly demonstrate that the miraculous life of a divine Jesus is a virtual impossibility. The Mythicist Thesis is possible but has a major flaw, namely the lack of sufficient motive. The Rumor Thesis presumes that Paul and the Gospel authors were gullible idiots who couldn't tell fact from fiction; but from what little we can discern, that seems most unlikely. The Roman Conspiracy Thesis stretches the bounds of plausibility, and does so with no discernable evidence; it is just "an interesting hypothesis," one that conveniently assuages the Jewish Lob-by. The Hallucination Thesis is actually quite plausible—the second most-likely scenario, I would say. But the Antagonism Thesis is by far the most credible analysis. It best accounts for all the known facts, and identifies an actual and fact-based motive for the whole construction. All signs point to a Jesus Hoax.

Critiquing Antagonism

What, then, is the counter reply to the Antagonism Thesis? The basic elements of it have been around for over a century. Obviously, it had been considered before and apparently rejected, since none of the recent Jesus skeptics defend it. What would they say in reply, to challenge that thesis?

In fact, I have raised this question with a number of experts, precise-ly so that I could gauge the strength of the thesis. Let me mention their comments and then offer my responses.

"It's not clear that all the Gospel authors, apart from Matthew, were Jews. John certainly was not."

As I've replied earlier, the Gospel of Mark was written for a Gentile audience and thus takes on the superficial appearance of a Gentile work. There is a strong consensus that Mark himself was Jewish. The extensive OT references in all four Gospels argue strongly for Jewish authorship, given that no one else—no Gentiles—of that time would have had such knowledge. There is no real evidence that Luke was a Gentile save his name, but as we know from Paul, it was not unheard of for Jews to change to Gentile names. The scattered anti-Jewish statements in all the Gospels—especially John—more reflect an internal Jewish battle over ideology than an external, Gentile attack. Paul is clearly and obviously Jewish, although some skeptics, such as Robert Price, argue that the letters weren't even written by a "Paul" but by a much latter Gentile Christian, such as Marcion. This is a very fringe view, but even if true, it doesn't undermine my thesis; it just shifts priority for the hoax to the Gospels. The letters then simply become late-added "substantiation," also fraudulent, by some duped Gentile.

"You are making sweeping generalizations. Not all Jews opposed Rome, and not all NT writers and characters are necessarily Jewish."

On the first point, of course, as I stated, many Jews acquiesced to Roman rule. Probably a large majority accepted it, even if begrudgingly. But the elite Jews were surely incensed, and there was certainly a substantial minority of Zealots and others violently opposed. My thesis doesn't require that all or even most Jews opposed Rome, only that a small band—Paul and friends—did so, and acted on that basis. Regarding the NT writers, that's addressed above. Regarding the characters in the story—Jesus, Mary, Joseph, et al—we can only go by the words written down, and the text is conclusive: all were Jews.

One knowledgeable colleague whom I contacted—a man cited as one of the "20 most influential living Christians" a few years ago—listed a number of specific problems for any such hoax theory:

- *Needs a motive.* Discussed above. The motive was revenge against Rome, and an attempt to undermine its support by confusing and corrupting the masses.

- *The Gospels are "rooted in history."* Of course, as intelligent fraudsters, the authors would include as much factual information as they could, in order to enhance the respectability of the document. But not so much that someone could easily ferret out the falsehood.

- *The Gospels have "self-damaging" material, such as cowardly disciples and women at the tomb, and numerous inconsistencies, which wouldn't have happened in a hoax.* Given that we had semi-independent fraudsters—Paul, Mark working after his death, Matthew and Luke working in evident disagreement—it's not at all surprising that some would incorporate storylines that would be contradicted by the others. In fact, it's almost inevitable. And the inclusion of women in the story is ideal if one is aiming at the Gentile masses, half of whom are female. One could argue that Christianity is the first religion in history to specifically target women equally as men.

- *The depiction of Jesus as Messiah conflicts with Jewish expectations of the time.* Certainly, and that's why the majority of the Pharisees opposed Paul's gang. Paul didn't concoct his hoax for the Jews; it was strictly for the 'benefit' of the gullible Gentiles.[4]

- *The Gospels include material that could be falsified by opponents.* True, if anyone had the time, money, and energy to track down all possible witnesses and to visit all relevant sites. But they generally took place in obscure locations (apart from events in Jerusalem). They had a verifiable core—a historical Jesus with a real crucifixion. And they weren't widely circulated for years or decades after the alleged events. Who would have

---

[4] Paul famously declared himself to be "Apostle to the Gentiles" (Rom 11:13, Gal 1:16).

bothered to refute the miracles, for example, at that point? Paul and company knew that their lie was safe.

- *There are no ancient opponents of Christianity who argue that Jesus was a hoax.* Generally true, but that's probably because the story had a true and verifiable core—the historical Jesus. Either that, or the critics just didn't know enough to make that charge. Then why didn't they simply say that the miracles were fabricated? First, they may well have believed in miracles themselves. But secondly, they would have had no basis for making such a claim, given the nature of miracles and the dearth of physical evidence available to writers in, say, the 300s or 400s, or indeed any time prior to the modern scientific era.

- *These are a tall order for any hoax theory to fill!* I have plausible and reasonable replies to all the above concerns. Therefore: Order fulfilled!

There is another popular response that needs to be addressed: *Who would die for a lie?* That is, why would Paul and the others undergo persecution, harassment, and risk of imprisonment or death for their hoax? I think there's a clear answer here: as Jews, they were all, already, under persecution by the Romans. As extremist, fanatical Jews, they were willing to do anything, and suffer any punishment, in order to help "Israel." And the more their nascent movement seemed to catch on, the harder they would have been willing to push it. Gentiles have a hard time understanding this, but Jews, like Arab and Muslim extremists, are quite willing to die *for their cause*—not for the lie itself, but for the cause that it represented. The lie was the means, not the end.

Regarding specifically the idea that Jesus was a revolutionary Zealot rather than a Son of God, Christian apologists have another ready reply: *"That's an old and discredited thesis, put forth by the likes of S. G. F. Brandon in the 1960s. No one accepts that idea anymore".*[5]

---

[5] This line was recently resurrected with the publication of Aslan's controversial book *Zealot* (2013). See my discussion in Appendix B.

This is worth examining for a moment. Samuel George Frederick Brandon was a British professor of religion who died in 1971. In his books *Jesus and the Zealots* (1967) and *The Trial of Jesus* (1968) he indeed argued that Jesus was a Zealot. He certainly made some observations that are consistent with my Antagonism Thesis. He rightly understood that the Jewish Christians' main aim was "the restoration of Israel's freedom and sovereignty," and that therefore, they would have been "instinctively hostile to the Gentiles" who wanted to join the church.[6] Later he correctly notes that "the end which that 'gospel' [of the Jewish Christians] had in view, namely, the vindication of Israel, implied both an overthrow of Rome and the punishment of the Gentiles".[7] That's exactly right, but he never considers the possibility that the Jews actively lied precisely in order to deceive the detested Gentiles, as a means to overthrow Rome.

Midway through *Jesus and the Zealots*, Brandon offers a concise explanation for why the 'revolution' thesis—precursor of antagonism—is not well-received today:

> The mere idea that the Jewish Christians might have countenanced violent resistance to the Romans provokes an instinctive rejection in the minds of most people today, inured as they are to a long-established tradition that the original disciples must have been quiet and peaceable men, if not actually pacifists. But, on analysis, that tradition is based upon no clear and irrefutable New Testament evidence. ... [A] parallel series can also be produced indicating an opposite attitude, such as "I have not come to bring peace but a sword"...[8]

In his other book, Brandon continues to develop the revolutionary angle: "Jesus' activity in Jerusalem coincided with an insurrection there, in which the Romans were directly involved".[9] And again later on, he adds, "Judaea was seething with unrest from the natural Jewish resentment of

---

[6] (1967: 169).
[7] (1967: 182).
[8] (1967: 202).
[9] (1968: 88).

the Roman yoke and the activities of the Zealots".[10] But even with all this acknowledgement, Brandon again never considers the possibility that the Jews lied to further their cause—and that changes everything.

In his analysis of Brandon, Robert Price hits the nail on the head, explaining where he went awry: "On Brandon's hypothesis, Christianity has mutated from a failed revolutionary movement…into a quietistic, Rome-accommodating faith community and sought desperately to hide their now-repudiated anti-Roman roots".[11] But the convergence of evidence does not support that view. There is no reason that the militant Jews would have given up; rather, they changed direction. Brandon's best defense is that the last Gospel, John, does indeed drop most all talk of revolution, as I noted previously. But that is better attributed to John's new, more intellectual audience than to any utter resignation on the part of the cabal.

The main point, though, is that the apologists never quite get around to explaining how exactly the Zealot thesis has been "discredited." And they can't. They can point to Jesus allegedly saying "love thy enemy" and "turn the other cheek," but that's about it. I will have more to say on this shortly.

---

[10] (1968: 101).
[11] Price (2014: 129).

Chapter 8

CHALLENGES AND CRITIQUES

My Antagonism Thesis—the idea of a Jesus Hoax—has been in circulation for several years now, both formally and informally, in hard copy and online, and presented by myself in talks, debates, and podcasts.[1] It has attracted increasing attention, in part because of its controversial nature and in part because of its uniqueness; no one else—no other Christ mythicist or Jesus skeptic—has put forth a similar thesis, and no conventional Christian scholar has (to my knowledge) even entertained the idea, let alone refuted it. I can only assume that, for the skeptics, the topic is 'too hot to handle,' and for the conventional scholars, it is much more convenient and easier to let a sleeping dog lie; they have the advantage of the status quo, and can just roll along as usual, blithely ignoring the possibility that Jesus is a hoax, conceived and conducted by Paul and his cabal.

Therefore, in a sense, I have captured the entire territory; there is no competition and there is no formal refutation. If my thesis continues to grow in popularity, of course, at some point the orthodox academics will have to address it, much to their dismay. But that day lies somewhere in the future. For now, they are safe in their quiet little ivory (or ecclesiastical) towers, churning out the same Jesus material, over and over, without ever addressing the fundamental questions at hand. This suits almost all parties just fine—except those interested in the truth.

But despite all this, some people have indeed taken it upon themselves to critique the Jesus Hoax: non-Christian academics, knowledgeable laymen, Christian fundamentalists, non-partisan researchers and even a few partisan ones. Christianity is an interesting subject, not the least because "everyone is an expert"—or at least, everyone has an opinion, sometimes well-informed, sometimes not. Thus, in a book such as this, I felt it was important to dedicate some space to my critics, and then to

---

[1] My first formal, public presentation of the thesis was in January 2014, in a debate with a Catholic theologian at my campus of the University of Michigan. Attendance was huge—said to be among the largest such events ever on my campus.

respond to them. Below and in the next chapter, I will cite nearly two dozen of the most prevalent criticisms of my Antagonism Thesis, along with a brief analysis and rebuttal. Naturally, some of these are more 'intellectual' and sophisticated than others, and some may appear rather petty and simple-minded, but still, these are the thoughts and reactions that people have, and therefore they ought to be addressed.

I have organized the critiques into three categories: (1) *Ad hominems*—personal attacks on myself; (2) *Consequentialist*—defending Christianity based on past or present consequences; and (3) *Theoretical*—arguments of a theoretical nature about my assertions.

Ad Hominem Critiques

I will start with the pettiest complaints, mostly to get them out of the way so that we can move on to more substantial issues. In general, I must point out that *ad hominem* attacks are a classic logical fallacy; that is, it does nothing to my argument to attack me personally, or my character, or my motives. I can be good, bad, or neutral; friendly, nasty, or anti-social—none of this affects the strength of my argument, which stands or falls on its own merits. Attacking me may make someone feel good, but it has no bearing on my case.

That said, let's see what more than a few people have had to say.

> (1) "Jews hate Christianity, communists hate Christianity, Marxists hate Christianity, atheists hate Christianity, leftists hate Christianity…these must be *you!*"

Actually, I am here condensing several complaints into one—the basic idea is that "X hates Christianity" and "you hate Christianity," therefore, "You are X," where X is something bad. First, this is logically invalid; it is the equivalent to saying, "Apples are red, firetrucks are red, therefore, apples are firetrucks." It obviously makes no sense.

Second, it is not even true that I "hate" Christianity. Generally, I don't "hate" people or things; that is a juvenile way of thinking. I do, however, strongly dislike being lied to, being deceived, being censored, and being coerced. I wouldn't even say that I "hate" Paul or his cabal for what they did; in fact, I have to hand it to them; it was a remarkably clever and effective hoax. And their masterful lying is truly impressive to behold. They did what they had to do under the circumstances. What is more annoying to me personally is people today, who (a) unquestioningly accept such nonsense, (b) oppose open discussion, (c) are utterly close-minded, even in the face of compelling evidence, and (d) who would slander those who *are* open-minded or skeptical.

Be that as it may, I understand the intuition here: I am taking a position on an issue that has, historically, been taken primarily by despised groups (Jews, Marxists, communists, atheists, leftists—depending on your point of view). It is therefore plausible that I am one of them. However, I can assure the reader that I am none of these. I addressed 'Jew' and 'atheist' in Chapter 1. Marx was a Jewish intellectual who is, in my opinion, highly overrated; I have never been a fan of his. Communism is typically affiliated with Marx but it has roots that go back to Plato; I can endorse much of the Platonic view but virtually none of the Marxist. And 'leftist' is so vague, and has been distorted so badly in recent years, that it has become almost meaningless; personally, I lean left on some issues, right on others, and down the middle on many.

But still…I can understand the hesitation that others may feel, not wanting to endorse a Hoax thesis for fear of even being associated with certain despised groups. This again is another logical fallacy, called "Poisoning the Well": *Don't adopt position X because then you will be associated with all those nasty 'position-Xers'*. It is more of a rhetorical tactic to keep said critic from building a following. And on some people, it works—sad to say. I would hope that most people have enough self-confidence and enough moral backbone to resist such tactics.

(2) "What is your motivation here? It cannot be good…"

My motive is a quest for truth, for honest inquiry, and for discarding false and detrimental ideas in favor of those that may lift us up as a people. It could be said that I have a lot of "gall" to raise such issues; perhaps so. But clearly it takes some firm commitment to the truth in order to pursue unconventional or unpopular ideas. I would hope people see my motives as positive and inspirational.

(3) "You must hate White people."

Far from the case. As a White European-American myself, I have nothing but the best wishes for my fellow Whites. This critic obviously equates Christianity with Whites and thus sees a disparagement of one as a disparagement of the other. Once again, this is illogical. It's like saying someone hates Blacks because they hate hip-hop music (or vice versa); it's nonsense. And, as above, 'hate' is such a juvenile word that I reject any such usage. Yes, I dislike Christianity because it is a hoax and a bogus story that has damaged millions, if not billions of people over the past two millennia, and has led to what surely must be hundreds of thousands of needless deaths. And yes, it is true that most Christians, historically, have been White; but today, by my rough estimate, there are significantly more non-White Christians in the world than White.[2] Christianity is no longer a 'White' religion, and it hasn't been for perhaps 100 years now.

(4) "You want to destroy belief in God."

This is related to the "you must be an atheist" complaint above. But again, this is untrue. As I explained in Chapter 1, there are many characteristics of God that are rational and justifiable, but the moral qualities are not among these—that God is good, loving, just, benevolent, etc. (because of the Problem of Evil). I am all for a limited, rational conception of God, but I would argue against any form of a moral God. So the above complaint is simply false.

(5) "There is some heavy Jew-bashing here. Sounds pretty anti-Semitic to me."

This is an odd situation: one minute I am charged with being a Jew (because both they and I "hate Christians"—see above) and the next minute I'm charged with being a Jew-basher—all because my thesis criticizes a literal handful of Jews who have been dead for 2,000 years. It seems unlikely that I can be both, unless I am a "self-hating Jew"; but of course, I

---

[2] Only the US and Russia have significant numbers of White Christians. The other largest Christian populations—Brazil, Mexico, Philippines, Nigeria, China, Congo—are virtually all non-White.

am none of these. My entire focus here is on history and what did or did not happen long ago. Just because I claim that a handful of Jews lied to the public two thousand years ago, this has no necessary connection to Jews in general or Jews today.

People are overly sensitive these days, particularly about Jews, probably because we hear so much about them and anti-Semitism in the media. It can't reasonably have anything to do with World War Two or the Holocaust, since that ended nearly 80 years ago and almost all the actual victims are now gone—despite the fact that the media and Hollywood are working hard to continually remind the public of Jewish suffering during the war and of the evils of Nazism. I see no good reason why Jews should continue to merit special sensitivity.

One can sense in all these *ad hominem* attacks a common theme: the critic encounters my Hoax thesis, is shocked, and feels personally offended—typically because he or she is a true believer. As a result, he or she responds emotionally rather than rationally, and lashes out at "the messenger" with slanders and insults. This is unfortunate but understandable.

Consequentialist Critiques

"Consequentialism" is a long-standing and highly-respected theory of ethics, dating back at least to British philosophers J. S. Mill and Jeremy Bentham in the 18th century. It claims that a given action can be judged ethically only by its consequences—specifically, actions are good if they lead to beneficial results, such as greater overall happiness. Conversely, actions can be judged as bad if they decrease wellbeing or lead to negative outcomes.

Several of my critics have argued against my Hoax thesis based on negative consequences; in other words, by my discussing or promoting it, it will lead to bad outcomes. In principle, this is a valid form of ethical argumentation. But note that *it does not argue against the validity of the theory itself.* One can accept or admit that a given theory is perhaps true, but also believe that if we discuss it out loud, then bad things will happen. These are two distinct things: the *truth of a theory*, and then its *consequences*.

The theory of evolution is a good example. It is one thing to argue that the theory itself—comprised of natural selection, survival of the fittest, etc.—is true, and another thing altogether to argue that it would have bad consequences (diminished belief in God or the Bible, being "related to monkeys," etc.). Consequences, good or bad, are not a criterion for truth or falsehood.

Here are half-a-dozen consequentialist critiques:

(6) "Without Christianity, Whites will turn liberal."

This assumes (a) that Christianity is not liberal, and (b) liberal is bad. This begs a question: What exactly is 'liberal? By most definitions, it is an outlook or belief-system based on the idea of progress, of the basic goodness of humanity, the autonomy of the individual, and the defense of individual rights and liberties. 'Liberal' derives from the Latin *liber*, or 'free.' As such, all these seem like good things; who is prepared to argue that they are bad?

Given its cult-like nature, it is true that Christianity is not liberal. There is no individual freedom there, no freedom of independent thought, no freedom of action. Everything is specified, up front, in the Bible; it is fixed in stone, for all time. Perhaps there is some comfort in having "eternal laws" to live by, but if they are fake laws, what good is that?

The critic clearly wants Whites (only Whites?) to stay, or become, "non-liberal"—meaning, presumably, "conservative." But even granting that 'conservative' is a good thing, are we prepared to accept anything, even a hoax, in order to coerce people to become that? Are there not other, better reasons and arguments in favor of conservatism? If there are, then use those. If not, then abandon it.

(7) "Whites can't live without Christianity. And anyway, they can 'bend' it in their favor."

First, "Whites" have lived without Christianity for some 1 million years, ever since early European humans became light-skinned due to their northerly climate. Two thousand years of Christian culture are a short-term aberration, a mere blip on the timeline of humanity. Pagan cultures, values, and traditions seemed to have served Europeans quite well, for tens of thousands of years. There is no reason they can't do so again in the future.

As to 'bending' Christianity, what is the point of that? To get rid of the bad, Judaic parts? To introduce something new? To 'spin' it in a certain way? Then it is no longer true Christianity, is it? At that point, we are more or less inventing a new theology; if this is the plan, let's do it right, from scratch, and not based on some bogus Jewish ideology.

(8) "The Hoax Theory would 'unify enemy goyim'."

This is a strange comment, which I have seen in a few different variations. The meaning is not entirely clear, but apparently the concern is that certain Gentile groups compose an 'enemy faction' that risks being unified and empowered by the threat posed by a Jesus Hoax thesis. Presumably, the 'enemy goyim' are the Christian Zionists, who are said to number up to 40 million in the USA. Being close-minded, fundamentalist, and unpersuadable, but faced with the Hoax charge, they might become galvanized in their pro-Christian and (especially) pro-Zionist, pro-Jewish beliefs. And this would be bad because the army of Christian Zionists—who outnumber American Jews by a factor of five, at least—could make things worse for Gentiles trying to undermine both the Christian ideology and the Jewish-Zionist Lobby.

To some degree, this might be true; promoting my Hoax thesis could galvanize Christian (and Jewish) opponents, and make things worse, or the task harder—at least, in the near term. Perhaps so. Any threatened opponent tends to toughen up when faced with a serious threat. But what is the alternative? Let the hoax continue on, unchallenged? Neglect to call out the central Jewish role? I don't see these as viable alternatives.

(9) "Christianity allowed Europeans to conquer the world."

It is true that a nominally 'Christian' Europe coincided with the great progress and great achievements of the Renaissance, the Enlightenment, and the Industrial Revolution. 'Christian' artists produced great art, 'Christian' musicians produced great music, 'Christian' writers produced great books. Europeans, via their colonial powers and military technology, in a sense did indeed "conquer the world." Just one Christian nation, Great Britain, in 1920, alone governed about 25% of global humanity.

But I would argue that all this occurred in spite of, not because of, Christianity. The Christian religion correlates with the great successes of Europe, but as we know, correlation is not causation. I would argue that all those same achievements, and likely more, would have occurred had no Christian hoax ever been invented. The greatness of Greece and Rome were just the beginning, only precursors to what could have been accomplished, had the Europe mindset not become derailed by Judeo-Christian manipulations and disputes. We can never prove this one way or the other, of course, but there is really no argument for the idea that Christianity was in any way essential to the cultural or social achievements of Europe.

(10) "The best neighbors (or best people, etc.) are Christians."

This was largely addressed back in Chapter 1, as the second of two initial charges that needed to be dismissed. The whole matter is a subjective judgment call, one that is partly self-reinforcing. If you are already a Christian, then of course, you will naturally see Christians as the best neighbors, best colleagues, best people, etc. But not always; a Catholic may not feel so sanguine about a Lutheran neighbor. A fundamentalist Baptist may never get along with a Presbyterian coworker.

The implication here is that *Christianity makes people better*. This is a striking claim; but is it true? To answer this, we would need a viable measure of 'better' and then seek out some objective data to test that claim. And even if we could show that Christians are somehow 'better' (less criminal, friendlier, happier, more productive, more successful), how could we know that it was the Christianity that made them that way? It could be the reverse: that the 'better people' are drawn to Christianity —perhaps by default, or for lack of other alternatives.

The situation is analogous to the Santa Claus scenario: that fear of punishment, or bribery with treats, keeps one "good." It works on small children because they are not really rational beings; but it is an insult for mature adults. If someone can only be made 'better' (more moral, nicer, etc.) by the carrot-and-stick approach of heaven and hell, or because "Jesus said it," or "Paul said it"—not to mention that it all is a hoax in the first place—then such a morality is scarcely worth having. There are a number of other mature, rational ethical theories that can make people better, and if these were taught from youth, they would certainly have a more beneficial effect on humanity than a Jewish hoax. Remember: People were good, noble, and moral long before a Jesus of Nazareth ever walked the Earth.

> (11) "Christian ideology led to the quest for universal laws of nature, which in turn led to modern science and modern technology."

This is a very interesting suggestion, which, as far as I know, originated with the historian Lynn White. He wrote an important article in 1967,[3] arguing for a two-part thesis: (1) The biblical creation story led to the idea of "natural theology," which is the quest to understand God through studying nature—a nature that he created. This in turn led to modern science. (2) The dominion mandate of Genesis led to the notion of morality through action ('dominating' action) in the physical world, which necessitated the development of modern tools and technology. Thus, White credits Christianity with being the source and motivating power behind both science and modern technology. Unfortunately, as he goes on to argue, these have led in turn to widespread destruction of the environment, and therefore Christianity is ultimately to blame for the ecological crisis, on his view.

It is a fascinating theory, but there are many arguments against it, which I can't elaborate here. On the face of it, it seems absurd: that Christianity could inspire the emergence of a scientific-technological society that would, in practice, be deeply opposed to supernatural theology of most any kind. And then there is the question, as White understood, of whether these wonderful inventions—science and technology—are a blessing or a curse; in the present day, events seem to be favoring the latter.[4]

In any case, this contention, like all the consequentialist arguments above, do nothing to refute my basic Antagonism (Hoax) Thesis. That the consequences are good, bad, or neutral says nothing about the truth value of my thesis.

---

[3] "The historical roots of our ecologic crisis." See White (1967).
[4] See my book *The Metaphysics of Technology* (2015) for an extended critique.

Theoretical Critiques

These are, generally, the most sophisticated critiques of my view. They directly challenge one or more of my central contentions.

> (12) "Jesus Christ is knowable only through introspection, not rationally or objectively. Therefore, your Hoax thesis is power less to prove the non-existence of the Son of God."

This is a more advanced version of one of the defenses that I examined in Chapter 1: the idea that Jesus is knowable only via faith, not reason. Here, it is not mere 'faith' that is required to know Jesus, but 'introspection'—presumably a kind of direct, immediate perception or intuition.

My answer here is similar to what I said in the first chapter; our entire Western civilization was built upon objective rationality, not faith, not intuition, not introspection, not subjective feelings, not personal truths or personal realities. I'm not saying that these are worthless, only that they cannot serve as the basis for an interpersonal society or civilization. You may "know" Jesus "in your heart," which is fine for you, but that does nothing for me personally, and more importantly, it provides no evidence or argumentation for your case (or against mine). People can have introspected "knowledge" about all kinds of non-existent things: spirits, demons, aliens, fairies, ghosts, deceased relatives, and so on. None of this argues against my thesis.

> (13) "The problem is not Christianity per se but the 'Jewish subversion' of Christianity. 'Original' Christianity is as true and valid as ever."

This is quite a popular reply, again coming in many variations. On this view, Jesus—likely a Gentile, though still the Son of God—had an original, noble, and uplifting message for humanity, but the poor fellow was hounded and persecuted by the nasty Jews, who ultimately succeeded in getting him crucified. Then later, after his death, they distorted his message (in some unspecified way) to serve Jewish interests (in some unspecified way). They managed to document their version of his ideas in the Pauline letters and Gospels, and the other, original set of teachings was subsumed and mostly lost to history.

This again is a clever hypothesis, which accepts about half of my Hoax thesis. Paul and the Gospel writers were shifty, lying, deceitful Jews who are to be blamed for altering or even constructing a 'negative' version of Christianity that caused harm to future believers. But there are some huge problems here: What exactly was the 'original' Christianity? How can we reliably separate that part out from the evil Jewish distortions? And how exactly did the 'new' version benefit them?

We must keep in mind that *everything* we think we know about Jesus and his message comes from Jewish documents: the Pauline letters and the four Gospels. There is no other source. It's not like we have a secret 'true' gospel of Jesus, or some independent version of his teaching. We have nothing. Even the so-called 'lost gospels' or 'gnostic gospels' date from a century or more later in time, and thus are generally worthless—unless they can plausibly lay claim to having had access to some secret, original teaching (that now is lost, conveniently).

Some people try to compare the words put into Jesus' mouth in the Gospels with other ideas pronounced by Paul or his cabal. For example, we read in 1 Tim (2:11):

> Let a woman learn in silence with all submission. And I do not permit a woman to teach or to have authority over a man, but to be in silence.

Paul says something very similar in 1 Corinthians:

> Women should be silent in the churches. For they are not permitted to speak, but should be subordinate, as the [Jewish] Law also says. (14:34)

But some could argue that Jesus never said anything like this; in fact, he (allegedly) held women in high esteem. Therefore, they say, this was a Jewish distortion.[5] But of course, *all* "Jesus' words" are *already* a "Jew-

---

[5] In the case of the role of women, it's a bit more complicated: I think Paul had a typical patriarchal outlook, and he assumed, probably correctly, that the Gentile masses did too. The later Gospel writers, however, seemed to soften their

ish distortion." Jesus' words are either (on the benign view) a Jewish se-lection and interpretation of what Jesus said, or (on the Hoax thesis) a total construction of what he said. We have no original transcript, no original recording, to compare what he "really" said with the words in the Gospels.

The other approach some take is to point out how Jesus' words in the Gospels differ, or conflict with, the Old Testament. In this way, they say, Jesus' teachings "correct" or "universalize" God's message in the OT. Post-Christian Jews adhere to the fallacious and defective view of God's word, whereas Christians adhere to the proper or correct version. But again, this is a ridiculous claim; how can we know what is "proper" or "correct"? Maybe if God appeared today, he could tell us. But short of that, we have literally no way to know.

By contrast, on my Hoax thesis, the explanation is clear: the devia-tions from the OT introduced by Paul and the cabal are there *strictly to appeal to the Gentiles*. The ideology of the NT is targeted at Gentiles, not Jews. It would have made no sense for Jesus to simply reiterate OT ideas, to just regurgitate ancient Judaism. That would have never appealed to the Gentile masses. It had to be different in certain key ways—universal, 'mythological,' ethereal—that would appear non-Jewish. Furthermore, Paul had no concern about introducing bizarre, defective, and even soul-destroying ideas into the Gentiles' heads; he likely detested them, as did all Jews. And he certainly wanted to rule over them, as did all Jews. Hence his new theology had to serve that purpose, and therefore to oppose Ro-man rule and the Roman worldview, if he was to achieve his goals.

The critic who wants to make the above point needs to show us, clearly and concisely, (a) the 'original' Jesus-version of Christianity, and (b) the distorted, Jewish version. And then he needs to explain *how he knows this*, given that Jews wrote both the original and the distortion. And then he needs to show that the 'original' version, too, is not a hoax. We could well be dealing with an original hoax that was later altered and supplemented by additional layers of hoax. Suffice it to say that this critic has a lot of work to do, to make a compelling case.

---

stance a bit, allowing women like Mary Magdalene and others to play a small role in the Jesus story. They likely assumed that this would better draw in the female Gentiles.

(14) "The Hoax theory is irrelevant because it is unknowable and
unverifiable."

This is a clever assertion. The critic is effectively pulling from the philosophy of Karl Popper, who famously demanded that, for a theory to be
"scientific," it had to be *falsifiable*; that is, conceivably proven wrong.
Any theory that is irrefutable is unscientific, and therefore unworthy of
consideration, according to Popper.[6]

Now, it is true, as I admitted at the start of this book, that my view is
unprovable. But so is the Christian view. We are both 'unknowable' and
'unverifiable'—at least, as things stand today. In theory, some new evidence could emerge, some long-lost document, that would bolster my or
their case. Maybe even sufficient to serve as 'proof.' But until that day
comes, we are stuck with the data that we have.

In the meantime, we are left with *plausibility arguments*: What is
most likely, given what we know? Who has the burden of proof? What
does the existing scientific evidence have to say? All these things point in
my favor.

(15) "What makes you think that *Paul* was a real person? If he was
fictitious, then, no hoax."

This is an interesting argument: that Paul was not a real individual man,
but perhaps a collection of individuals working under a pen name, or
possibly even mythical himself. With no Paul, there can be no "artful
liar" (as I call him), and thus no Jesus hoax—or so the critic claims.

First, consider this quotation from Christian scholar and university
chemist John Oakes:

> As far as I know, there is not a single reputable scholar, in-
> cluding atheists, Jews, Muslims, skeptics or anyone from
> any background who is a historian or scholar, who doubts
> that Paul was a real person. Even the real fringe people who
> (against all scholarly evidence) doubt the reality of Jesus—
> even they do not have the nerve to claim that Paul was not

---

[6] See Popper's famous book *Conjectures and Refutations* (1963).

a real person… Evidence for the reality of Paul comes from the dozens of writers who quoted him within a generation of his death. Every single Christian source agrees that he was a real person…

To say that they were deceived that Paul was an apostle and that he was a real person is to verge on irrationality. There is not a single example of an opponent of Christianity in the first two or three centuries who doubted his reality. It would have been like doubting that Seneca or Ovid or Cicero lived. Bart Ehrman, one of the biggest critics of the reliability of the Bible, has debated unscholarly atheists who claim that Paul is not real and struggled to not laugh at his atheist friends for making the foolish and unfounded claim that Paul was not a real person.[7]

Granted, Oakes is a Jesus-believer, but he has authored a dozen books on the subject and thus has at least some standing to make such a claim.

But what are the alternatives? I think there are only two: (1) "Paul" was really a collection of individual Jews, writing under his name. But this only modifies my hoax thesis. Now there are many anonymous Jewish hoaxers instead of a single one. My basic theory still holds, under modified form. (2) "Paul" was a mythical figure made up later in time. But Acts is virtually a biography of Paul, and is standardly dated to the mid-80s. The First Epistle of Clement mentions Paul, and was likely written in the 90s AD. Ignatius' Epistle to the Romans also mentions Paul, and probably dates to ca. 105 AD. So who made up "Paul," and when? The only plausible culprit is Marcion (85-160 AD), but he could not have constructed a Paul myth at those early dates—which occurred either before he was born or while just in his teens. So, who did it? And why? Until we can answer these questions, we don't have a viable counter-view.

And even if there was no historical Paul, what about the Gospel writers? Were they, too, mythical figures? *All* of them? Invented when, and by whom? This implies that *none* of the Gospels can be dated to the 1st century AD—can this be sustained? I don't think so. If *any* of the

---

[7] Dated 2015. Posted here: www.dtodayarchive.org/bible-study/hot-topics/item-7103-q-is-there-any-historical-evidence-that-paul-was-a-real-person

Gospels date to 70-100 AD, and had Jewish authors, then my hoax thesis is still maintained. Only now it is just "the cabal" who fooled the world.

(16) "Paul believed in a 'celestial' Jesus, not an earthly one."

This idea is notably promoted by Jesus mythicist Richard Carrier, one of the more active and better-qualified skeptics. This is worth a bit of an elaboration; Carrier is largely on the right track in his writing, but, sadly, he always stops just short of drawing the logical conclusion.

Let me start with what he gets right, in his book *On the Historicity of Jesus* (2014). He repeatedly observes, correctly, that there is extensive "fabrication," "inventing," and yes, "lying" going on with the NT writers. For example:

- "John has run wild with authorial gluttony, freely changing everything and inventing whatever he wants. By modern standards, he is lying." (p. 491)
- "John has clearly 'inserted' this figure into these stories… In plain terms, that's simply a lie." (p. 500)
- "The Gospels generally afford us no evidence whatever for discerning a historical Jesus. Because of their extensive use of fabrication and literary invention…we cannot know if anything in them has any historical basis…" (p. 506)
- "[The Gospel writers] are mythographers; novelists; propagandists. They are deliberately inventing what they present in their texts." (p. 509)

All this is completely correct and well-said. But then when it comes to an explanation, a reason for all this, Carrier stumbles. He says that a given Gospel "becomes considerably more powerful and effective if it is also taken literally" (p. 507), and that "such historicizing also gave the church hierarchies more control over doctrine." But to what end? Was that the whole motive—power and control, for its own sake? The Gospel writers "had a different agenda" (what?), for "preaching, teaching, and propaganda" (to what end?). The writers "are doing it *for a reason* (even if we can't always discern what that is)" (p. 509). Really? Why can't we discern this? With a knowledge of the history and conventional motives of Jewish action, at least one possibility becomes quite clear—a Jesus hoax.

But not for Carrier. The entire construction of the Jesus "lie" occurred "not as a result of any organized conspiracy, but simply from independent scribes and authors widely sharing similar assumptions and motives" (p. 609). Motives such as…*what?* And how can he be so sure that there was no "conspiracy"? Does he say this to avoid being called a "conspiracy theorist"?

Carrier furthermore denies the existence of even a historical Jesus, the ordinary rabbi. As he sees it, Paul hallucinated a "cosmic" or "celestial" Jesus—later to be called "Jesus in outer space." This accords with my Hallucination Thesis. But against this, Paul says, time and again, that his Jesus was a real, flesh-and-blood man, one who really lived and really died on the cross. Consider what Paul says in Galatians. Jesus was "raised from the dead" (and thus obviously was once alive); he was "crucified" and "died"; he was Abraham's "offspring", and indeed was "born of a woman" (4:4). All these can only apply to a physical human being.

Or look at 1 Thessalonians, where Paul again says that Jesus was "raised from the dead," and that "the Jews killed Jesus" (2:15). Or in Romans, where Jesus "descended from David according to the flesh" (1:3). And again we find phrases like "raised from the dead," "by his blood," and "body of Christ"—all of which can only apply to a living, breathing human.

Thus, we see that it is unlikely that Jesus was merely a "celestial" being. But more to the point, even if he was, there was still a Jewish hoax—if not by Paul, who was mentally ill, then by his followers, who were not.

> (17) "Why pick on Jesus? Why not Moses, or King David, or
>   King Solomon? Maybe they were the original hoaxes."

It is true, as I discussed in Chapter 2, that these very early figures in Jewish history are quite possibly mythical in nature. Moses allegedly lived around 1300 BC, but we have zero corroborating evidence for him. King David is supposed to have reigned circa 1000 BC, but again, most scholars doubt his actual existence. David's alleged son, King Solomon (reign ca. 950 BC) seems to be slightly more plausible as a real person, but again, so little is known that we are hard pressed to make firm conclusions. Therefore, it is certainly possible, even likely, that someone "made up" all three figures to add some glory to the ancient Hebrews, and thus they were a kind of hoax. But if so, they hoaxed *only themselves*; no one else really cares if any of these three figures were real, except orthodox Jews. Perhaps someday, a scholar will write a book titled "The Moses Hoax"; but for now, our focus is on the vastly more important Jesus.

> (18) "Your Hoax theory is irrelevant because it is now *history*; generations have accepted Christianity as true, and it is built into the fabric of Western Civilization."

Is it too late for my thesis? Has history settled the matter? Obviously, I cannot undo 2,000 years of history, nor do I attempt to. It is clear that Christianity is indeed "history" and that it has been, to some degree, built into our civilization. But all this is irrelevant to my claim. In principle, it doesn't matter if Jesus the man lived 2,000 years ago, or 200 years ago, or 20 years ago; if someone took his real life and constructed a fable based on a kernel of truth, and then passed that off as reality, then we are being hoaxed. It is certainly a more *tragic* hoax, given that it has persisted for two millennia, but the length of time actually makes my thesis *more* relevant, not less. A 20-year hoax is almost certainly less consequential than a 2,000-year hoax.

> (19) "The lack of documented Jesus miracles is not a problem because miracles were commonplace at that time. It was simply not necessary to record such events."

This is a rather stunning objection, and one made by a PhD'd former professor, no less.[8] In response to this issue, he said this:

> The most obviously fallacious is the claim that if Jesus really worked miracles, it would have been headline news and recorded in all the contemporaneous sources and later the

---

[8] Who shall remain nameless, to protect his reputation. His comments were posted on an essay by an author making a similar argument as I have made.

history books. That is, of course, ridiculous. Accounts of alleged miracles and supernatural events, especially healings, are ubiquitous in most cultures. There are so many of them that only a minuscule minority are written down and remembered.

Everything hinges here on the phrase "accounts of." He may be correct, that there were many "accounts of" or "reports of" miracles back then; many people in those days were alleged "magicians" who could work wonders. If it is merely "accounts," then he may have a point. But the good doctor goes on to undermine his own credibility by saying this:

> No small number of people in today's Morocco are doing things as outlandish as many of Jesus's miracles, if my informants can be believed. There are people who teleport to Mecca or Algeria, others who stop or reverse time, still others who feed multitudes by miraculously pulling vast quantities of food out of the air. ... Telepathy, clairvoyance, and precognition abound. And miracle healings, of course, are a dime a dozen.

Really? Has anyone captured any of this on a cellphone video? I suspect not. Until then, call me skeptical.

(20) "Jews have long hated Christians and Christianity. So how can Christianity be a Jewish plot?"

There is a lot to unpack here in this short critique. First, we need to remind ourselves that, if history is any guide, that Jews hate *everybody*—recall the discussion in Chapter 4. That was a historical study, but there are reasons to believe that, just has Judaism has not changed its fundamental outlook, that the Jewish worldview has not fundamentally changed either. Jewish supremacism is as robust as ever, and the Jewish mania for wealth and power over others is, if anything, more intense than in past centuries. Obviously there are exceptions, and there are many varieties of 'hate,' but still, by and large, Jews seem to have a built-in antipathy to all non-Jewish people. If you are White, or Christian, you sense it as a hatred against Whites or Christians; but you don't realize that the same (or similar) feelings are projected against all Gentiles. This is the first point to keep in mind.

Next, we need to recall the context of Paul's actions. He was going against the orthodox elite Jews in claiming that Jesus was (a) the Messiah (albeit a dead-and-risen one), and (b) Jesus was to save *everyone*, Jew and Gentile alike. Both of these points were anathema to the orthodoxy. This alone was enough for the elites to hate Paul and his invented theology, not to mention his 'Jesus.' This hatred was enough for Paul and his cabal to claim that the Jews "killed" (or wanted to kill) Jesus—or rather, the 'Jesus-concept'.[9] Paul and his band were a tiny minority, vastly outnumbered by orthodox Jews who were his opponents or outright enemies; no doubt, to him, "the Jews" were the enemy, even though he was one of them.

Thus, anyone who joined the nascent Christian movement—mostly Jews at first, then gradually more Gentiles, and eventually only Gentiles—were automatically hated by the orthodox Jews. As Christianity became, over several decades, a wholly Gentile movement, there was thus a double reason for Jews to hate them: as Gentiles, and as Christians.

Naturally, this hatred was eventually reciprocated, which is why, beginning with Melito of Sardis (ca. 150 AD), Tertullian (ca. 190), and Hippolytus (ca. 200), we find evidence of "Christian anti-Semitism" among major church figures. This attitude reached a kind of peak with Gregory of Nyssa, Jerome, and especially Chrysostom, around the year 375; it has persisted ever since, to varying degrees.[10]

But the critic implies that this holds in the present day, where the situation is somewhat different. For the approximately one-third of Jews who are religious, the attitude is the same: they harbor a secret (or open) detestation of both Gentiles and Christians, and especially Gentile Christians. But for the two-thirds of Jews who are secular or non-Judaic, they generally manifest the in-built hatred of Gentiles at a racial level, and they embody the longstanding attitude of Jewish supremacy; these can exist apart from religious considerations. Furthermore, given that wealthy secular Jews are dominant in both media and the political

---

[9] See 1 Thes 2:15, Mk 10:33, Lk 22:2, and Jn 7:1.
[10] See especially the work of Martin Luther (2020), and the Catholic essays of the late 19th century, as reproduced in Dalton (2022: 147-194).

sphere, we see both entertainment and governmental policy that manifests itself as anti-Christian: rigorous separation of church and state, mocking or abuse of Christian values (such as Jews being pro-abortion), and cultural intrusion (such as eliminating "Merry Christmas," etc.).

And then there are two further issues at play. First, Jews (secular and religious) seem to loathe and fear so-called "Christian nationalism," which is a kind of right-wing political movement that seeks to restore or create a nation based on Christian teachings and values, but which is, almost by default, heavily White and frequently anti-Semitic. Such a movement implicitly or explicitly excludes Jews from positions of power, and hence they (Jews) are reflexively opposed to it. Second is the general feeling, apparently shared by many Jews, that Whites are their greatest rivals in the struggle for power and control—which indeed seems true, given that Whites have repeatedly beaten back Jewish influence over the centuries; we need only recall the dozens of expulsions of Jews from Europe, or the German National Socialist era. Thus, strictly on a power-struggle basis, Jews instinctively 'hate' Whites, especially White Christians.

Regarding Christianity itself, secular Jews generally laugh at its stupidity. But at the same time, they realize that it works to their benefit, both via Christian Zionists and via the famous pacifistic Christian tendencies ("turn the other cheek," "love thy enemy," etc.). So on the one hand, they snicker and mock Christians, but on the other, they like what it does for them. Hence it is a kind of love-hate relationship. Overall, the situation is quite complicated, as I noted above.

The bottom line: Christianity is indeed a "Jewish plot" precisely *because* of Jewish hatred. It is the culmination of Jewish hatred, manifest as its very opposite—Christian "love." This is precisely what Nietzsche recognized long ago:

> Out of the trunk of that tree of vengeance and hatred, Jewish hatred—the deepest and most sublime hatred, that is, a hatred which creates ideals and transforms values, something whose like has never existed on earth—from that grew something just as incomparable, a *new love* [i.e. Christian 'love'], the deepest and most sublime of all the

forms of love: —from what other trunk could it have grown?

However, one should not assume that this love arose essentially as the denial of that thirst for vengeance, as the opposite of Jewish hatred! No: the reverse is the truth! This love grew out of that hatred, as its crown, as the victorious crown unfolding itself wider and wider in the purest brightness and sunshine, which, so to speak, was seeking for the kingdom of light and height, the goal of that hate… This Jesus of Nazareth, the living evangelist of love, the "Savior" bringing holiness and victory to the poor, to the sick, to the sinners—was he not that very seduction in its most terrible and most irresistible form, the seduction and detour to exactly those *Jewish* values and innovations in ideals?[11]

It was this hatred—hatred for Rome, hatred for Gentiles in general—that drove Paul and his cabal to construct a monumental lie for the benefit of "Israel." Nietzsche understood this over a century ago; and yet today, we act shocked at such a notion.

> (21) "Absence of evidence is not evidence of absence. That is, just because we have no corroborating (non-Christian) evidence on Jesus from the years zero to 90 AD, that doesn't mean he didn't exist."

Consider this scenario. Say I am out working in my yard, and my neighbor comes over and says, "Hey, hi! Say, did you know that a pack of wild wolves is roaming through the neighborhood?" To this, I am likely to say something like "Wow, really? That seems mighty unlikely to me. In fact, I would bet $100 that there are no wolves in the neighborhood. Do you have any evidence?" "Well, no. But you know, absence of evidence is not evidence of absence."

Does saying this help or hurt my neighbor's case? Does it help or hurt *my* contention that there are no wolves? Clearly, this is bad news for him; if he expects me to believe something extremely unusual and un-

---

[11] *On the Genealogy of Morals* I.8.

likely, then he needs to provide the evidence. As I explained in Chapter 1, he has the burden of proof. And in the *absence* of evidence, his assertion has no credibility. If in fact there were a pack of wolves in the neighborhood, we would expect actual evidence: paw prints in the dirt, wolf droppings, dead animal carcasses, video or audio recordings, corroborating witnesses, and so on. In the absence of evidence, I have no reason whatsoever to believe the claim. Sometimes, the absence of evidence *is* evidence of absence.

The same is true with Jesus, Son of God. He is not just your run-of-the-mill miracle worker (if there ever was such a thing); no—this is the *Son of God*, or perhaps *God himself*, come to Earth, working dramatic and unmistakable miracles. There were many opportunities, with literally thousands of witnesses, and dozens of capable, literate scholars, Jewish and Gentile, who might have documented something, anything, on the Son of God. But *no one* wrote *anything*. Here, the absence of evidence is extremely telling; here, it *is* evidence of absence.

> (22) "How could so many people be fooled for so long? It doesn't
>   seem possible."

Actually, there have been several famous examples in history when many people, even many smart people, have been fooled for a very long time. The ancient Greeks, as brilliant as they were, initiated a number of false beliefs that were sustained for centuries. For example, it was long held that the stars rotated around the Earth affixed to a cosmic or celestial sphere—a view held by Plato, Eudoxus, and Aristotle, among others.[12] And everyone believed it; what could be more obvious than that the stars, which rotate around us each night, in fixed constellations, were attached to a gigantic sphere? This fact was taken for granted well into the 1500s, nearly 2,000 years after it was introduced. But it was totally and completely false.

Another famed Greek philosopher, Empedocles, determined that all material objects were composed of four basic elements: fire, air, earth, and water. And these were pushed and pulled by two forces that he called

---

[12] See Plato's *Timaeus* 33b, 36c-d and Aristotle's *Metaphysics* 1073b18-1074a15.

'love' (attraction) and 'strife' (repulsion). So compelling was this notion that it held as true until the time of Robert Boyle in the late 1600s.

Then we have witchcraft. Witches have been condemned and burned since at least 300 BC, and during the peak period in Europe—from 1450 to 1750—some 500,000 were killed. Thousands of people, mostly young women, were drowned or burned alive simply because someone—almost certainly a Christian—was *absolutely positive* that they were witches. Imagine how sure you would have to be of your "facts" in order to burn a young girl alive at the stake; and yet, they did it, over and over. (I doubt that there's a hell, but if there is, those people are in it.)

Finally, consider the document known as the Donation of Constantine. This was an alleged declaration by Emperor Constantine who supposedly "donated" his entire Roman Empire to the Catholic Church in the year 315 AD. (Constantine was the first Roman emperor to convert to Christianity, in 312). But the document surfaced only in the 700s, when it was used as justification for the Church to maintain complete rule over Europe. It was held as true and valid for about seven centuries, until Lorenzo Valla proved that it was a forgery in 1440. But by then, the Church had a stranglehold on power and no longer really needed ancient justification. It did, however, serve to spur reformers like Martin Luther, who would found the anti-Catholic Protestant movement in the early-1500s.

In all these cases, millions of people were fooled, deceived, or otherwise attached to false beliefs for centuries. At the time, they were dead-certain that they were correct; but in fact, they were dead wrong. It is no surprise that millions or billions could still be wrong about religion. In fact, it is virtually guaranteed.

CHAPTER 9

IS THE NEW TESTAMENT PRO-ROMAN?

Back in Chapter 5, I addressed the likely truth of the Jesus story. I argued that Paul and his cabal had a two-part motive: to undermine Roman rule, and to morally and psychologically weaken the detested Gentile masses. In a brilliant flash of insight, Paul realized that he could do both at once, through a god-man Jesus who promised everyone eternal life in heaven, if only they followed his "way." The Jesus-message, as relayed by Paul and his fellow Jews, included an exhortation for permanent celibacy (even in marriage) along with numerous explicit and subtle calls for rebellion. I touched on this again in Chapter 7, with my "Roman Conspiracy" thesis.

But the idea that the NT was somehow anti-Rome, or a call to revolt against it, has raised a number of complaints from critics, which I will put in the form of a 23rd and final critique:

> (23) "Paul is *pro-Roman*, not anti-Roman. So are the Gospels. Just look at all the pro-Roman passages, and the famous pacifism of Christianity. Therefore, the 'hoax' cannot have been intended to undermine Rome or rebel against it; Christianity supports Rome!"

This is an important point, one that I hear incessantly, in various forms. But it is extremely weak in justification. The critic's basic idea is that Christianity is all about loving your neighbor (and your enemy), turning the other cheek to wrongs, being a good "lamb," being chaste, being meek, turning away from worldly concerns. All these things favor Rome. By contrast, on my Antagonism Thesis, Paul and cabal are agitating *against* Rome. Let's compare the textual evidence on both sides and see what we can conclude.

First, on the allegedly "pro-Roman" side of my critic: When we search the NT for relevant pro-Roman passages, we actually find few—they are *famous*, but few in number. In the letters of Paul, we find a few apparently pro-Roman sentiments, but almost exclusively in *one book*: Romans. And then, almost exclusively in *one chapter*: 13. Here is Rom (13:1-7):

> Let everyone be subject to the governing authorities, for there is no authority except that which God has established. The authorities that exist have been established by God. Consequently, whoever rebels against the authority is rebelling against what God has instituted, and those who do so will bring judgment on themselves. For rulers hold no terror for those who do right, but for those who do wrong. Do you want to be free from fear of the one in authority? Then do what is right and you will be commended. For the one in authority is God's servant for your good. But if you do wrong, be afraid, for rulers do not bear the sword for no reason. They are God's servants, agents of wrath to bring punishment on the wrongdoer. Therefore, it is necessary to submit to the authorities, not only because of possible punishment but also as a matter of conscience. This is also why you pay taxes, for the authorities are God's servants, who give their full time to governing. Give to everyone what you owe them: If you owe taxes, pay taxes; if revenue, then revenue; if respect, then respect; if honor, then honor.

So who, exactly, are "the authorities" that we are supposed to respect? Romans was written around the year 57, when Nero was emperor. Why didn't Paul say "Nero"? Why didn't he say "emperor" or "Rome"? On the other hand, the Jerusalem Jews had a local Jewish ruler: Herod Agrippa II. And he was the nominal leader of all Jews, no matter where they resided. It is far more likely that Paul would defer to a Jewish king than to a Roman emperor, which is perhaps why he cleverly said only "authorities." Paul is far more likely to be *pro-Jewish* here than he is to be pro-Roman.

And even if he does mean "Nero" here, all he is really saying is, "Follow the law, don't make waves, lay low." And this, only to his fellow Jews in Rome—nowhere else. We must recall that the whole premise of the Jesus Hoax is that Paul is trying a new tactic: not open confrontation with Rome, but a subtle undermining of the Gentiles with his new, pro-Jewish religion. To that end, of course, you will pay your taxes and avoid overt trouble. We have better, subtler plans, says Paul.

Paul then goes on to cite the Old Testament morality:

> The commandments, "You shall not commit adultery," "You shall not murder," "You shall not steal," "You shall not covet," and whatever other command there may be, are summed up in this one command: "Love your neighbor as yourself." Love does no harm to a neighbor. Therefore love is the fulfillment of the law.

Of course, we recall that, since the OT is exclusively aimed at Jews, that "the neighbor" is exclusively *your fellow Jew*—not a Roman, not a Greek, not a pagan. There is no "love" here for the Romans, only for the fellow down-trodden Jews.

And that's virtually all that we find in Paul. There is one other passage in Galatians that is sometimes cited, but this again is a repeat of above: "You shall love your neighbor as yourself" (5:14). But once more, this is the Jewish neighbor, no one else. Apart from this repeat, we find no other pro-Roman passages in Paul. The critic is invited to search for others, and to make his argument. In any case, we need to compare these few lines to the many anti-Roman or rebellious passages from Paul, which I will do shortly.

But turn now to the Gospels; where are their "pro-Roman" passages? In Mark, we find *one*: the famous "Render unto Caesar":

> Jesus said to them, "Render to Caesar the things that are Caesar's, and to God the things that are God's" (Mark 12:17).

Is this supposed to be an impressive statement of some kind? Is that the best that Jesus can come up with? Obviously, "Caesar" (again, why not "emperor" or "Rome" or "Tiberius"?) is the ruler, and of course, you need to give him his due—otherwise he will crush you. This is obvious. But this says nothing about not also hating him and his rule, and working against him and the detested Gentile masses. Those two things are quite compatible. This is all we find in Mark.

What about Luke? There we find the stripped-down version of the famous Sermon on the Mount, in contrast to the much longer account in Matthew. Luke records just a couple ostensibly pro-Roman lines by Jesus: "love your enemies" (6:27), turn the other cheek (6:29), "judge not" (6:37)—that's it. The longer Matthew Sermon simply repeats these three (5:44; 5:39; 7:1) and adds nothing more. But this gospel does include the example of Jesus healing the centurion's servant (8:5-13), which is supposed to imply…what? That Jesus loves centurions? Or their servants? Is this (bogus) miracle supposed to serve as a profoundly pro-Roman message? Lastly in Matthew, we have the incident where Jesus is apprehended *by his fellow Jews* (26:47-56). A follower then draws his sword and slices off the ear of one of the apprehending Jewish slaves. Jesus replies, "Put your sword back into its place; for all who take the sword will perish by the sword" (26:52). So Jesus doesn't want Jews stabbing other Jews; how is this a pro-Roman message? And yet, this is constantly cited as "proof" or "evidence" of the Gospels' pro-Roman stance. It is nonsense.

Apart from these few statements—which do little or nothing for the critic's case—there is *nothing*. Nothing more in Luke or Matthew, nothing at all in John.

Now, let's compare these to the many anti-Roman or rebellious passages, beginning with Paul. Again, these are in roughly chronological order:

- Jesus will "deliver us from the present evil age." (Gal 1:4)
- Turn away from "weak and beggarly elemental spirits" of Rome. (Gal 4:8)
- "Do not submit to the yoke of slavery." (Gal 5:1)
- No victory "unless the rebellion comes first." (1 Thes 2:3)
- Put on the "breastplate of faith," "helmet of hope." (1 Thes 5:8)
- Jesus is not coming "unless rebellion comes first." (2 Thes 2:3)
- Salvation will come "to the Jews first." (Rom 1:16)
- When "the full number of Gentiles come in" then "all Israel will be saved." (Rom 11:25)
- Put on "the armor of light." (Rom 13:12)

- Paul will say anything "to win obedience from the Gentiles." (Rom 15:18)
- With luck, "the God of peace will soon crush Satan [i.e. Rome]." (Rom 16:20)
- "God chose the foolish…the weak…the low and despised…to bring to nothing the things that are [i.e. Roman rule]." (1 Cor 1:26-28)
- "Rulers of this age [i.e. Romans] are doomed to pass away." (1 Cor 2:6)
- "The [coming] kingdom of God…consists in power." (1 Cor 4:20)
- "The form of this world is passing away." (1 Cor 7:31)
- The "end" comes when God "destroys every rule and every authority and power." (1 Cor 15:24)
- "[Jesus'] power is made perfect in weakness." (2 Cor 12:9)
- "Put on the whole armor of God…against the world rulers of this present darkness… the breastplate of righteousness… the shield of faith… the helmet of salvation…the sword of the Spirit." (Eph 6:11)

Here we find numerous explicit and veiled references to the need to revolt, to destroy the worldly powers, to defeat Satan, put on "armor," and to bring "evil" Rome "to nothing." This will free the Gentiles, of course, but it will save "the Jews first."

Since this is a kind of revolt or rebellion against "Satan," who is powerful, we can expect to pay a price; we will need to *suffer* (for "the Jews first," of course). Again, Paul:

- "We rejoice in our sufferings…" (Rom 5:3)
- We will be "heirs with Christ," but only "provided we suffer with him, in order that we may also be glorified with him." (Rom 8:17)
- "All who desire to live a godly life in Christ Jesus will be persecuted." (2 Tim 3:12)

Paul then died, the Jews revolted, and they lost badly. Then in short order came the Gospel of Mark, who, freshly coming off defeat, had to down-

 The Jesus Hoax

play such rebellious talk while maintaining the morale of the troops by promising ultimate victory in the end. He wrote:

- We need to bide our time; the "kingdom of God" is now "like a grain of mustard seed," which grows in time to "the greatest of all shrubs." (4:30; also Lk 13)
- Jesus says, "Whoever loses his life for my sake will save it." (8:35; also Jn 12)
- "The kingdom of God [will] come with power." (9:1)
- The Romans are now "first," but keep a stiff lip; "The many that are first will be last, and the last will be first." (10:31; also Mt 19 and Lk 13)
- At some point, we can expect great turmoil: "Nation will rise up against nation." (13:8; also Mt 24 and Lk 21)

Some 15 years pass, and then appear Matthew and Luke. They are now ready to accelerate talk of resistance and rebellion, of struggle and death:

- "The meek shall inherit the earth." (Mt 5:5) Note that this is *not* passive; the meek will *rule*.
- "Brother will deliver up brother to death." (Mt 10:21; also Lk 12)
- Jesus: "I have not come to bring peace, but a sword." (Mt 10:34) A remarkable admission.
- Jesus: "I have come to set a man against his father." (Mt 10:35)
- Jesus: "He who loses his life for my sake will find." (Mt 10:39)
- Jesus: "He who is not with me is against me." (Mt 12:30) A classic, cult-like demand.
- All who abandon their families "will inherit eternal life." (Mt 19:29)
- The Gospel will be preached and then, "the end will come." (Mt 24:14)—in victory.

And then some passages unique to Luke:

- "The devil," aka Rome, rules "all the kingdoms of the world." (Lk 4:5)

- Jesus: "I came to cast fire upon the earth." (Lk 12:49)—Christ, the great destroyer.
- Jesus: "I came to give not peace, but division." (Lk 12:51)—divide and conquer.
- A follower must "hate his own father, mother, wife, children…" (Lk 14:26)
- Jesus: "Bring my enemies here and slay them before me." (Lk 19:27) Yes, I know, this is a parable—but a parable *of Jesus.*
- Jesus, at the Last Supper: "Let he who has no sword, sell his cloak and buy one." (Lk 22:36)—arm yourselves, brothers.

I would also note here that, according to Luke, that Jesus actually seemed to *not* want us to pay our taxes: In dragging Jesus before Pontius Pilate, the Jewish priests say, "We have found this man subverting our nation. He opposes payment of taxes to Caesar and claims to be Messiah, a king" (23:2). So much for "rendering unto Caesar"!

Then comes the Gospel of John, which, being more esoteric and intellectual, has very little in the way of incitement to rebellion. John understood that his more intellectual readers would not be the ones armed with sword and shield. He is content to indicate that "Jesus" is the only path forward: "No one comes to the Father except through me [Jesus]" (14:6); and "apart from me, you can do nothing" (15:5)—again, classic cultish programming.

Lastly we have the Book of Revelation, likely written about the same time as John (around 95 AD). This is perhaps the most profoundly anti-Rome book in the entire NT; references to "a beast rising out of the sea" (13:1) and "a great harlot" (17:1) by the name of Babylon (17:5) are widely understood as metaphors for the Roman Empire.

In chapter 13 we read of the beast arising from the sea, a beast with "ten horns and seven heads"—the heads, we later discover, refer to the famous Seven Hills of Rome, and the horns are the many kings which serve the emperor. "The whole earth followed the beast [of Rome] with wonder… Who is like the beast, and who can fight against it"? (13:3-4) —so great was the power of Rome.

Then in chapter 17, where we read of "the great harlot who is seated upon many waters [seas ruled by Rome], with whom the kings of the earth have committed fornication [by yielding to Rome's power]" (17:1-

2). The woman has written on her forehead "Babylon the great, mother of harlots and of earth's abomination"—recalling that Babylon was long hated by the Jews for their capture of Jerusalem in 586 BC. The 'new Babylon' was Rome, another faraway power that had managed to capture Jerusalem and, once again, to destroy the famed Jewish Temple. The harlot sits upon the beast with seven heads: "the seven heads are seven hills on which the woman is seated" (17:9). "The woman that you saw is the great city which has dominion over the kings of the earth" (17:18)—the analogy could hardly be clearer.

The prophecy, of course, is that Babylon the harlot will fall: "Fallen, fallen is Babylon the great! It has become a dwelling place of demons… [where] all nations have drunk the wine of her impure passion… [and] the merchants have grown rich with the wealth of her wantonness" (18:2-3). The Jewish God will have his revenge "and she shall be burned with fire." Revelation is thus a fitting ending to a thoroughly anti-Rome testament.

So, how do the two sides stack up? On the pro-Roman side, we have:

- one paragraph (of dubious value) of Paul, from Romans.
- one passage (of dubious value) in Mark ("render unto Caesar").
- "Love your enemies", "turn the other cheek," "judge not"—in Matthew and Luke.
- And "perish by the sword"; but this applies to fellow Jews.

On the anti-Roman side, we have:

- 18 passages by Paul, across several letters.
- Paul's glorification of suffering.
- 5 passages in Mark.
- 14 passages (more, with duplicates) in Matthew and Luke.
- Rome as a beast and harlot in Revelation.

Now, obviously it's not just a numbers game, but still, I think it is clear that the preponderance of evidence is on the anti-Roman side. There simply is not much to be said for the opposing view. And yet it is amazing how many people, even well-educated ones, will automatically assume the contrary, based on a very superficial reading of the text.

CHAPTER 10

WHAT NEXT?

> For two thousand years, an abiding faith in Jesus' resurrection has displayed enormous power, but because of its utter groundlessness, we must now acknowledge that it has all along been a worldwide historical hoax.
> — G. Lüdemann (2004: 190)

So: Whither Christianity? It seems to be done for, at least as a credible theology. The lies, the manipulations, and the deceit that have been conducted by Paul and the Gospel writers, by the early Church Fathers (who likely couldn't have known better), and by modern defenders (who can and should) is utterly appalling. The reader is invited to review any recent book by a current "scholar of Christianity"; he will find incredible gyrations, excuses, twisting and turning, stretched interpretations, hoop-jumping, misrepresentation—and an absolute avoidance of the most crucial questions. Our scholars will bend over backward, and then some, to sustain an unsustainable fable of a Jewish god-man who came to Earth, born of a virgin, who worked miracles, died on a cross, and then was bodily resurrected. He then roamed the world for 40 days,[1] only to "ascend to heaven" and never be seen or heard from again. In the face of such absurdity, our scholars betray themselves as naïve dupes or utter fools.[2]

Christianity offers nothing of substance to thinking people; the morality is a warmed-over Jewish morality, distorted by Paul for his malicious ends. The much older value system of Greece and Rome was far superior. The "Christian" God is just the Jewish God, Yahweh, with his

---

[1] Acts (1:3). The number 40, incidentally, betrays more Jewish mystical numerology. It appears several times in the OT: Gen (7:12), Ex (24:18), Deut (8:2, 9:18), and 1 Kings (19:8).

[2] Bizarrely, though, Christians seem more than happy to be fools. As Paul says, "We are fools for Christ" (1 Cor 4:10). It is hard to know what to say in response to such willful ignorance.

nasty, vengeful side hidden from sight; rest assured, Yahweh's anger is still there, and still directed at "the enemies of Israel" by his "chosen," who still roam the Earth and exert vast and disproportionate influence across the globe.

In the US, Christianity is on the decline and is increasingly non-White. As of 2021, just 63% of all Americans self-identified as Christian, versus 78% in 2007—a loss of more than 1 percentage point per year. Conversely, Americans who claim "no religion" are up from 16% in 2007 to 29% today.

Racially, the decline has been heaviest among Whites. The percentage of all Americans who identify as "White Christian" has declined from 65% of the total population in the mid-1990s to about 42% today. Or if we look at it by racial group, 70% of American Whites call themselves Christian, versus 77% of Latinos and 79% of Blacks. Thus we see that Christianity is both declining and browning.

The religion is declining even more rapidly in its nominal homeland of Europe. While significant numbers of Europeans still call themselves Christian—between 40% and 80%, among Western Europe—these are inflated figures; the number of serious, church-attending believers is far lower: a maximum of 35-40% in Italy and Portugal, down to 9-10% in Belgium, Denmark, Finland, and Sweden. And the picture is even starker among European youth, aged 16 to 29. Apart from Poland, the number of regularly-attending youths lies in the range of 5-10%. In seven countries, more than 50% of youth "never" attend church.[3] Worse, the number of youths who profess "no religion" at all generally ranges from 35% (Austria, Slovenia) to as high as 91% in Czech Republic.[4] The future generations have little interest in this "religion of love"; they want something real, something credible, something valuable—not mindless manipulation.

On the positive side, Christianity is expected to make gains in the global South and East, such that, by one estimate, it will hold its global share of religious commitment steady at around 31%. As always, Christianity's brightest prospects are among the poorest and least-educated of humanity. Perhaps they view that as a virtue; for me, it is sheer exploitation of the least-able and most vulnerable portion of the global population.

---

[3] Czech Republic, Netherlands, Spain, UK, Belgium, France, and Hungary.
[4] With two exceptions: Poland and Lithuania, where less than 25% are "no religion."

Looking Ahead

Given all this, given the compelling account of a malicious Jesus hoax perpetrated upon Gentiles of the world, a question frequently arises: What next? Where are we heading? What should we do now? I think there is a two-part answer here: *What next for religion*, and then *What next for society at large*. I will address the former here and defer the latter until the end of this chapter.

As to religion, the first question is: Do we need religion at all? Religion, after all, is a process by which we are connected to the beyond, to divinity, to the gods; the word 'religion' derives from the Latin *re-ligio*, meaning 'a re-binding' or 'binding back to.' Religion, by definition, binds us to the gods; it also, historically, binds us to an entire religious bureaucracy: a ruling clergy, a religious hierarchy, dogmatic teachings, tithing, vague promises and vague threats. And because it is so subjective and unverifiable, it can be extremely hard to separate 'valid' religions from mere cults; for example, are Scientology and Mormonism real religions? What about Jehovah's Witnesses? Or the Amish? Or the "Unification Church," also known as 'Moonies'? Can anyone make up their own religion? Why or why not? We have no good answers to these questions.

One could make a good case that any 'modern' religion should revere real things, like the sun, or the Earth. Some have named the earth-goddess Gaia as a possible source of worship. Here, it is fairly obvious: if we don't honor and protect the global biosphere, we won't survive very long. If personifying the Earth as Gaia aids in this process, then perhaps we should do it. Solar religions are ancient, dating back at least to Akhenaten's *atenism*—worship of the sun, the *aten*—in Egypt in the 1300s BC.[5] The sun is the energy- and life-source for everything on the planet; if there is one thing in this universe that we should honor, that is it.

Interestingly, famed British writer D. H. Lawrence, in his insightful commentary on the Book of Revelation titled *Apocalypse* (1931), proposed precisely a kind of sun-worship, and even cosmos-worship, as a replacement for a defective Christianity. In some remarkable passages, he wrote:

---

[5] See my discussion in Chapter 5.

Who says the sun cannot speak to me! The sun has a great blazing consciousness, and I have a little blazing consciousness. …

There is an eternal vital correspondence between our blood and the sun: there is an eternal vital correspondence between our nerves and the moon. If we get out of contact and harmony with the sun and moon, then both turn into great dragons of destruction against us. The sun is a great source of blood-vitality, it streams strength to us. But once we resist the sun, and say: It is a mere ball of gas!—then the very streaming vitality of sunshine turns into subtle disintegrative force in us, and undoes us. The same with the moon, the planets, the great stars. They are either our makers or our unmakers. There is no escape.

We and the cosmos are one. The cosmos is a vast living body, of which we are parts. The sun is a great heart whose tremors run though our smallest veins. … Now all this is *literally* true, as men knew in the great past, and as they will know again. …

When I hear modern people complaining of being lonely, then I know what has happened. They have lost the cosmos. … What we lack is cosmic life, the sun in us and the moon in us. … We can only get the sun by a sort of worship: and the same the moon. By *going forth* to worship the sun, worship that is felt in the blood. (1931/1995, chap. 5: pp. 76-78)

He closes the book with these thoughts:

Christ's way of loving your neighbor leads to the hideous anomaly [in Revelation] of having to live by sheer resistance to your neighbor, in the end. The Apocalypse, strange book, makes this clear. …. It shows us the Christian in relation to the State, to the world, to the cosmos. It shows him in mad hostility to all of them, having, in the end, to will the destruction of them all. … [T]he Apocalypse destroys the sun and the stars, the world, and all kings and all rulers…

> [But] what we [really] want is to destroy our false, in-
> organic connections, especially those related to money, and
> reestablish the living organic connections, with the cosmos,
> the sun and earth, with mankind and nation and family.
> Start with the sun, and the rest will slowly, slowly happen.
> (chap. 23: pp. 148-149)

For Lawrence, the dark, destructive, and "thoroughly Jewish" picture in Revelation is the logical end of Judeo-Christian thinking.

Notable in sun- or earth-religions is the fact that we do not really need to pray to them, ask forgiveness, beseech them, request personal favors, and so on. It is more a recognition of appreciation and gratitude for their existence, and for ours—so precarious in a vast universe. One does not 'pray to the sun' so that it will rise tomorrow; that will happen, no matter what we do. Rather, as Lawrence suggests, it is a recognition and celebration of the miracle (if I can use that word) of being.

But what about the afterlife? Much of the power of Christianity is the carrot and stick: heaven or hell. That keeps many people in line, and keeps them coming back every Sunday. But again, there is virtually no reason to think that any such things exist—or if they do, that our eternal destination is a function of a handful of thoughts or actions in this life. And why just two destinations? That was a Jewish invention, designed for maximum manipulation.[6] Why not three, or four, or a thousand destinations, depending on how well we live our lives?

Many are likely unaware that Plato advocated a kind of merit-based reincarnation. On his view, we strive for goodness and wisdom in this life, to be rewarded by the gods with the best chance for an even better life the next time around. In his "Myth of Er," Plato depicts a kind of judgment in the afterlife, one in which everyone is compelled to choose their next life, but where the best and wisest are 'first in line,' and thus can chose the best possible lives. The foolish or wicked are last, and they are left with only poor choices. Thus, virtue indeed leads to a kind of 'heaven,' albeit in the form of a (temporary) excellent next life; and the

---

[6] Notably, *the Jews themselves* don't believe this. In OT Judaism, the afterlife is a kind of pit or place underground—Sheol or Hades—where everyone goes, good or bad. There is no rebirth and no salvation. Heaven and hell are only for the gullible Goyim.

foolish or evil get the 'hell' of a (temporary) life of pain or suffering. This is a far better guide to the afterlife than any Jewish formulation.[7]

As an aside, I note that Socrates had a different view. For him, the afterlife was one of two alternatives: either a place where we all go, or a nothingness. The former would be wonderful, he said, because it would be like a grand, eternal party—a chance to meet and talk with all the great thinkers of the past (and future). The latter wouldn't be so bad either; he described it as a blissful quietude, something like when we have a great night's sleep—total calm, no bad dreams, no nightmares, and the time passes in an instant. All of eternity could be like that: perfect calm, passing in an instant. Either way, says Socrates—eternal party or perfect sleep—death is nothing to fear. In fact, it is actually "a good thing": the completion of our being on this earth.[8]

Once we abandon the destructive Christian myth, all sorts of options open up to us. Some may wish to revive other ancient religions: the Greek or Roman pantheon served us well for many centuries and could do so again. European peoples may wish to resurrect beliefs centered on Wotan or Odin, which are long and venerable mythologies. Conservative groups, like Richard Spencer's "Alexandria" project, are trying to reimagine and reinvent a new Eurocentric theological system; and the National Alliance has put forth an intriguing theology, "cosmotheism," based on the Greek notion that the universe itself is God (typically referred to as pantheism). Even forms of ancient animism are viable; I myself have argued for the metaphysical truth of panpsychism, a system that sees mind or awareness in all animals, all plants, and even in inanimate objects.[9] All such systems have their virtues, and none the drawbacks of a malicious Judeo-Christianity.

Again, we must remind ourselves: Humanity thrived and prospered for thousands of years before anyone ever heard of Judaism or Christianity. We can thrive and prosper again.

---

[7] See *Republic* (614b-621b).
[8] See Plato's *Apology* (40c-41b).
[9] See my *Panpsychism in the West* (2017), revised edition. For a good anthology of several views, see Seager (2020).

Some Final Questions Answered

At this point, I think I have addressed nearly all issues, concerns, and criticisms that most people could raise against my Hoax thesis. But there are a few remaining comments and questions that some have raised, so let me take a moment to briefly respond to these directly; most of these points have been touched on previously, but I want to give my skeptical readers a few final words.

Question: *"You insist that the lack of* contemporaneous *evidence is damning. But we don't have contemporaneous evidence for many figures in history, all of whom are accepted as real. So why do you hold a double standard for Jesus?"*

Answer: Jesus is unlike every other figure in history. He is (allegedly) not just a man, not a ruler or emperor, but the Son of God, or a demi-god, or God himself. The standard is ridiculously high here—meaning, it is absolutely absurd to think that God himself came to Earth in human form, worked miracles before thousands, and no one from those events bothered to write a single word. Far lesser figures than the Son of God have left extensive contemporaneous evidence, in addition to later, and perhaps better, sources. If it happened for them, why not for God himself? Could God not ensure that contemporaneous evidence survived? Or did he do the opposite, and made it vanish? If so, why?

Question: *"Okay, as a Christian I've read and absorbed your whole shocking message. What am I supposed to do about all this now?"*

Answer: First, try to confirm as much of the evidence cited here as possible. Check my quotations, pull out your Bible and confirm the passages I cite. Satisfy yourself that I have given you a straight story. Next, go to your local church leader and confront them with the evidence (or lack thereof). Their response will confirm everything you need to know. Then, make it clear to them that *you have been swindled*. Tell them you want your money back. And your time. And your life—everything that you've invested, and lost, in the most famous hoax in history.

Then consider alternatives, such as those I sketched out above. It will take some time and effort, some searching and reading, but there is a vast collected body of wisdom out there, and it far surpasses the simple-minded absurdities of the Christian story.

Question: *"Lots of Christians actually don't take the Bible literally. For them, the miracles and all that other stuff are just stories intended to give lessons in morality. They don't really believe that they happened. So why isn't it ok to just accept that sort of 'minimalist' Christianity?"*

Answer: If you allow that the miracles aren't real, how do you know that the rest isn't real? Where can we draw the line between fact and fiction? We have almost no reason to believe that *any* of it is real. The most important miracle of all was the resurrection—was that one, too, just a story? If so, the whole basis for Christianity goes down the drain. Then it's just some guy saying, "be kind to the poor," "help your neighbor," "love God," etc. And we don't need a church and a religion to tell us that!

And what were those guys thinking—Matthew, Mark, Luke, and John—who wrote that fiction about the miracles? Did they *know* they were writing fiction? But they sold it as truth; why did they lie? These are precisely the questions I've tried to answer here in this book. Any way we look at it, a stripped-down or minimalist Christianity makes no sense; it still essentially involves a Jewish hoax at its core.

Question: *"What about all the OT prophecies fulfilled in the NT? Isn't that proof of divine origins of the Bible?"*

Answer: One thing is clear: When you have extensive knowledge of the prophecies, you can bake their realization right into the text that you are constructing. Paul and the Gospel writers were very well versed in OT theology, and they knew exactly when and how to include ideas from the OT that would seem compelling or prophetic for their Jesus. And this is not to mention the actual historical events that Jesus "predicted" in the year 30, when you are writing his lines in the year 80 or 90. The prophecy game was rigged from the start.

Question: *"Why do you accept the idea of an historical Jesus? Why not just call the whole thing a hoax?"*

Answer: Paul needed a kernel of truth for his hoax. What better way than to take a real person who was really crucified for his pro-Jewish, anti-Roman activities, and turn him into God? This makes complete sense. Other than this, neither I nor anyone else has evidence for a historical Jesus. The execution of a minor insurrectionist rabbi would not be expected to leave any documentary trail, and he didn't.

Question: *"Why is all this even important? It was so long ago, and no one really knows what happened back then."*

Answer: Even for those who aren't religious, it should still be clear that any forgery that holds the belief of three-quarters of Americans, and one-third of all humanity, is a matter of greatest importance. Those in academic or intellectual circles, or those agnostic or atheist readers out there, may find all this much ado about nothing. But we can easily forget how seriously some people take the Bible. Roughly 42% of Americans believe in Biblical creationism, and about the same number think Jesus will return to Earth by 2050. About 53% of all Americans say that religion is "very important" in their lives. Let there be no doubt: this is a subject of greatest importance.

For those who don't take religion all that seriously, many of them see church as more of a social club than anything else. But even so, who above age six would be happy to join a 'Santa Claus Club' or an 'Easter Bunny Club'? Christians need to own up to the fact that they have been swindled, and then see if anything can be salvaged of their religion. By all means, keep the social club, do charity work, help the poor—just dump the bogus metaphysics.

Question: *"I've read all your points, and even though I have nothing to say in reply, I frankly don't care. You have your opinion, I have mine, and I'm never going to change my mind."*

Answer: Then good luck to you, my friend!

Society at Large: Media, Government, Hollywood

As I noted above, the second aspect of "What next?" relates to society at large. So let me expand and modernize our discussion here to include aspects of the Jesus hoax, and its cause, as they relate to larger spheres of contemporary life.

A critically-thinking reader may bring to mind this pertinent question: Why haven't we heard anything about all this before? Surely, if the case were so compelling, one might say, we would have seen it in movies, or heard news stories about it, or had it taught in schools. And yet nowhere—not even in our universities—do we hear this matter discussed. Why is that?

This is an enlightening question. We need to ask this: Who would have an incentive to examine the truth on this whole subject? Christians, obviously not. No one in the Christian elite wants people to explore the truth, even though it's highly likely that many of them do know it. Once you have an organization in place, salaries to pay, mortgages, monthly bills, and taxes, you need the whole business to keep functioning. Christians have every reason to sustain the hoax, not get to the bottom of it.

Jews have no interest in the truth here, either. As the 'bad guys' in the hoax story, Paul and friends threaten to cast a negative light on all Jews, past and present. This is particularly true when we look at the millennia-long history of critical comments on the Jews, as discussed in Chapter 4. Any widespread unearthing of these facts would require a lot of subtle explaining, to say the least. Rather than admit to a Jewish lie, present-day Jews would rather not bring up the subject at all. Particularly so, when millions of Christian Zionists are ideologically on their side. It's simply a no-win situation for Jews, and so they let that sleeping dog lie.

One might think that Muslims would be eager to criticize Jews and Christianity, and to expose any hoax. Yes and no. Islam, of course, is part of the Abrahamic lineage and thus is ultimately wedded to Judeo-Christianity, whether it likes it or not. Muslim monotheism derives ultimately from Judaic monotheism, just as it does for Christianity. All the Abrahamic religions worship the Jewish God; Muslims simply changed his name.

Islam furthermore accepts Jesus as a "prophet" and even grants him a kind of divine status—though they disavow his resurrection. The Quran has a number of interesting passages on him. Jesus ("Isa") performs miracles, but only with Allah's "permission" (III.49, V.110). Jews neither killed nor crucified him (IV.157), and so he did not die a martyr's death. In a particularly impressive miracle, the Quran states that the infant Jesus spoke *immediately upon birth*: "He said: 'Surely I am a servant of Allah; He has given me the Book and made me a prophet, and He has made me blessed...'" (XIX.30-31). Muslims therefore cannot accept either a mythicist Jesus nor even a merely historical Jesus; they need a semi-divine miracle man as well.

Governments are nominally neutral on religion, especially in the United States with its famous "separation of church and state." They should, therefore, have an interest only in historical truth. When they draft school curricula for millions of public-school children, it's clear that they should at least present a mythicist alternative to traditional orthodoxy, as one line of thinking. But such information has yet to appear in any public text, to my knowledge.

But there are deeper reasons, I think, for why they avoid criticizing Christianity. Governments everywhere want compliant populations. They want citizens who will respect authority without question, follow the laws, accept its power, and not be too inquisitive. They like people who simply have faith in government, and who more or less blindly trust them. And in Christianity, rulers have found an ideology that can serve their interests. They can play up the 'peaceable Jesus' storyline—love thy neighbor, turn the other cheek, Jesus as "our paschal lamb" (1 Cor 5:7) or our "shepherd" (Jn 10:11), followers as "sheep," (Mk 6:34, Jn 21:15)—while directing any militant undertones toward the "devil" of their choosing. Governments have no interest in turning over that applecart.

An additional factor, perhaps even more important, is the role of the Jewish lobby in Western governments. Since the Jews themselves have no interest in exposing this story, they use their influence in government to make sure that *the government* has no interest either. Governments are routinely pressured to pass "hate speech" laws, censorship laws, and "disinformation" laws that can be used against anyone, even degreed scholars and academics, who raise inconvenient topics.

Colleges and universities fare somewhat better than most institutions, occasionally having panels or speakers who challenge the Christian view. But the Antagonism Thesis is particularly difficult to discuss since it casts blame on Jews, and any negative talk about them risks ostracism or worse, even in our "liberal" and "free speech" universities. This, thanks to the dominating role played by Jews, at least in American universities; they are vastly overrepresented in most educational institutions, certainly within the academic ranks but more importantly in positions of leadership (deans, chairs, provosts, chancellors) and on boards of regents. Not long ago, it was noted that all eight presidents of the American Ivy League schools were Jews; this is a remarkable fact, but one that cannot be stated out loud, thanks to pressure from the Lobby.

What about our irreverent media and Hollywood filmmakers—those who are so willing to commit sacrilege against any social norm or moral standard? Again, I suspect this has something to do with the extensive role played by Jewish Americans. It is uncontroversial that Hollywood has been dominated by Jews for decades; a relatively recent article in the *LA Times* cites Jewish heads of nearly every major Hollywood studio.[10] And it's not just the movie business. All the major media and news conglomerates have a heavy Jewish presence in top management. If they should decide that Jewish malevolence at the heart of the Christian story "looks bad," then they obviously won't bring it up at all—not in the news, not on TV, not in books.[11]

Sometimes, of course, we do hear about the Jesus controversy in our media. But always in carefully crafted ways. A good example came during Easter 2017, in an article on the British website Guardian.com, written by Cambridge University professor Simon Gathercole.[12] The subtitle notes that "some claim that Jesus is just an idea, rather than a real historical figure." "But," it adds, "there is a good deal of written evidence for his existence." Gathercole says that evidence for an historical Jesus is "long-established and widespread." "Within a few decades"—if 60 to 80 years counts as "a few decades"—Jesus is "mentioned by Jewish and Roman historians"—actually, *one* Jewish (Josephus) and *one* Roman (Tacitus), for a total of about ten sentences. The evidence, says Gathercole, "is early and detailed," citing Paul's letters and the Gospels. But we

---

[10] "How Jewish is Hollywood?", by Joel Stein (Dec 19, 2008).

[11] For an interesting analysis of the role of Jews in the media and in government, see Dalton (2023: 353-366).

[12] www.theguardian.com/world/2017/apr/14/what-is-the-historical-evidence-that-jesus-christ-lived-and-died

have seen the many problems with those, and in any case they don't count as independent evidence. "It is also difficult to imagine why Christian writers would invent such a thoroughly Jewish savior in a time and place where there was strong suspicion of Judaism." Actually, not difficult at all: the "Christian" writers were Jews who were trying to build an anti-Roman church based on a Jewish God and a Jewish savior. They just had to make sure that the enemy was "the devil" and not "Rome."

When asked about the present controversy over Jesus' existence, Gathercole cites only the Frenchman Michel Onfray, and deftly avoids mention of any other skeptic. He cites two pseudo-skeptics—Maurice Casey and Bart Ehrman—as declaring any mythicist approach to be "pseudo-scholarship." When asked about any archeological evidence for Jesus, he offers a few confusing words about Cleopatra and the Shroud of Turin, only to conclude that "the documents [Epistles, Gospels, Josephus, Tacitus] form the most significant evidence"—which is a virtual admission of failure. As Gathercole well knows, *there is no physical evidence*. In the end, he never makes clear the distinction between the historical Jesus (the man) and the biblical Jesus (the Christ). We can accept the man, even if there is very little actual evidence, but we cannot accept any of the miraculous biblical account. And the man alone, as I've said repeatedly, means the end of Christianity.

Speaking of Bart Ehrman, he is repeatedly held up by the media as some kind of neutral and scholarly skeptic on the topic of Christianity. But what we find instead is a safe critic, someone who knows his bounds and which topics to address—and not to address. During Easter 2023, for example, he wrote an opinion piece for CNN, examining the different "lessons" from Good Friday (death on the cross) and Easter Sunday (resurrection).[13] He laments the focus on the resurrection and eternal life rather than on "the day of suffering and death that the Savior willingly experienced for others." For him, the death on the cross demonstrates the "life of service" and of self-sacrifice for others: "strangers, foreigners, followers of other religions." Be like the "peaceable Jesus," says Ehrman; we should "not be violent, not seek revenge, not return evil for evil."

---

[13] "The messages of Good Friday and Easter are not the same." CNN (9 April 2023).

This is a very politically-correct determination, surely as pleasing to corrupt government officials as it is to the Jewish Lobby. But Ehrman's essay fails on several counts. It fails theologically; Jesus wasn't crucified because he "served others" but because he was a heretic (to the orthodox Jews) and a rabble-rousing seditionist (to the Romans). Is that the example we should follow? Be a heretic and seditionist?

But mostly Ehrman fails in what he assumes to be true, and in what he does not tell us. He assumes a divine Jesus existed (no talk of mythicism here). He assumes the Gospels should be taken at face value and not as fables or lies. He assumes that his readers are largely ignorant, acritical simpletons. He tells us nothing about the many problems with the NT account of Jesus: the evidence, the chronology, the absurdities, the logical impossibilities. He says nothing about the Jewish propensities for domination and misanthropy that underlie the entire Bible, Old Testament and New—which is especially galling, considering his plea for "selflessness" and for "not dominating others." What hypocrisy! Learn selflessness and humility from a Bible written by the masters of domination and hatred—or so says Bart Ehrman. This is what passes for popular commentary in our mass media today.

What Next?

As I have argued throughout this book, the key to understanding the Jesus Hoax is to understand the Jewish mindset and Jewish values—their worldview, in effect. These things, I said, are guided by two central characteristics: (1) control and domination ('dominion') and (2) misanthropy, or hatred of non-Jews. Both of these are captured in the notion of *Jewish supremacy*: that Jews believe they have a God-given right to rule over others, *all* others, who are seen as lowly and detestable. Under the conditions of Roman rule in Palestine 2,000 years ago, this became the driving force for Paul and friends to create a hoax, one that would both undermine foreign rule and weaken the Gentile masses. It was a brilliant plan, and given a few centuries, it worked.

But as important as religion is to individual people, it is less so on the contemporary world stage—at least, in the Western world. Western nations are not theocracies; we have generally relegated theology to a peripheral role, and governments, by and large, try to stay out of such issues. Western politicians don't generally cite the Bible in support of a given policy; they don't typically condemn opponents as "the devil." Generally speaking, we in the West live in societies with religious freedom (more or less) but with secular management.

Unfortunately, though, the Western nations—especially the US—have large, wealthy, and active Jewish lobbies who still seem to embody those ancient prejudices and that ancient sense of Jewish supremacy. Obviously there are individual exceptions, but that notwithstanding, the 'power Jews' in America and the West are almost uniformly of the supremacist variety. In the US, they are hugely influential at the highest levels of government. The AIPAC lobby is the most feared and most obeyed; Jewish money dominates both Republican and Democrat politicians; and both Congress and the president 'religiously' enact policies and laws that are pro-Jewish and pro-Israel.

The level of control and genuflection is frankly astonishing. Here is proof: In mid-2023, an Indian-American congresswoman made an off-hand comment that "Israel is a racist state"—which is true; it is defined as a Jewish state. But by simply stating the truth, she was rebuked in writing by 40 of her colleagues. Worse, within *two days*, the US House, which can stalemate on critical national issues for months, approved a "non-binding" resolution defending Israel. The resolution reads, in full:

> Resolved by the House of Representatives (the Senate concurring), That it is the sense of Congress that— (1) the State of Israel is not a racist or apartheid state; (2) Congress rejects all forms of antisemitism and xenophobia; and (3) the United States will always be a staunch partner and supporter of Israel.

This obsequious resolution was approved by a vote of 412 to 9 (with 14 voting 'present,' or abstaining). Therefore it is clear that precisely 95% of the House (412/435) is firmly in Israel's pocket. Similar previous votes in the US Senate have passed 100-0. These same congressmen will reflexively vote in favor of Israel's or the Lobby's interests—whether on financial aid to Israel, political cover for Israeli crimes against humanity, 'hate speech' laws, confirming compliant political appointees, even conducting favorable foreign military operations. To put it bluntly: American foreign policy, and much of its domestic policy, is an enactment of Jewish supremacism. And through American military power, Jews have effectively achieved their dream of world domination.

This has been true for at least 20 years, although rarely spoken. One exception was the former prime minister of Malaysia, Mahathir Mohamad, who said in 2003, upon the launching of the American war on Iraq: "Today, Jews rule the world by proxy. They get others to fight and die for them".[14] He reconfirmed this thought in 2016:

> I believe I am speaking the truth. You look at America; it is totally dedicated to supporting Israel, even when Israel commits international crimes. In fact, candidates for election need to inform the Jewish Lobby that they support Israel. … What I said is that the Jews are ruling the world by proxy. If you refuse to see the evidence, then I cannot help you. … America is very much under Jewish influence.[15]

So it seems that the driving force behind the Jesus Hoax affects not only religion but major policy actions by the Western nations and therefore, indirectly, much of the globe. Europe lives in terror of the Judeo-American goliath, and thus does its bidding. Lesser nations live in perpetual fear that the goliath may declare them "enemy combatants" or "rogue nations" and launch covert attacks or drone strikes against them. Having sold its soul, America has become a bloodthirsty villain, a zombie nation, one that is hated and feared worldwide.

But even a goliath has his limits. As the war in Ukraine plays out, it increasingly looks like a losing situation for the US, NATO, Europe, and the West—quite possibly a catastrophic loss. We see from a history of Europe that Jewish groups, upon gaining a modicum of power and wealth, consistently over-play their hands; they overreach, they miscalculate, they display a blind arrogance and utter lack of humility. Eventually, these things lead them to disaster—and another "Holocaust" ensues. That time may be approaching once again.

---

[14] AP, 17 October 2003.

[15] "Former Asian leader won't stop claiming Jews 'rule the world'." *Washington Post* (27 June 2016).

So: What to do? At this point, education and enlightenment are the orders of the day. A vast majority of people in the West, in the US and Europe, are either (a) blinded by Christian theology, or (b) ignorant of the root causes of their (and the world's) troubles. It takes a bit of work, a bit of searching, but there are excellent sources available—books, writers, publishers, bloggers—who are willing to speak the truth. A good guide is to look for those sources that are censored or banned by the orthodoxy; that's a fairly sure sign that you are close to the truth. The faster that a counter-narrative can be circulated—whether on religion, politics, racism, identity politics—the faster that the tide will turn.

But all this leads us far afield. Here, my topic is Christianity, and on this matter, I rest my case. By all accounts, and despite protests to the contrary, Christianity indeed seems to be a "cleverly devised myth" (2 Pet 1:16)—a lie, a hoax—foisted upon the innocent and gullible masses simply for the benefit of Israel and the Jews. Jesus perhaps spoke the truth when he said, "I was sent only to the lost sheep of Israel" (Mt 15:24), and a few true words even slipped from Paul's mouth, as he was awaiting "the full number of Gentiles [to] come in" so that "all Israel will be saved" (Rom 11:26). And again a few chapters later, when he said, "For I tell you that Christ's life of service was on behalf of the Jews…" (Rom 15:8). But it's in the Gospel of John that we read one of the bluntest statements of truth, wherein Jesus says, "You [Gentiles] worship what you do not know; we worship what we know, for salvation is of the Jews" (4:22). We know what we are doing, say the Jews; you Gentile Christians don't even know what you're worshipping—which in fact is us and our God. But that's okay. Just leave everything to us; "salvation is of the Jews."

But it is Paul who is really the star of this show. Paul comes across as a masterly and artful liar—one of the all-time greats in world history, a man who can lie with impunity about the soul, the afterlife, God, everything. This unprincipled scoundrel, who admits to being "all things to all men," would do anything or say anything to win his "kingdom of God" here on Earth. His mournful cries of "I do not lie!" are revealed as nothing other than an inveterate liar caught in the act.

Let me close by citing Nietzsche again. At the end of *Antichrist,* he unleashes his full fury on the lying, world-maligning, soul-destroying Saint Paul:

Then Paul appeared—Paul, the chandala hatred against Rome, against 'the world,' become flesh, become genius, the Jew, the *eternal* Wandering Jew *par excellence*. What he guessed was how one could use the little sectarian Christian movement apart from Judaism to kindle a 'world fire'; how, with the symbol of 'God on the cross,' one could unite all who lay at the bottom, all who were secretly rebellious, the whole inheritance of anarchistic agitation in the Empire, into a tremendous power. "Salvation is of the Jews."

Christianity as a formula with which to outbid the subterranean cults of all kinds, those of Osiris, of the Great Mother, of Mithras, for example—*and* to unite them: in this insight lies the genius of Paul. His instinct was so sure in this that he took the ideas with which these chandala religions fascinated, and, with ruthless violence, he put them into the mouth of the 'Savior' whom he had invented, and not only into his mouth—he *made* something out of him that a priest of Mithras too could understand.

This was his moment at Damascus: he comprehended that he *needed* the belief in immortality to deprive 'the world' of value, that the concept of 'hell' would become master even over Rome—that with 'the beyond' one *kills life*. (sec. 58)

With his fabricated "Jesus" and his fabricated "afterlife," Paul drained all value from this world, the real world. It turned believers into weak and subservient sheep, ones whose lives are oriented around the manufactured sayings of a marginal rabbi and of prayer to Jehovah, the invisible God of the Jews. It took a few hundred years, but when enough people fell for the hoax, it helped to bring down the Roman Empire.

And what a colossal loss it was. Everything was there, in Greece and Rome, all the groundwork was laid, ready for a thousand-year flowering of a great and noble civilization. But then along came Christianity:

Greeks! Romans! The nobility of instinct, the taste, the methodical research, the genius of organization and administration, the faith in, the *will* to, man's future, the great Yes to all things, become visible in the *imperium Romanum,*

> visible for all the senses, the grand style no longer mere art but become reality, truth, *life*. And not buried overnight by a natural catastrophe, not trampled down by Teutons and other buffaloes, but ruined by cunning, stealthy, invisible, anemic vampires. Not vanquished—merely drained. Hidden vengefulness, petty envy become master. Everything miserable that suffers from itself, that is afflicted with bad feelings, the whole ghetto-world of the soul *on top* all at once. (sec. 59)

The Jewish-Christians were vampires, bloodsuckers, parasites, whose only purpose was to bleed the strong:

> Parasitism as the *only* practice of the church, with its ideal of anemia, of 'holiness,' draining all blood, all love, all hope for life; 'the beyond' as the will to negate every reality; *the cross* as the mark of recognition for the most subterranean conspiracy that ever existed—against health, beauty, whatever has turned out well, courage, spirit, graciousness of the soul, *against life itself.*
>
> This eternal indictment of Christianity I will write on all walls, wherever there are walls—I have letters to make even the blind see. I call Christianity the one great curse, the one great innermost corruption, the one great instinct of revenge, for which no means is too poisonous, too stealthy, too subterranean, too *small*—I call it the one immortal blot on mankind. (sec. 62)

This immortal blot still holds sway today; and after two thousand years, it cannot but degrade society, weighing us down, blocking us from attaining that which we are capable of, that which was only hinted at in the greatness of Athens and Rome. And all for the salvation of the Jews.

Jesus saves. I truly believe this. Jesus—the *real* Jesus, and his *real* story—will someday save us from a two-thousand-year-old nightmare. As he himself said, "you will know the truth, and the truth will set you free" (Jn 8:31). When that happens, then he really will deserve his title as the most famous man in history.

APPENDIX A

The 36 Miracles of Jesus

#	Category	Miracle	Mark	Matt	Luke	John
1	Dead	Raises Jairus' daughter	5:21, 35	9:18, 23	8:40, 49	
2	Dead	Raises a Widow's Son in Nain			7:11-17	
3	Dead	Raises Lazarus from dead				11:1-45
4	Healing	Drives Out an Evil Spirit at synagogue	1:21-27		4:31-36	
5	Healing	Heals Peter's Mother-in-Law	1:29-31	8:14-15	4:38-39	
6	Healing	Heals Many Sick at Evening	1:32-34	8:16-17	4:40-41	
7	Healing	Cleanses a Man With Leprosy	1:40-45	8:1-4	5:12-14	
8	Healing	Restores Sight to Bartimaeus	10:46-52	20:29-34	18:35-43	
9	Healing	Heals a Paralytic	2:3-12	9:1-8	5:17-26	
10	Healing	Heals a Man's Withered Hand	3:1-6	12:9-14	6:6-11	
11	Healing	Casts Demons from 2 men into herd of Pigs	5:1-20	8:28-33	8:26-39	
12	Healing	Heals a bleeding woman in the Crowd	5:25-34	9:20-22	8:42-48	
13	Healing	Heals Many Sick in Gennesaret	6:53-56	14:34-36		
14	Healing	Heals Demon-Possessed gentile girl	7:24-30	15:21-28		
15	Healing	Heals a Blind Man at Bethsaida	8:22-26			
16	Healing	Heals a Boy with a Demon	9:14-29	17:14-20	9:37-43	
17	Healing	Heals Centurion's servant		8:5-13	7:1-10	
18	Healing	Heals Two Blind Men		9:27-31		
19	Healing	Heals a Man Unable to Speak		9:32-34		
20	Healing	Heals a Blind, Mute Demoniac		12:22-23	11:14-23	
21	Healing	Heals a Crippled Woman			13:10-17	
22	Healing	Heals a Man With Dropsy on the Sabbath			14:1-6	
23	Healing	Cleanses Ten Lepers			17:11-19	
24	Healing	Heals a Servant's Severed Ear			22:50-51	
25	Healing	Heals an Official's Son at Capernaum				4:43-54
26	Healing	Heals an Invalid at Bethesda				5:1-15
27	Healing	Heals a Man Born Blind				9:1-12
28	Nature	Jesus Withers the Fig Tree	11:12-14	21:18-22		
29	Nature	Jesus Calms a Storm	4:35-41	8:23-27	8:22-25	
30	Nature	Jesus Feeds 5,000 (5 loaves, 2 fish)	6:30-44	14:13-21	9:10-17	6:1-15
31	Nature	Walks on water	6:45-52	14:22-33		6:16-21
32	Nature	Jesus Feeds 4,000 (7 loaves, "a few" fish)	8:1-13	15:32-39		
33	Nature	First Miraculous Catch of Fish			5:1-11	
34	Nature	Miraculous Temple Tax in a Fish's Mouth		17:24-27		
35	Nature	Water into wine				2:1-11
36	Nature	Second Miraculous Catch of Fish				21:4-11

Total miracles: 19   22   21   8

The Jesus Hoax

APPENDIX B

A Critique of Aslan's *Zealot*

The idea that Jesus was a rebel against the Roman Empire is an old one. It goes back at least to Reimarus' work in the 1770s, and was repeated in the 1960s by S. G. F. Brandon in such books as *Jesus and the Zealots*. Recently it has been articulated again, in Reza Aslan's book *Zealot*. *Zealot* has a superficial resemblance to the Antagonism Thesis that I have promoted in this book, and so I feel compelled to give a short analysis and critique. Despite points of agreement, Aslan misses entirely the main thrust of the present book.

As always with such books, we should start with the author. Aslan is a Muslim-turned-Christian-turned-Muslim who has a PhD in modern sociology, and now teaches creative writing at UC-Riverside. He has published two prior books on religion with major (non-academic) publishers, and thus has some claim to expertise, although certainly an unconventional one.

On the positive side, Aslan views Jesus in strictly an historical sense, as a Jewish man who rebelled violently against Roman rule and against those elite Jews who acquiesced. The late BC and early AD period, he says, was a time of upheaval and revolt by the various Jewish tribes. Jesus was part of this ferment, and sought to drive out the Romans and reestablish Jewish rule according to Judaic orthodoxy. As a zealot, he was eventually arrested and crucified. Following his death, his followers—the 11 apostles, Paul, and a few others like Mark and Luke—constructed a version of his life that fit their particular needs. All this is consistent with my own thesis.

But there are several points of divergence from my approach, and several independent weaknesses to Aslan's book. Consider the divergences first. Of the Gospels, Aslan rightly says "the gospels are not, nor were they ever meant to be, an historical documentation of Jesus' life. These are not eyewitness accounts of Jesus' words and deed recorded by people who knew him" (p. xxvi)—which is true. He notes their pseudepigraphal nature, but immediately adds that such works "should by no means be thought of as forgeries." He does not explain why. If the accounts are known to be false but are portrayed as true, and published un-der a false name, *then that is a forgery*. Aslan doesn't consider this op-tion because he relies on the Gospels as mostly literal truth, in contradic-tion to his view just quoted.

Later he repeats the same mistake, entirely neglecting the possibility of forgery. "All of Jesus' miracle stories were embellished with the pas-sage of time and convoluted with Christological significance, and thus none of them can be historically validated" (p. 104)—true, but that's be-cause they are fictional constructions, which he does not admit, or even consider.

Paul does not appear in the book until very late, and then plays only a relatively minor role. He correctly notes that Paul's Jesus is "almost wholly of his own making," but never quite manages to place any blame on Paul at all. On Aslan's reading, Paul is always an innocent and upright fellow, just doing his best to build a church as he sees fit. Paul never lied. In Aslan's world, no one has any malicious intent, no one ever does any-thing bad or wrong, no one is to blame for anything.

There are structural problems as well. Aslan rehashes in great detail the New Testament account of things, in a very novel-like format, as if everything mentioned there is reliable and true. He rehashes Josephus' *The Jewish War* and *Antiquities of the Jews* in further detail, again ac-cepting virtually everything as written. He doesn't consider the view of either fellow skeptics or critics, except in a lengthy, disconnected, and highly unconventional "Notes" section at the end of book, which does not relate to any specific "notes" in the text at all.

His scholarship is also in question. Apart from Biblical passages, there are almost no exact quotations (source plus page number) in the entire book, "notes" included. The citations he does have are mostly of the lazy sort—simple reference to a book or article title, with no details or quotation. His most important and obvious predecessor, S. G. F. Bran-don, is almost invisible; one listing in the bibliography, and two passing mentions in the notes. This is very poor scholarship. There is likewise no mention of major scholars of the skeptical stance: nothing on Price, Thompson, Wells, or Doherty, not even the likes of Bart Ehrman. There is no mention of Nietzsche at all.

Granted the book is aimed at a popular audience, but it reads too much like a fictional novel to really be taken seriously. It's filled with unsubstantiated assertions, speculations, and flat claims of fact that are highly questionable. His portrayal of events reads like a soap opera—which perhaps it is, but at least Aslan should admit as much. Instead he casts it as the likely truth.

This is a shame because the general thesis is correct: Jesus was almost certainly just a man, a Jewish rabbi, who advocated for the poor and oppressed, and got himself killed. Beyond this mere skeleton of a life, we can say almost nothing about the real Jesus—and yet Aslan offers page after page of what Jesus "said" or "did."

The many weaknesses allow critics to pick the book apart while avoiding the valid central theme. One critical reviewer, Craig Evans, claims that Aslan "heavily relies on an outdated and discredited thesis"[1]—the Zealot thesis—but without telling us why or how it is "outdated" and "discredited." Just because it's old, that doesn't make it "outdated." And it can only become "discredited" by argumentation and a superior theory, which I think does not exist. Certainly the biblical account, with its myriad inconsistencies, incoherencies, and patent falsehoods, is no superior theory; not even close.

---

[1] *Christianity Today*, August 2013.

APPENDIX C

Pliny's Letter to Trajan
(ca. 112 AD)

It is my practice, my lord, to refer to you all matters concerning which I am in doubt. For who can better give guidance to my hesitation or inform my ignorance? I have never participated in trials of Christians. I therefore do not know what offenses it is the practice to punish or investigate, and to what extent. And I have been not a little hesitant as to whether there should be any distinction on account of age or no difference between the very young and the more mature; whether pardon is to be granted for repentance, or, if a man has once been a Christian, it does him no good to have ceased to be one; whether the name itself, even without offenses, or only the offenses associated with the name are to be punished.

Meanwhile, in the case of those who were denounced to me as Christians, I have observed the following procedure: I interrogated these as to whether they were Christians; those who confessed I interrogated a second and a third time, threatening them with punishment; those who persisted I ordered executed. For I had no doubt that, whatever the nature of their creed, stubbornness and inflexible obstinacy surely deserve to be punished. There were others possessed of the same folly; but because they were Roman citizens, I signed an order for them to be transferred to Rome.

Soon accusations spread, as usually happens, because of the proceedings going on, and several incidents occurred. An anonymous document was published containing the names of many persons. Those who denied that they were or had been Christians, when they invoked the gods in words dictated by me, offered prayer with incense and wine to your image, which I had ordered to be brought for this purpose together with statues of the gods, and moreover cursed Christ—none of which those who are really Christians, it is said, can be forced to do—these I thought should be discharged. Others named by the informer declared that they were Christians, but then denied it, asserting that they had been but had ceased to be, some three years before, others many years, some as much as 25 years. They all worshipped your image and the statues of the gods, and cursed Christ.

They asserted, however, that the sum and substance of their fault or error had been that they were accustomed to meet on a fixed day before dawn and sing responsively a hymn to Christ as to a god, and to bind themselves by oath—not to some crime, but not to commit fraud, theft, or adultery, not falsify their trust, nor to refuse to return a trust when called upon to do so. When this was over, it was their custom to depart and to assemble again to partake of food—but ordinary and innocent food. Even this, they affirmed, they had ceased to do after my edict by which, in accordance with your instructions, I had forbidden political associations. Accordingly, I judged it even more necessary to find out what the truth was by torturing two female slaves who were called deaconesses. But I discovered nothing else but depraved, excessive superstition.

I therefore postponed the investigation and hastened to consult you. For the matter seemed to me to warrant consulting you, especially because of the number involved. For many persons of every age, every rank, and also of both sexes are and will be endangered. For the contagion of this superstition has spread not only to the cities but also to the villages and farms. But it seems possible to check and cure it. It is certainly quite clear that the temples, which had been almost deserted, have begun to be frequented, that the established religious rites, long neglected, are being resumed, and that from everywhere sacrificial animals are coming, for which until now very few purchasers could be found. Hence it is easy to imagine what a multitude of people can be reformed if an opportunity for repentance is afforded.

BIBLIOGRAPHY

Archer, G. 1982. *Encyclopedia of Bible Difficulties*. Zondervan.

Aslan, R. 2013. *Zealot: The Life and Times of Jesus of Nazareth*. Random House.

Atwill, J. 2005. *Caesar's Messiah*. Createspace.

Barbiero, F. 2010. *The Secret Society of Moses*. Simon & Schuster / Inner Traditions.

Bauckham, R. 2006. *Jesus and the Eyewitnesses*. W. B. Eerdmans.

Ben-Sasson, H. 1976. *A History of the Jewish People*. Harvard University Press.

Bischoff, E. 2023. *The Book of the Shulchan Aruch*. Castle Hill.

Blomberg, C. 1987. *The Historical Reliability of the Gospels*. Inter-Varsity Press.

Blomberg, C. 1997. *Jesus and the Gospels*. Broadman & Holman.

Bock, D. and D. Wallace. 2007. *Dethroning Jesus: Exposing Popular Culture's Quest to Unseat the Biblical Christ*. Thomas Nelson.

Boyarin, D. 2001. "The Gospel of the Memra." *The Harvard Theological Review* 94(3): 243-284.

Brandon, S. 1967. *Jesus and the Zealots*. Manchester University Press.

Brandon, S. 1968. *The Trial of Jesus*. Batsford.

Brodie, T. 2012. *Beyond the Quest for the Historical Jesus*. Sheffield Phoenix Press.

Bultmann, R. 1958. *Jesus Christ and Mythology*. Scribner's Sons.

Burkett, D. 2002. *An Introduction to the New Testament and the Origins of Christianity*. Cambridge University Press.

Carotta, F. 2005. *Jesus was Caesar: On the Julian Origin of Christianity*. Aspekt.

Carrier, R. 2014. *On the Historicity of Jesus*. Sheffield Phoenix Press.

Carrier, R. 2020. *Jesus from Outer Space*. Pitchstone.

Carroll, J. 2001. *Constantine's Sword*. Houghton Mifflin.

Coogan, M. 2007. *New Oxford Annotated Bible* (3rd ed.). Oxford University Press.

Crossan, J. 1991. *The Historical Jesus: The Life of a Mediterranean Jewish Peasant*. HarperOne.

Crossan, J. 1994. *Jesus: A Revolutionary Biography*. Harper.

Dalton, T. 2020. *Debating the Holocaust* (4th ed.). Castle Hill.

Dalton, T. 2022. *Classic Essays on the Jewish Question*. Clemens & Blair.

Dalton, T. 2023. *The Steep Climb: Essays on the Jewish Question*. Clemens & Blair.

Davis, H. 2018. *Creating Christianity*. Independent.

Detering, H. 1995/2003. *The Falsified Paul*. Translated in *Journal of Higher Criticism* 10(2). Later published as *The Fabricated Paul* (2018).

Dever, W. 2003. *Who Were the Early Israelites and Where Did They Come From?* W. B. Eerdmans.

Devi, S. 2015. *Son of God, Son of the Sun* (D. Skrbina, ed.). Creative Fire Press.

Doherty, E. 1999. *The Jesus Puzzle*. Canadian Humanist Publications.

Doherty, E. 2001. *Challenging the Verdict*. Age of Reason Publications.

Drews, A. 1909/1998. *The Christ Myth*. Prometheus.

Dunn, J. (ed.). 1992. *Jews and Christians*. Mohr.

Ehrman, B. 2003. *Lost Christianities*. Oxford University Press.

Ehrman, B. 2011. *Forged: Writing in the Name of God.* HarperOne.

Ehrman, B. 2012. *Did Jesus Exist?* HarperOne.

Ehrman, B. 2018. *The Triumph of Christianity*. Simon & Schuster.

Einhorn, L. 2016. *A Shift in Time*. Perseus Distribution.

Eisenman, R. 1997. *James, the Brother of Jesus*. Viking.

Evans, C. 2006. *Fabricating Jesus*. IVP Books.

Evans, C. 2012. *Jesus and his World: The Archaeological Evidence*. Westminster John Knox.

Evans, C. 2020. *Jesus and the Manuscripts*. Hendrickson.

Fairchild, M. 1999. "Paul's pre-Christian zealot associations." *New Testament Studies* 45: 514-532.

Feldman, L. 1958. "Philo-semitism among ancient intellectuals." *Tradition* 1(1): 27-39.

Feldman, L. 1988. "Pro-Jewish intimations in anti-Jewish remarks cited in Josephus' *Against Apion*." *The Jewish Quarterly Review* 3-4: 187-251.

Feldman, L. 1991. "The enigma of Horace's thirtieth sabbath." *Scripta Classica Israelica* 10: 87-112.

Feldman, L. 1993. *Jew and Gentile in the Ancient World.* Princeton University Press.

Finkelstein, I. and N. Silberman. 2001. *The Bible Unearthed*. Free Press.

Frazer, J. 1890/1998. *The Golden Bough*. Oxford University Press.

Freke, T. 2001. *Jesus and the Lost Goddess*. Three Rivers Press.

Gabba, E. 1984. "The growth of anti-Judaism or the Greek attitude toward the Jews." In *Cambridge History of Judaism* (vol 2), Cambridge University Press.

Gmirkin, R. 2006. *Berossus and Genesis, Manetho and Exodus*. T&T Clark.

Goebbels, J. 2019. *Goebbels on the Jews*. Castle Hill.

Goguel, M. 1926. *Jesus the Nazarene*. D. Appleton.

Grant, M. 1973. *The Jews in the Roman World*. Scribner.

Habermas, G. 1996. *The Historical Jesus: Ancient Evidence for the Life of Christ*. College Press.

Habermas, G. 2004. *The Case for the Resurrection of Jesus*. Kregel.

Harpur, T. 2004. *The Pagan Christ*. Thomas Allen and Son.

Hertzberg, A. 1968. *The French Enlightenment and the Jews*. Columbia University Press.

Herzog, Ze'ev. 1999. "Deconstructing the walls of Jericho." *Ha'aretz Magazine* (Oct 29).

Hitler, A. 2017. *Mein Kampf* (T. Dalton, trans.) Clemens & Blair.

Homer. 1990. *The Iliad* (R. Fagles, trans.). Penguin.

Hopkins, K. 1998. "Christian number and its implications." *Journal of Early Christian Studies* 6(2): 185-226.

Horsley, R. 1985. *Bandits, Prophets, and Messiahs: Popular Movements at the Time of Jesus*. Winston.

Hume, D. 1778/1991. *Dialogues Concerning Natural Religion*. Routledge.

Kant, I. 1798/1978. *Anthropology*. Southern Illinois University Press.

Kant, I. 1997. *Lectures on Ethics*. Cambridge University Press.

Keener, C. 2011. *Miracles: The Credibility of the New Testament Accounts*. Baker.

Kersten, H. and E. Gruber. 1992/1994. *The Jesus Conspiracy*. Element Books.

Kirsch, J. 2004. *God against the Gods: The History of the War between Monotheism and Polytheism*. Viking Compass.

Kitchen, K. 2003. *On the Reliability of the Old Testament*. W. B. Eerdmans.

Komoszewski, J. and D. Bock (eds.) 2019. *Jesus, Skepticism & The Problem of History*. Zondervan.

Kulikowski, M. 2016. *The Triumph of Empire*. Harvard University Press.

Kulikowski, M. 2019. *The Tragedy of Empire*. Belknap.

Landsborough, D. 1987. "St Paul and temporal lobe epilepsy." *Journal of Neurology, Neurosurgery, and Psychiatry* 50: 659-664.

Lataster, R. 2013. *There Was No Jesus, There is no God*. Createspace.

Lataster, R. 2019. *Questioning the Historicity of Jesus*. Brill.

Lawrence, D. H. 1931/1995. *Apocalypse and the Writings on Revelation*. Penguin.

Lindemann, A. 1997. *Esau's Tears*. Cambridge University Press.

Loftus, J., ed. 2022. *Varieties of Jesus Mythicism*. Hypatia.

Lüdemann, G. 2001. *Jesus After 2,000 Years*. Prometheus.

Lüdemann, G. 2002. *Paul, The Founder of Christianity*. Prometheus.

Lüdemann, G. 2004. *The Resurrection of Christ*. Prometheus

Luther, M. 2020. *On the Jews and Their Lies*. Clemens & Blair.

Maccoby, H. 1980. *Revolution in Judaea*. Taplinger.

Maccoby, H. 1986. *Mythmaker: Paul and the Invention of Christianity*. Harper & Row.

Mackie, J. 1955. "Evil and omnipotence." *Mind* 64(254): 200-212.

Martin, M. 1991. *The Case against Christianity*. Temple University Press.

Meier, J. 1991. *A Marginal Jew: Rethinking the Historical Jesus*. Doubleday.

Murray, E. at al. 2012. "The Role of Psychotic Disorders in Religious History Considered." *The Journal of Neuropsychiatry* 24(4): 410-416.

Nietzsche, F. 1881/1997. *Daybreak* (R. Hollingdale, trans.). Cambridge University Press.

Nietzsche, F. 1887/1967. *On the Genealogy of Morals* (Kaufmann and Hollingdale, trans.). Vintage Books.

Nietzsche, F. 1888/2006. *Antichrist* (A. Ludovici, trans.). Barnes and Noble.

Onfray, M. 2007. *The Atheist Manifesto.* Melbourne University Press.

Osterer, H. 2012. *Legacy.* Oxford University Press.

Pitre, B. 2016. *The Case for Jesus.* Image.

Plutarch. 1998. *Greek Lives* (R. Waterfield, trans.). Oxford University Press.

Popper, K. 1963. *Conjectures and Refutations.* Routledge.

Price, R. 2000. *Deconstructing Jesus.* Prometheus.

Price, R. 2003. *The Incredible Shrinking Son of Man.* Prometheus.

Price, R. 2007. *Jesus is Dead.* American Atheist Press.

Price, R. 2012. *The Christ-Myth Theory and its Problems.* American Atheist Press.

Price, R. 2014. *Killing History.* Prometheus.

Reimarus, H. 1778/1970. *Fragments.* Fortress Press.

Roetzel, C. 1999. *Paul: The Man and the Myth.* T&T Clark.

Salibi, K. 1992/2007. *Who Was Jesus? Conspiracy in Jerusalem.* Tauris Parke.

Schafer, P. 1997. *Judeophobia.* Harvard University Press.

Schopenhauer, A. 1819/1966. *World as Will and Representation.* Dover.

Schopenhauer, A. 1851/1974. *Parerga and Paralipomena* (vol 2). Oxford University Press.

Schweitzer, A. 1906/2001. *The Quest of the Historical Jesus.* Fortress Press.

Seager, W. 2020. *The Routledge Handbook of Panpsychism.* Routledge.

Seland, T. 2002. "Saul of Tarsus and early Zealotism." *Biblica* 83: 449-471.

Skrbina, D. 2015. *The Metaphysics of Technology.* Routledge.

Skrbina, D. 2017. *Panpsychism in the West* (revised edition). MIT Press.

Sheldon, R. 1998. "Jesus, the security risk." *Small Wars and Insurgencies* 9(2): 1-37.

Smiles, V. 2002. "The concept of 'zeal' in second-temple Judaism." *Catholic Biblical Quarterly* 64: 282-299.

Stark, R. 2011. *The Triumph of Christianity.* HarperOne.

Statlow, M. 2008. "Theophrastus' Jewish philosophers." *Journal of Jewish Studies*, 59(1): 1-20.

Stern, M. 1974. *Greek and Latin Authors on Jews and Judaism* (vol 1). Israel Academy of Sciences and Humanities.

Stern, M. 1980. *Greek and Latin Authors on Jews and Judaism* (vol 2). Israel Academy of Sciences and Humanities.

Strauss, D. 1835/1970. *The Life of Jesus.* Scholarly Press.

Strobel, L. 1998. *The Case for Christ.* Zondervan.

Suetonius. 1957. *The Twelve Caesars.* Penguin.

Tabor, J. 2012. *Paul and Jesus.* Simon & Schuster.

Tabor, J. and S. Jacobovici. 2012. *The Jesus Discovery.* Simon & Schuster.

Tabor, J. 2018. "The quest for the historical Paul." Online: www.jamestabor.com

Tacitus. 2012. *Annals*. Penguin.

Thompson, T. 2005. *The Messiah Myth*. Basic Books.

Valliant, J. and W. Fahy. 2018. *Creating Christ: How Roman Emperors Invented Christianity*. Crossroad Press.

Van Voorst, R. 2000. *Jesus Outside the New Testament*. W. B. Eerdmans.

Vermes, G. 2004. *Authentic Gospels of Jesus*. Penguin.

Voskuilen, T. 2005. "Operation Messiah: Did Christianity start as a Roman psychological counterinsurgency operation?" *Small Wars and Insurgencies* 16(2): 192-215.

Voskuilen, T. and R. Sheldon. 2008. *Operation Messiah*. Vallentine Mitchell.

Wallace, D. 2011. *Revisiting the Corruption of the New Testament*. Kregel.

Walsh, R. 2021. *Origins of Early Christian Literature*. Cambridge University Press.

Wells, G. 1975. *Did Jesus Exist?* Prometheus.

White, L. 1967. "The historical roots of our ecologic crisis." *Science* 155: 1203-1207.

Wright, N. 1996. *The Original Jesus: The Life and Vision of a Revolutionary*. W. B. Eerdmans.

Yosef, O. 2010. "Gentiles exist only to serve Jews." *Jerusalem Post* (Oct 18).

INDEX